American Media
of World War II

MW01134654

For three generations of Americans, World War II has been a touchstone for the understanding of conflict and of America's role in global affairs. But if World War II helped shape the perception of war for Americans, American media in turn shape the understanding and memory of World War II. Concentrating on key popular films, television series, and digital games from the last two decades, this book explores the critical influence that World War II continues to exert on a generation of Americans born over thirty years after the conflict ended. It explains how the war was configured in the media of the wartime generation and how it came to be repurposed by their progeny, the Baby Boomers. In doing so, it identifies the framework underpinning the mediation of World War II memory in the current generation's media and develops a model that provides insight into the strategies of representation that shape the American perspective of war in general.

Debra Ramsay teaches and researches in film and media in the UK and is currently a researcher at the University of Glasgow, UK.

Routledge Research in Cultural and Media Studies

For a full list of titles in this series, please visit www.routledge.com

American Media and the Memory of World War II

Debra Ramsay

Routledge
Taylor & Francis Group

NEW YORK AND LONDON

First published 2015
by Routledge
711 Third Avenue, New York, NY 10017, USA

and by Routledge
2 Park Square, Milton Park, Abingdon, Oxfordshire OX14 4RN

First issued in paperback 2017

*Routledge is an imprint of the Taylor & Francis Group,
an informa business*

Library of Congress Cataloging-in-Publication Data

Ramsay, Debra, 1965–
    American media and the memory of World War II / Debra Ramsay.
        pages cm. — (Routledge research in cultural and media studies; 71)
    Includes bibliographical references and index.
    1. World War, 1939–1945—Motion pictures and the war.   2. World War, 1939–1945—Mass media and the war.   3. Collective memory—United States.   4. Mass media and public opinion—United States.   I. Title.
    D743.23.R365 2015
    791.43'6584053—dc23
    2014039391

ISBN 13: 978-1-138-05704-3 (pbk)
ISBN 13: 978-1-138-80552-1 (hbk)

Typeset in Sabon
by Apex CoVantage, LLC

For Warwick. Because the sun rises in your eyes, and always will.

Contents

Figures*

*All screenshots.

Acknowledgments

Material from *Now You Know: Reactions After Seeing* Saving Private Ryan, Jesse Kornbluth and Linda Sunshine, eds., compiled by America Online and DreamWorks (New York: Newmarket Press, 1999), is reproduced here with the permission of AOL.

I am indebted to Andrew Hoskins for permission to use material from the unpublished manuscript of *iMemory: Why the Past Is All Over* (Cambridge, MA: MIT Press, forthcoming).

Parts of Chapter 4 appeared in an article in *InMedia*, 4 (November 2013), entitled "Television's 'True Stories': How Memory Became Documentary in *Band of Brothers* and *The Pacific*," and are reproduced here with permission.

An adaptation of Chapter 5 was previously published in *Cinema Journal*, 54, no. 2, in an article entitled "Brutal Games: The First Person Shooter and Cultural Story of World War II," and is used here with permission.

I am indebted to Paul Grainge for the astute observations and insights that shaped this project from the outset. Thanks also to Jake Smith, for valuable suggestions just when I needed them. I am also thankful to Robert Burgoyne and Mark Gallagher, who provided comments on an early version of this manuscript. Special acknowledgment must go to Roberta Pearson, for seeing the big picture and pointing out which pieces were missing, as well as for unwavering support and advice, not to mention a ride on an actual World War II tank. Thanks also to long-suffering friends and family, who went through more discussions about war and trauma than most people should ever have to.

Most especially, thanks to my husband, Warwick Ramsay, without whose sacrifices, belief, patience, unique perspective, and sense of humor this book would not exist.

Introduction
Objects on the Shelf and Long-Running Stories

On the shelves of our homes, as in the wider cultural sphere, old and new media products jostle for space. Books might sit alongside DVDs (digital video discs) of films, and box sets of television series might be balanced against PlayStation games. Even transformed into digital form, films occupy space on hard drives or in cloud storage alongside folders containing photographs or journal articles saved for reading on tablets or smartphones. No event of significance, either private or public, is confined to representation in any one medium, and large-scale events, such as wars or catastrophes, cascade through time and across media of all kinds. In just one household, for example, World War II could be represented in DVDs of *The Longest Day* (Ken Annakin, Andrew Marton, Bernhard Wicki, 1962) and *Saving Private Ryan* (Steven Spielberg, 1998), Blu-ray box sets of the television series *The Pacific* (HBO, DreamWorks, Playtone, 2010), Xbox games from the *Call of Duty* franchise (Activision, 2003–present) and Tom Brokaw's (1998) book *The Greatest Generation*. Memories of World War II, like memories of all other events, are shaped, shared, and given meaning through mediated objects such as these. The memory of World War II is a dynamic composite constructed by a range of media operating in combination that nevertheless retains an essential mnemonic identity.

This book is concerned with how interactions among media shape the formulation of massive and complex structures of memory and with how such structures evolve through time. It sets out to explore the intersections between structures of mediated memory and generational perceptions of war. War plays a major role in the ongoing development of the American national identity, and media in turn play a major role in shaping mnemonic structures of war. There are a number of such structures to choose from, including those related to the war in Vietnam or the events of September 11, 2001, but this book focuses on World War II, partly because this conflict stretches across the media of three key generations whose members all share the same mediascape today: the wartime generation, sometimes referred to as the Greatest Generation, their progeny the Baby Boomers, and the current generation. This book begins by explaining the concept of transmedia and transgenerational mnemonic structures, situating it within current understandings of media and memory. It moves on to establish how the mnemonic structure of World War II evolved in the wartime generation's media and was repurposed in that of the Baby Boomers. Its primary focus, however, is in mapping the points of continuity and contradiction in representations of World War II from the last two decades in the three media industries whose products are most likely to be found on the shelves, either actual or virtual, of the majority of American homes today: film, television, and digital games.

During the course of this book, it will become clear that the mediated structure of World War II memory is complex and many faceted, filled with contradictions as well as continuities. Comprised of extended networks of texts related to specific historical events, mediated structures do not evolve neatly, nor do they develop in a neat, linear fashion. To understand the configuration of World War II in today's media, therefore, I begin by outlining some of the public and academic debates concerning memory and media that occurred in the final two decades of the twentieth century, not with the advent of the war itself. I explain the significance of the transmedia structure of World War II to debates concerning media and memory, and provide a context for how the relationship between media and memory is configured and understood in today's mediascape, before moving on to briefly outline the approach adopted in this book.

According to Mariana Torgovnick (2005, 2), the way in which war is remembered "intensifies patterns found in memory work more generally." In the final decade of the last millennium, general concerns regarding the relationship between memory and media coalesced around the commemoration and memorialization of World War II. The conflict features prominently in what Andreas Huyssen (1995, 5) refers to as a "memory boom of unprecedented proportions" that began in the 1980s and accelerated through the 1990s. Brought about by the complex convergence of a series of political, technological, social, and cultural factors, the so-called boom in memory manifested in the public sphere through a proliferation of new museums and memorials appearing across the world, including the Holocaust Memorial Museum on the National Mall in Washington and the Nagasaki Atomic Bomb Museum in Japan, together with a series of disagreements and controversies in the academy and in popular media regarding different views on how the past should be recalled and commemorated. Examples include the Textbook Wars in East Asia, initiated by the formation of a nationalist group in Japan that campaigned for the rewriting of school textbooks to minimize or excise details of any atrocities committed by Japan during the Asia-Pacific conflict (particularly those pertaining to the so-called comfort women), as well as debates concerning the construction of the Holocaust Memorial in Berlin, which began in the 1980s and continued well into the first decade of the new millennium.[1] Academic discussions about the role and significance of individual recollection, often revolving around the relationship between history and memory, paralleled those in the public arena.[2]

Not only was World War II the only source of historical trauma prompting new public responses during the 1990s, but the war received a great deal of attention because the decade marked a series of semicentennials of significant dates from the war.[3]

The sense that the generation that had directly experienced World War II would not survive long into the new millennium lent a particular urgency and resonance to the commemoration of the fiftieth anniversaries of dates such as the D-Day landings in Normandy (June 6, 1944); the liberation of Paris (August 1944) and of the concentration camps, such as Buchenwald (April 8, 1945), Bergen-Belsen (April 15, 1945), and Dachau (April 29, 1945); and the surrender of Germany (May 8, 1945) and Japan (August 15, 1945). Both Jay Winter (2000) and Gavriel Rosenfeld (2009) identify the shift in generations as a significant factor in facilitating the memory boom, as the progeny of the wartime generation, the so-called Baby Boomers, reached maturity with a desire to explore the past, the power to implement that desire in the public sphere, and, in the US and Europe in particular, the prosperity required to memorialize the past. The awareness in the Baby Boomer generation of the impending mortality of the previous generation created a drive to somehow preserve the memoires and memories of their elders and fed into a burgeoning interest in the memory of trauma to the extent that Jay Winter (2000) attributes the memory boom at least in part to the "belated but real acceptance that among us, within our families, there are men and women overwhelmed by traumatic recollection."

The recollection of traumatic memories of World War II in particular gave the memory boom an additional depth and impetus, in that it connected the memories of individuals and families with widespread national and international movements of commemoration, which were in turn facilitated by political factors (Winter 2000). The fall of the Eastern bloc, for example, finally opened the way for the confrontation of painful historical legacies from World War II. During the immediate postwar years, the pressures of recovery pushed aside memories of the war. Later, as Rosenfeld (2009) points out, comfortable national narratives emphasizing triumphalism or victimization allowed for an avoidance of accountability for the suffering of others. In the 1990s, however, European countries such as France and Sweden began to acknowledge the history of collaboration during German occupation, which had previously been smoothed over by more palatable narratives of victimhood. In the same decade in Asia, Japan faced demands for the recognition of atrocities committed during the war, as well as claims for restitution. Even in the US, where the memory of World War II supposedly holds fewer moral ambiguities, the dropping of the two atomic bombs, together with the previously "hidden" history of the Japanese internment camps in operation during the war, were the subjects of passionate debates that played out in the media—points I will explore in a little more detail later in this introduction. The various ways of recalling and reconstituting memories of World War II direct attention to intersections of processes of commemoration, individual memories of trauma, and media.

Projects to collect the testimony of survivors, particularly of the Holocaust, fueled a growing interest in the memory of trauma in general, raised questions regarding the role of individual memory in history, and challenged the value of historiography itself as an adequate form of representation for such an event.[4] Although the issue of how the Holocaust should be represented has always been a topic of moral and ethical deliberation, both the opening of the US Holocaust Memorial Museum and the release of Steven Spielberg's *Schindler's List* in 1993 became focal points for disputes over who has the right to represent the event and in what medium.[5] As a result of such controversies, discussions on Holocaust memory featured heavily in American newspapers and periodicals throughout the 1990s.[6] Despite its undeniable bearing and significance on the forms of historical trauma associated with World War II, the Holocaust is nevertheless only one aspect of a global conflict that affected the wartime generation in innumerable ways. During the 1990s, the complex array of memories associated with World War II coalesced in the media coverage of another group of survivors: the veterans.

The figure of the veteran took center stage in the coverage of the fiftieth anniversary of D-Day in Normandy, as well as in the celebrations commemorating the end of the war in the US. Of all the dates and events from World War II, June 6, 1944 has taken on special significance in American remembrance, a topic I examine in more detail in Chapter 3. For now, however, it is enough to bear in mind that the date has become synonymous with a national narrative about the war that focuses primarily on the sacrifices made by US citizen soldiers. Public interest in the D-Day ceremonies of 1994 was facilitated through extensive coverage of the events on the major US television networks: ABC, CBS, and NBC. Satellite television news network CNN also provided live coverage as the day progressed. Cable channels such as AMC offered a festival of World War II films throughout the day. Even the Travel Channel offered a one-hour special to mark the anniversary, *Tours of Remembrance: A World War II Journey*, which followed veterans on their return visits to Europe.[7] The anniversary of the surrender of the Japanese at the end of the war a year later received similar coverage. The plethora of news footage, documentaries, books, and classic war films that circulate around dates of commemoration demonstrates the complex blend of fictional and factual media texts that work in combination to formulate memories of World War II. The combination of individual testimony with archival or official material on television creates what Andrew Hoskins and Ben O'Loughlin (2010, 108) describe as a "fusion of human and media memory that seem[s] to produce the ultimate history-in-the-present." The figure of the veteran soldier functions as a literal embodiment of "history-in-the-present" by bringing individual memory to bear on historical narratives and transforming both into mediated memory, as demonstrated by controversies regarding the ways in which two specific narratives of World War II history were recalled and memorialized in the 1990s —the first concerning the detonation of the two atomic bombs, the second relating to the internment of the Japanese in camps across the US during World War II. The public arguments relating to these specific issues demonstrate that in addition to the centrality of the veteran in the media coverage of commemorative events, veterans feature prominently in determining what aspects of the war are remembered and commemorated.

The first dispute began because of a proposed exhibition by the Smithsonian National Air and Space Museum to mark the semicentennial of the end of the war with Japan. In what became known as the Enola Gay controversy, several veterans' organizations protested at the inclusion of material indicating the impact on the Japanese of the atomic bombings of Hiroshima and Nagasaki.[8] The proposed exhibit was consequently cancelled and later replaced by a revised version without the contentious material. The second controversy arose over the transformation of Manzanar, one of the largest internment camps for the Japanese in America, into a national historic monument in 1992. The proposal caused a furor over the use of phrases such as "concentration camp" and elicited a series of protests from local veteran groups.[9] Both controversies illustrate the discursive struggles for equilibrium between history and the individual memory of the veteran in representations of the past, while the media coverage devoted to the anniversaries and associated discourse confirms the status of the veteran as a central figure in the remembrance of the war and the importance of World War II as news in the 1990s. As Gavriel Rosenfeld (2009, 141) puts it, with media "getting into the act and devoting attention to covering controversies over monuments, museums, trials, truth commissions, and reparation payments around the world, memory became virtually inescapable in everyday life."

Media, however, did far more than "get into the act" during the memory boom. Media technologies featured prominently in the discussions concerning how the past is accessed, preserved, represented, and understood. The introduction of digital technologies, such as the spread of the World Wide Web throughout the 1990s, brought about a seismic shift in practices of producing, sharing, and storing information, together with a reevaluation of previously held notions of spatial and temporal boundaries. In addition to the proliferation of digital media, the television industry experienced a boom of its own during the 1990s, particularly in the US where subscribers to cable networks went from four million to fifty-seven million in 1993 (Bertman 1998, 4). The confluence of the development and proliferation of media technologies and platforms, the need to preserve the memories of the wartime generation, and the disputes regarding memorialization intensified ongoing debates on the relationship between media and memory.[10]

For some observers, the ubiquity and commercial accessibility of the past in mass mediated forms in the 1990s, whether related to World War II or other conflicts and historical moments, was not an indication of a memory boom but of a crisis of memory. According to Stephen Bertman (1998, 4), for example, the rapid dissemination of digital and electronic media technologies "keeps pictures, sounds, and data continually coursing on a nonstop, high-speed track, saturating our environment with instancy." For Pierre Nora (1996, 2) in such a frantic and ephemeral mediascape, the "thin film of current events" displaces memory, or the "legacy of what people knew intimately." Andreas Huyssen (1995, 2), however, suggests that media be regarded as "neither apocalypse nor panacea" for memory. Huyssen (1995) proposes that the 1990s be viewed as both a memory boom *and* a period of cultural amnesia. To understand the transformation of memory in response to new media technologies, mass-market consumerism, and the shifting practices and politics of continuously evolving media industries, Huyssen argues that it is essential to acknowledge that different mediated texts operate simultaneously in the same mediascape (2000, 29). The implications of the concurrent circulation of mediated texts for the mediation of memory are a central concern of this book. The ways in which media combine to produce notions of the past have not been fully considered in studies of media and memory. What does it mean for memory when a conflict such as World War II spills out across diverse media? How do interactions between media industries shape the memory of the war, and what intertextual relationships occur between mediations that occupy the same public and private spaces?

The variety of media represented on the shelves of an average home is a small indication of the number of ways in which an individual might choose to encounter and build a relationship with the past. Studies of media and memory that select individual media forms or texts and discuss them in isolation therefore risk missing out on what Andrew Martin (2006, 107) calls "the long-running nature of the story—in other words, how the production of cultural meanings builds upon preexisting narratives, just as a long-running television series does." The plethora of memorials, museums, newspaper articles, books, documentaries, films, and websites devoted to the memory of World War II and the Holocaust that appeared during the 1990s did not emerge into a vacuum but took their places in a preexisting, interconnected, and continuously evolving network of texts, paratexts, and intertexts. Concentrating only on representations of the war in one specific medium such as film or print media, or at a specific moment in time, thus risks missing out not only on the "long-running story" of the war but also on the multitude of ways in which individuals might construct their own meanings and memories of the conflict. Bearing in mind Marianna Torgovnick's point that the memory of conflict concentrates the principles generally at work in memory practices, exploring the ongoing evolution of World War II across American media and through time illuminates some of the dynamics at work in the production of mediated memory in general.

My approach in this book is to consider memory and media as fundamentally integrated, a position I explain in more detail in Chapter 1, along with the theoretical stance the book takes and the use of terminology. Media technologies have a long history of being associated with both memory "booms" and memory "busts," a topic explored in more detail in Chapter 1, but most theorists agree that it is difficult, if not impossible, to separate memory from its mediation. José van Dijck (2007, 16), for example, argues that media "invariably and inherently shape our personal memories, warranting the term 'mediation'." Media, of course, are also intrinsically connected to cultural, social, economic and political structures—relationships that lead to the idea of memory making as a negotiation or struggle for meaning. Such struggles occur both at the level of individuals, in the negotiation between personal identity and society as explored by José van Dijck (2007), and also at national level, as different versions of the past compete for a place in history and memory in the formulation of national identity, as investigated by Marita Sturken's analysis of "cultural memory" (1997). Neither position, however, fully considers how media work in combination to construct continually evolving configurations of the past. Recent theories of media ecologies, such as the approach advocated by Andrew Hoskins (forthcoming), recognize memory as operating in an environment in a continual state of flux and focus on analyzing the relationships between the key components of that environment. This book adopts a similarly holistic view of media and memory, but my interest lies not so much with exploring the state of the mediascape at a single point in time as with mapping how patterns of representation accumulate and circulate over time. I am therefore interested in exploring the procedural and diachronic dimensions of the mediation of memory and in doing so by drawing on a systems theoretical approach that considers memory not as a faculty of storage or even as an act of decoding the remains of the past, but as an ongoing process of categorizing and recategorizing cultural data relating to the past, present, and future. One of the key purposes of this book is to develop a model that can be used to understand the evolution and relationship to memory of vast networks of interrelated, repurposed mediated material, such as the network of representations associated with World War II.

To return to the mediated objects that so many of us have on our shelves, it is highly unlikely that all of them will be the products of one specific time frame. Old and new media texts and industries are in constant interaction, and the products of the past persist, sometimes in different forms, in the present. In one sense, the books, films, and television series that circulate in our mediascape offer in material form what sociologist Karl Mannheim (1952, 298) referred to as the "stratification of experience"—the articulation of reactions to and interpretations of a generation's experiences through various institutions and mechanisms. One of the pivotal ways in which individuals encounter the discursive material that shaped their predecessors' perspectives of themselves and of their world is through media. The concept of generations and of generational media consequently offers a useful perspective on how the system of memory evolves over time. As with memory, there are a range of different approaches to the concept of generations, and I explore these in more detail in Chapter 1, but following on from Mannheim's foundational work on generations, most sociologists agree that cultural data plays a crucial, if somewhat undefined role, in the formation of generational identity. Judith Burnett (2010, 48, table 3.1), for example, identifies "shared cultures and systems of identification" as key to the development of generational identity but does not explain the mechanisms by means of which cultural data is shared or identified. Similarly, Barry Schwartz (1996, 911) recognizes the existence of a "publicly visible discourse that flows through the organizations and institutions of the social world" but that only very generally acknowledges the involvement of media in allowing for the circulation of cultural material from past to present.

In contrast, a study conducted by Ingrid Volkmer (2006) suggests that even with the proviso that mass media are distributed, interpreted, and valued differently around the world, it is nonetheless possible to speak of "media generations," as people of different ages and vastly different social contexts share experiences of key moments through the dominant technologies of communication available at the time. In Volkmer's approach, for example, the Baby Boomers are therefore identified as the Television Generation because television was new to the mediascape as this cohort came of age (6). Volkmer concentrates specifically on the impact of news media and establishes that they are instrumental in shaping "generational-specific worldviews" (ibid.). The study is useful in confirming the role of media in creating shared systems of identification and memory in generations, but by concentrating solely on news media, Volkmer's research explores only one facet of the vast range of texts and technologies that contribute to the mediation of memory. Although news media and documentaries are an important part of the mediated structure of World War II, this book is primarily concerned with representations of World War II that occupy the space between the fictional and factual, inasmuch as these representations are just as significant, if not more so, in revealing the interplay between media, memory and history. Whereas Volkmer is concerned with the effect of media on generational memory and identity, my interest lies in exploring how experiences, perceptions, and values are articulated as discursive constructs by media in the system of memory.

As I explain more comprehensively in Chapter 1, this book adopts a similar understanding of generations to that of Sofia Aboim and Pedro Vasconcelos (2014), who propose that generations are themselves constructs articulated by and through discursive cultural systems. Understanding generations as discursive cultural constructs allows for a far more dynamic perspective of the ways in which generational identity is formulated and develops over time. Generations are therefore not defined in this book through biological succession, nor are they understood as age cohorts or collectives, but instead they are considered as dynamic constructs that are shaped, like memory, through networks of mediated narratives, images, and belief systems. Because they are cultural constructs, generations are inextricably bound to the media technologies, industries, and texts that produce the discourse defining them. The three generations selected for this book have particularly powerful discursive presences that overlap with the structure of World War II memory. Because World War II features so heavily in the media of the wartime generation, it is part of what defines this generation. The unprecedented population growth of the postwar years led to the identification of the next generation as the Baby Boomers, whose cultural identity is marked by extreme social and cultural upheaval and is frequently articulated in contradistinction to that of their predecessors. There is as yet no widely accepted appellation for the current generation, but it is variously referred to as the Digital, Internet, or even Gamer Generation. Although this generation's cultural identity is still evolving, the significance of media technologies, rather than moments of conflict or upheaval, is evident in the discourse relating to the current generation.[11] In applying the concept of generations, I do not presuppose the existence of a homogeneous set of experiences or memories, nor do I imagine a unified response to media. During the course of this book, it will become clear that individuals encounter and interpret generations as discursive constructs and transmedia structures of memory as part of an ongoing process of individuation that connects self to society.

Given that memory emerged from the 1990s as the "historical signature of our generation," as Jay Winter (2000) puts it, and that World War II features so prominently in the configuration of that signature, representations of the conflict at the turn of the millennium are particularly appropriate for considering the ways in which media operate in constructing representations of the past. Furthermore, of all the wars in America's history, World War II alone offers what Michael Sherry (1995, 449) lists as the "the attractive combination of giant scale, moral clarity, American unity and total American victory." My interest lies in exploring the development of a discursive cultural structure of war that makes it "attractive," or at the very least persistently useful, as an ideological touchstone against which all subsequent conflicts that the US engaged in have been measured. The memory of the Holocaust is connected to the transmedia structure of World War II, but it is large enough to form a transmedia structure of its own and to warrant an entirely separate field of study. Because this book focuses on the mediation of the process of waging and remembering war in the US, it does not engage comprehensively with the mediated structure of Holocaust memory. This book explores the memory of World War II as a continually evolving, intricate mediated structure that operates as part of a system involving individuals, media industries, and their products. I concentrate on the nodes of connection between the system's component parts and utilize the discursive concept of generations as a means of tracking how the system of memory operates through time, rather than in specific moments of crisis.

The notion that the past is always reconfigured to serve the needs of the present is central to most studies of media and memory, but Barry Schwartz's (1996) work on the memory of Abraham Lincoln draws attention to the significance of continuity in representations of the past in order to distinguish it from the present and to reveal its usefulness as an ideological model for the present. Following on from Schwartz's work, this book is concerned not only with identifying changes in the mediated structure of World War II memory but also with exploring those elements that are resistant to change. This book therefore identifies an organizational framework running through the mediated structure of World War II memory, comprised of three key components. The first is the citizen soldier, a pivotal and persistent figure that nevertheless undergoes significant changes in the course of the evolution of the structure. The second is the development of an ideological narrative that identifies World War II as America's "good war." The third concerns the development of a distinctive esthetic identity for the conflict that in turn feeds into specific ideological and political perceptions of warfare. Tracking the evolution of the citizen soldier, the "good war" concept and the war as a visual construct across media and through time allows for an exploration of the relationships between media texts and industries and in turn reveals what these relationships mean for the current mediation of the memory of World War II.

Ultimately, this book seeks to answer the following questions: How is the mnemonic structure of World War II repurposed as it cycles through the media of each generation? More specifically, what continuities and changes emerge in the three central components of the structure—the citizen soldier, the war as a visual construct, and the notion of the "good war"? Most importantly, how are these three layers configured today, and what do they contribute to our understanding of the mediation of current conflicts?

PART I

The two opening chapters provide an overview of the theoretical field in which the book operates. Chapter 1 provides an outline of how the connection between memory and media in general has been theorized and briefly surveys approaches that understand memory as operating in an ecology. In this chapter, I draw on systems theory to establish an understanding of the system of memory as both procedural and diachronic. This chapter exposes a gap in the study of memory and media that relates specifically to the presence of fluid intertextual and intermedial networks that accrue around specific events such as moments of catastrophe or conflict. It establishes how this book develops the idea of transmedia structures in response to that gap. Chapter 1 ends by explaining the notion of generations as discursive cultural constructs and demonstrates how generations intersect with transmedia mnemonic structures.

Having outlined the concept of World War II as a transmedia, trans-generational structure in Chapter 1, I move on in Chapter 2 to establish the significance of the citizen soldier, the "good war," and the war as a visual construct in the media of the wartime generation, and their subsequent reconfiguration in the media of the Baby Boomers. Understanding the development of these three components is crucial to considering how the memory of World War II has evolved in the current mediascape and provides a bedrock for the case studies analyzed in the remaining chapters.

PART II

Part II concentrates on the continued evolution of the transmedia structure of the war in films, television series, and digital games of World War II from the last two decades. Given the significance of intertextuality and intermediality to this book's approach to mediated memory, although each chapter in this section focuses on key texts, analysis extends to the paratextual networks that accumulate around the selected case studies. Paratexts, according to Jonathan Gray (2010), are essential to understanding any text's meaning and cultural value. Gray defines a paratext as any text that "constructs, lives in, and can affect the running of the text" (6). Paratexts are also, as Gray points out, not necessarily tangible but may be also be constructed through accrued layers of meaning (ibid.). As will become clear as this book progresses, intangible paratexts such as star personas or brand identities are as crucial to understanding the evolution of the mediated structure of World War II as the more tangible paratexts, such as reviews or promotional material, and the texts themselves. Each chapter addresses specific historical and intellectual concerns, and each includes discussions of representations of World War II in both the European and Pacific theaters.

Chapter 3 focuses on cinema and begins with an analysis of Steven Spielberg's *Saving Private Ryan*, a film released at the apex of the memory boom in 1998. Both academic and popular commentators tend to regard cinema as perhaps the most culturally significant of all visual media. Marita Sturken (1997, 23), for example, argues that fiction films "supersede and overshadow documentary images and written texts." Although the remaining chapters challenge the idea of film as the dominant medium in the transmedia structure of the war, there can be no doubt that *Saving Private Ryan* casts a significant shadow over subsequent representations of World War II in visual media, to the extent that it can be understood as a "master mediation" of the war, as this chapter will show. This chapter is perhaps the most traditional in its approach, in that it uses textual analysis, but it also explores intertextual and intermedial relationships between the film and previous strategies of representation in American media in order to establish how *Saving Private Ryan* incorporates and recalibrates the citizen soldier, the "good war," and the war as a visual construct. *Saving Private*

Ryan reflects and perpetuates the centrality of D-Day in Normandy and the war in Europe in the transmedia structure of the war, but Clint Eastwood's diptych, *Flags of Our Fathers* and *Letters from Iwo Jima* (both released in 2006), shifts attention to the Pacific theater. Eastwood's films deal with Joe Rosenthal's photograph of the raising of the American flag during the battle for the island of Iwo Jima in 1945. They examine the relationship between public perceptions of warfare and traumatic memories of combat and demonstrate that the war in the Pacific is more difficult to accommodate in neat narratives of unambiguous military success.

Chapter 4 examines two television miniseries, *Band of Brothers* (2001) and *The Pacific* (2010), both coproductions of HBO, DreamWorks SKG, and Playtone, as industrial and thematic extensions of *Saving Private Ryan*. The influence of the commercial imperatives of the three producers on the construction of the citizen soldier, the "good war," and the visual construction of World War II in televisual narratives is the central concern of this chapter. This chapter demonstrates how HBO mobilizes the memorialization of World War II to augment its distinctive brand identity, first through carefully crafted connections between each series and commemorative events, and second through the marketing of both series in DVD and Blu-ray box sets as mementos of those events. Derek Kompare (2006) and Barbara Klinger (2006) are among those who acknowledge the impact of DVD and Blu-ray technology on practices of viewing and consuming film and television. Although the films discussed in the previous chapter are available in these formats, the box sets of *Band of Brothers* and *The Pacific* are particularly useful in considering how this form of digital technology recalibrates the relationship between television, memory, and history—an area previously underexamined in studies of media and memory.[12]

Chapter 5 turns to digital games, one of the fastest growing sectors of the entertainment industry. Despite the size of the markets and audiences they command, first-person shooters (FPSs) like the *Call of Duty* franchise (Activision, 2003–present) are at best ignored, at worst dismissed as having nothing to contribute to either memory or history—a perspective I challenge in this chapter. World War II has been the most prevalent of all conflicts used in digital wargaming in general since the development of computer games in the 1980s, and it has a long association with the FPS in particular, yet digital games do not feature significantly in discussions of World War II in media. With reference to the *Medal of Honor* series (EA Games, 1999–2014), which is heavily influenced by *Saving Private Ryan* and Steven Spielberg, but moving on to focus on *Call of Duty: World at War* (Activision, 2008), I explore what happens to the citizen soldier, the notion of the "good war," and the visual construction of the war when translated via a technology that simulates warfare and that introduces the notion of play to the memory of the war. Drawing on Paul Connerton's concept of habit memory (1989), this chapter shows that the FPS configures war memory in sometimes unexpected ways. More importantly, this chapter demonstrates how *World at War* engages with aspects of the memory of the conflict largely unexplored elsewhere in the transmedia structure of the war.

"War is hell," writes Vietnam veteran Tim O'Brien (1991, 77), "but that's not the half of it, because war is also mystery and terror and adventure and courage and discovery and holiness and pity and despair and longing and love. War is nasty, war is fun." Like the experience of warfare itself, the memories of a conflict on the scale of World War II can never be reduced to a single moment, emotion, or narrative or even to a collection of mediated objects on the shelf. This book acknowledges the ways in which a multi-faceted, intricate transmedia structure refracts the innumerable moments, emotions, and memories of World War II, questioning how media work together to produce an ongoing and "long-running story" of war in American generational memory.

NOTES

1. For a summary of the debates regarding the Textbook Wars, see Beal, Nozaki, and Yang (2001). For an overview of the debates on the Holocaust Memorial, see Cohen (1999a, 1999b) and also *BBC Monitoring*, "Press Cool on Berlin Memorial" (May 10, 2005).
2. Examples include Pierre Nora's work on the shifting roles of history and memory in France (1984–1992) and Huyssen (1995). For an overview of the burgeoning academic interest in memory, see Rosenfeld (2009) and Winter (2000).
3. Others include the recognition of past social injustices related to slavery and racism in the United States, with universities such as Yale acknowledging their reliance on the slave trade for scholarships and endowments, and the establishment of the Truth and Reconciliation Committee in South Africa to deal with the legacy of the apartheid regime.
4. The Fortunoff Video Archive for Holocaust Testimonies is one such project, as is Survivors of the Shoah, a project initiated by Steven Spielberg after the release of *Schindler's List* (1993).
5. See Loshitzky (1997) for a collection of essays about *Schindler's List*.
6. For a detailed breakdown of coverage of the Holocaust in the American press, see Carrol (1997).
7. For an overview of the programming offered on US television for June 6, 1994, see *LA Times*, "Coverage of Anniversary of D-Day Will Start in France" (June 6, 1994).
8. For a detailed description of the media coverage of this controversy, see Kishimoto (2004).
9. For a discussion of the legislative history involved in creating the Manzanar National Historic Site, see Hayashi (2003).
10. Anxieties over the perceived separation of "organic" or "lived" memory from "external" or artificial methods of recording the past are an intrinsic part of the history of both media and memory, as I explore in more detail in Chapter 1.
11. A survey conducted by the Pew Research Center (2010) in the US suggests that the current generation adopts technology as a "badge of generational identity" and identifies the use of media technologies as precisely what makes them distinctive from other generations.
12. I discuss the DVD and Blu-ray discs of *Flags of Our Fathers* and *Letters from Iwo Jima* in more detail in Ramsay (2013).

REFERENCES

Aboim, Sofia, and Pedro Vasconcelos. 2014. "From Political to Social Generations: A Critical Reappraisal of Mannheim's Classical Approach." *European Journal of Social Theory* 17, no. 2 (originally published online November 21, 2013): 165–183. DOI: 10.1177/1368431013509681

BBC Monitoring. 2005. "Press Cool on Berlin Memorial." *BBC* (News.bbc.co.uk, May 10). Accessed December 15, 2011. http://news.bbc.co.uk/1/hi/world/eu rope/4533463.stm

Beal, Tim, Yoshiko Nozaki, and Jian Yang. 2001. "Ghosts of the Past: The Japanese History Textbook Controversy." *New Zealand Journal of Asian Studies* 3, no. 2. (December): 177–188. Accessed December 15, 2011. www.nzasia.org.nz/down loads/NZJAS-Dec01/Textbook.pdf

Bertman, Stephen. 1998. *Hyperculture: The Human Cost of Speed.* Westport, CT: Praeger.

Brokaw, Tom. [1998] 2002. *The Greatest Generation.* London: Pimlico.

Burnett, Judith. 2010. *Generations: The Time Machine in Theory and Practice.* Farnham, UK and Burlington, VT: Ashgate.

Carrol, James. 1997. "Shoah in the News: Patterns and Meanings of News Coverage of the Holocaust." Discussion Paper D-27. Shorenstein Center on the Press, Politics and Public Policy, Harvard University, John F. Kennedy School of Government. Accessed November 11, 2011. www.hks.harvard.edu/presspol/publica tions/papers/discussion_papers/d27_carroll.pdf

Cohen, Roger. 1999a. "Berlin Holocaust Memorial Approved." *New York Times,* June 26. Accessed December 15, 2011. www.nytimes.com/1999/06/26/world/berlin-holocaust-memorial-approved.html

Cohen, Roger. 1999b. "Schroder Backs Design for a Vast Berlin Holocaust Memorial." *New York Times,* January 18. Accessed December 15, 2011. www.nytimes.com/1999/01/18/world/schroder-backs-design-for-a-vast-berlin-holocaust-mc morial.html?src=pm

Connerton, Paul. 1989. *How Societies Remember.* Cambridge: Cambridge University Press.

Gray, Jonathan. 2010. *Show Sold Separately: Promos, Spoilers, and Other Media Paratexts.* New York: New York University Press.

Hayashi, Robert T. 2003. "Transfigured Patterns: Contesting Memories at the Manzanar National Historic Site." *The Public Historian* 25, no. 4 (Fall): 51–71. www.jstor.org/stable/10.1525/tph.2003.25.4.51

Hoskins, Andrew. Forthcoming. *iMemory: Why the Past Is All Over.* Cambridge, MA: MIT Press.

Hoskins, Andrew, and Ben O'Loughlin. 2010. *War and Media.* Cambridge: Polity Press.

Huyssen, Andreas. 1995. *Twilight Memories: Marking Time in a Culture of Amnesia.* New York: Routledge.

Huyssen, Andreas. 2000. "Present Pasts: Media, Politics, Amnesia." *Public Culture* 12, no. 1 (Winter): 21–38. http://muse.jhu.edu/

Kishimoto, Kyoko. 2004. "Apologies for Atrocities: Commemorating the 50th Anniversary of World War II's End in the United States and Japan." *American Studies International* 42, nos. 2–3: 17–50. www.jstor.org/stable/41280073

Klinger, Barbara. 2006. *Beyond the Multiplex: Cinema, New Technologies and the Home.* Berkeley and Los Angeles: University of California Press.

Kompare, Derek. 2006. "Publishing Flow: DVD Box Sets and the Reconception of Television." *Television and New Media* 7: 335–360. DOI: 10.1177/1527476404270609

LA Times. 1994. "Coverage of Anniversary of D-Day Will Start in France," June 6. Accessed November 11, 2011. http://articles.latimes.com/1994-06-06/entertainment/ca-1069_1_world-war-ii-veterans

Loshitzky, Yosefa, ed. 1997. *Spielberg's Holocaust: Critical Perspectives*. Bloomington and Indianapolis: Indiana University Press.

Mannheim, Karl. 1952. "The Problem of Generations." In *Essays on the Sociology of Knowledge*, Paul Kecskemeti, ed.: 276–322. New York: Oxford University Press.

Martin, Andrew. 2006. "Popular Culture and Narratives of Insecurity." In *Rethinking Global Security: Media, Popular Culture, and the "War on Terror."* Andrew Martin and Patrice Petro, eds.: 104–116. New Brunswick, NJ: Rutgers University Press.

Nora, Pierre. 1996. *Realms of Memory: Conflicts and Divisions*. Vol. 1. Lawrence D. Kritzman, ed. Arthur Goldhammer, trans. New York: Columbia University Press.

O'Brien, Tim. 1991. *The Things They Carried*. London: Flamingo.

Pew Research Center. 2010. *Millennials, a Portrait of Generation Next: Confident. Connected. Open to Change*. Washington, DC: Pew Research Center (February). Accessed January 18, 2012. http://pewsocialtrends.org/files/2010/10/millennials-confident-connected-open-to-change.pdf

Ramsay, Debra. 2013. "Flagging up History: The Past as a DVD Bonus Feature." In *A Companion to the Historical Film*. Robert Rosenstone and Constantin Parvulescu, eds.: 54–70. Malden, MA: Wiley-Blackwell.

Rosenfeld, Gavriel D. 2009. "A Looming Crash or a Soft Landing? Forecasting the Future of the Memory 'Industry.'" *Journal of Modern History* 81 (March): 122–158. Accessed November 2, 2011. http://digitalcommons.fairfield.edu/history-facultypubs/11/

Schwartz, Barry. 1996. "Memory as a Cultural System: Abraham Lincoln in World War II." *American Sociological Review* 61, no. 5 (October): 908–927. Accessed September 16, 2014. www.barryschwartzonline.com/CulturalSystem.pdf

Sherry, Michael. 1995. *In the Shadow of War: The United States Since the 1930s*. New Haven, CT, and London: Yale University Press.

Sturken, Marita. 1997. *Tangled Memories: The Vietnam War, the AIDS Epidemic and the Politics of Remembering*. Berkeley: University of California Press.

Torgovnick, Marianna. 2005. *The War Complex: World War II in Our Time*. Chicago: University of Chicago Press.

Van Dijck, José. 2007. *Mediated Memories in the Digital Age*. Stanford, CA: Stanford University Press.

Volkmer, Ingrid, ed. 2006. *News in Public Memory*. New York: Peter Lang.

Winter, Jay. 2000. "The Generation of Memory: Reflections on the 'Memory Boom' in Contemporary Historical Studies." *The German Historical Institute* 27, no. 3 (Fall). Accessed September 16, 2011. www.ghi-dc.org/publications/ghipubs/bu/027/b27winterframe.html

Part I

1 Notes on Approach: Memory and Generations

As the focus of a range of different disciplines—psychology, sociology, history, media studies, to name just a few—it is perhaps unsurprising that there are manifold understandings of the concept of memory and a proliferation of terms associated with it. From Maurice Hallbwachs' (1952), notion of "collective memory" through Pierre Nora's (1996) "*lieux de mémoire*," Jan Assman's (1995) "cultural memory," Jeffrey Olick's (1999) idea of "collected memory," and the more recent notion of "connective memory" (Hoskins, 2011), to psychological understandings of "cognitive memory," "screen memory," and "traumatic memory," even this briefest survey of terms makes apparent the tangle of theories of memory and approaches to how we process the past. It is not my intention to provide a comprehensive overview of the field in this chapter, but because of the range of possible theories and perspectives, it is necessary to identify the approach to memory taken within this book and to explain the reasons for its implementation.[1] This chapter is divided into two sections. The first begins by considering very briefly some of the key ways in which the relationship between media and memory has been theorized. As established in the Introduction, I consider memory as a procedural and transmedial phenomenon. The understanding of memory as a process operating across media is explained in more detail in this chapter, and this approach is located within the broader spectrum of media and memory studies. As will also be clear from the Introduction, this book is concerned not only with how the process of memory making extends across media but also with how that process develops over time. One of the most effective ways of exploring the diachronic dimension of mediated memory is through generational mediascapes. As with memory, the concept of generations is understood in a number of different ways across a range of different disciplines.[2] Drawing primarily on the work of Sofia Aboim and Pedro Vasconcelos (2014), I consider generations not as stable entities with fixed boundaries and shared characteristics but as fluid and dynamic cultural constructs. The second section of this chapter explains how generations intersect with both media and memory, establishing what is meant by the term "mediascape." This chapter ultimately outlines the systems and structures of both memory and generations as they are understood in this book.

MEMORY AND MEDIA

Underlying most approaches to memory is the understanding that media play an essential role in the processes of memory making. According to Astrid Erll (2011, 116), media are so thoroughly imbricated in memory that the history of memory can be understood as the history of media. Even the earliest formal approaches to memory conceived of it in terms of the media available at the time. The Greek art of memory, or *ars memoriae*, as it is commonly known, for example, is known for its technique of locating elements that the practitioner wished to remember within the mental reconstruction of a place or architectural structure, but painting, sculpture, and inscriptions on wax tablets were also all invoked metaphorically as ways of improving recall.[3] Yet despite the intimate and long-standing connections between memory and media, the relationship between the two is not always harmonious. The introduction of new forms of media has at times initiated changes in processes of memory and prompted reevaluations of the relationship. Plato's observation that the advent of writing would herald the destruction of carefully cultivated memory practices is perhaps the earliest example of one such moment, as mnemonic aids went from internal practices of memorization to external methods of recording and storage (*Phaedrus* 1938, 274). At other times, media technologies have been heralded as the "savior" of memory and history, as Scott McQuire (1998, 124) describes a widespread perception of photography in the nineteenth century—a period when "the past was under threat and time itself seemed to be accelerating." The arrival of digital media, as briefly mentioned in the Introduction, signaled another series of reassessments of the relationship. Yet despite the attention such moments receive from scholars and other observers, they are relatively rare in the history of memory and media, as Geoffrey Bowker points out (2008, 2). Memory and media are so profoundly integrated that more recently theorists such as José van Dijck argue that the relationship between them is in fact mutually transformative (2007, 21). In van Dijck's model, which is also the perspective adopted within this book, mediated memory is understood as a dynamic process that blurs whatever lines are thought to exist between the public and the private and that facilitates the connection between self and culture in an ongoing integration of past, present, and future. When memory making is understood as an ongoing process, it becomes clear that media cannot be considered as impersonal mechanisms for simply recording and somehow storing the past.

Media technologies and industries are firmly enmeshed in consumerism, culture, and politics, relationships that exert pressures of their own on the formation of memory. Because the choices made by all of us as to which versions of the past we incorporate into our lives and through which media technologies more often than not involve commercial transactions, Barry Schwartz (1990) describes memory making as an activity in which individuals or groups of individuals have the resources to convince others what aspects of the past are worth remembering. Mass media texts in particular have consequently been criticized and marginalized in general critiques on commodity culture that see products of consumerism as empty of meaning, obscuring rather than facilitating the understanding of the past. Jean Baudrillard's (1997) notion of a "sale" of memory at the end of the last millennium is one example of the perception that the commodification of memory through mass media in particular leads to the loss of the past. However, a number of theorists have taken critiques of mass media to task. Two of these warrant further discussion as they touch on elements that are important for this book: Alison Landsberg and Marita Sturken.

Where Baudrilllard (1997) sees media producing spectral events and likens them to "phantom limbs . . . which hurt even when they are no longer there," Alison Landsberg (2004) sees mass media creating memories that are "worn" on the body like a prosthesis, enabling empathic connections across temporal, spatial, and cultural boundaries. In Landsberg's approach, mass media provide memories of moments outside an individual's direct experience and also potentially beyond his or her social and cultural milieu, allowing for the generation of empathy, which Landsberg defines as an "intellectual and emotional negotiation with the plight of the 'other'" (2004, 108). I return to touch on Landsberg's idea of empathy and prosthetic memory in Chapter 6, but for now it is enough to acknowledge that Landsberg advocates a progressive view of mass media by suggesting that they are crucial in allowing memories to be shared across national and temporal boundaries.

Marita Sturken, in turn, suggests that in a society in which the boundaries between commercialization, memory, culture, and art are irrevocably blurred, the dismissal of the products of consumerism as worthless is no longer a "viable option," if indeed it ever was, as Sturken points out (1997, 22–12). Sturken's notion of "tangled memories" is perhaps one of the more useful metaphors to apply to the process of memory making, inasmuch as it conjures up a network of interrelated texts and phenomena, although Sturken uses it specifically to describe the relationship between "cultural memory" and history, which she suggests is so occluded that it is practically impossible to distinguish between the two (5). Within Sturken's model, different versions of the past compete within the tangle of memory and history in a process by means of which national identity is "established, questioned and refigured" (13). Sturken's (1997) work is thus significant in acknowledging the role that mass media play in circulating narratives about the past that compete for a place in both history and memory and that contribute to the construction of national identities. The intimate connection between mass media texts and industries and ideas of history and national identity is a theme explored throughout this book, which proceeds from the work of both Landsberg (2004) and Sturken (1998) in its consideration of popular forms of media as particularly significant in the process of memory making.

However, although both Sturken and Landsberg are instrumental in countering critiques of the commodification of memory through mass media, the proliferation of digital technologies initiated further revisions of the understanding of the mediation of memory. Andrew Hoskins (forthcoming), for example, calls for a "conceptual shift" that moves away from what he identifies as the co-related and outdated paradigms of collective memory and mass media. To account for the ubiquity of media in today's world, Hoskins instead posits an approach that draws on Media Ecology. Although Media Ecology is a theoretical framework for the study of media first formalized in the 1970s, its attempt to account for relationships between media technologies and society can be useful in considering the implications of the current profligate spread of media. Media Ecology was first formalized in the 1970s by Neil Postman but owes much to Marshal McLuhan's (1964) well-worn principle that the technologies of media remake us and the world we live in. Postman (1970) explains how this school of thought, later identified as the North American tradition of Media Ecology, considers the study of each medium as the study of an environment or "complex message system which imposes on human beings certain ways of thinking, feeling, and behaving." As the word "imposes" suggests, the North American approach to the relationship between media systems and human beings is rooted in technological determinism. According to Michael Goddard (2011), however, more recent pathways by European theorists into media ecologies, rather than Media Ecology, regard the North American tradition as limited because it considers media as "parts of relatively stable environments from which normative ideas about human beings form the center." Matthew Fuller is a key figure in the European school. For Fuller, the use of the term "ecology" implies "dynamic systems in which any one part is always multiply connected, acting by virtue of those connections, and always variable, such that it can be regarded as a pattern rather than simply as an object" (2005, 4). Fuller's use of the concept of media ecologies here is very much as Hoskins (forthcoming) applies it in advocating a "holistic" approach to the study of media and memory, one that acknowledges that the mediated environment is undergoing constant change but that also attempts to account for the relationships among media industries, technologies, the objects, and texts they produce, as well as social institutions and individuals.

The idea of media environments functioning as complex systems is a recurring theme running through both schools of thought on media ecology, and it also surfaces in Hoskins' work. I want to explore systems theory in a little more detail because it cuts through the debates concerning the supposed stability of environments, as opposed to the dynamism of ecologies, and instead shifts attention onto the procedural nature of mediated memory. As will already be apparent from even this briefest of overviews of some of the central theories of memory and media, the field is infested with metaphor (memory as prosthetic limbs, as entangled networks, etc.)—some more useful than others—and systems theory is no different inasmuch as it takes the functionality of computerized memory for its allegory of memory.[4] Systems theory, as explained by Elena Esposito, understands memory as operating like a "computing device" that does not so much store or record data as implement a set of "procedures that generate the data again, and in a different way, each time" (2008, 184). I have already established that media cannot be considered as simple containers for memory, but systems theory allows us to move beyond the notion of storage completely and into an understanding of media as part of a system that constantly reworks and reconstitutes aspects of the past. Systems theory describes memory making as a "procedural capability realizing a constant re-categorization" (Esposito 2008, 185).

The process of constantly recategorizing sets of data is central to this book, which explores how particular constructs of memory are reformulated not only across various media but also through time. The idea that memory is always reconstructed to serve the needs of the present is central to most theories of memory, but understanding the mediation of memory as a process of continual recategorization allows for a far more nuanced perspective of the relationship between past, present, and future. As this book progresses, it will become apparent that aspects of the past are not only reformulated in response to the needs of the present but that they may also exert pressures of their own as they are repurposed. Unlike Sturken, therefore, I am not so much concerned with how different versions of the past compete for a place in history but rather with how they combine to create continually evolving mnemonic configurations. I draw on the perspective of media ecologies, as well as on José van Dijck's work, to acknowledge the significance of mutually transformative relationships among media industries, technologies, and texts, as well as individuals and their sociohistoric contexts. This book is concerned with how these relationships feed into the procedural capabilities of the system of memory to generate patterns through which we interpret and understand the past.

The way in which patterns of representation circulate through the system of memory and media is, as Astrid Erll observes, an area of memory studies that is only just beginning to be investigated, although Erll puts forward Aby Warburg's work as an early example of the examination of how particular aspects of the past might "travel" across media and through time (2011, 143). Warburg tracked the recurrence of specific symbols from the Ancient Greeks through to the Renaissance and identified what he referred to as "pathos formulas," or focal points for intense emotion.[5] While specific symbols have undoubted longevity and ongoing significance, as products of memory systems they offer a concentrated but essentially limited understanding of the evolution of larger patterns of recollection. Frederick Bartlett's (1932) notion of psychological "schema" is perhaps more useful as a starting point for understanding the processes of reformulation that characterize the operation of memory as a system. Bartlett identified schema as "living, momentary" arrangements or "organized settings" (a term Bartlett preferred) that come into play in individual responses to changing situations and environments ([1932] 1955, 201). Bartlett's theory resonates, albeit very distantly, with systems approaches in that it works against the idea that memory operates as an inert storage "faculty" and suggests instead that memory is an active and integrative process with a myriad different components ([1932] 1955, 12–13).

Traces of Bartlett's concept of organized settings or configurations of memory can be found in the idea of media templates. According to Jenny Kitzinger (2000, 61), media templates function as a kind of "rhetorical shorthand" by recalling an event in the past in order to shape the understanding of an event that is perceived as similar in the present and to guide discussions in the future. Similar to Bartlett's schema, in Kitzinger's view, templates are not stable, fixed constructs. Although templates provide a structure of meaning through which to interpret present events, they are also retrospectively reframed by the present; as Kitzinger puts it, "osmosis occurs in both directions" (69). Kitzinger focuses on the narratives constructed in news media, but Andrew Hoskins (2004) suggests that images operate in a similar fashion. For Hoskins, certain images function as "visual prompts" that are "instantly and widely recognizable as representing a particular event or moment in history" (2004, 6). Hoskins calls these images "flash-frames" and argues that they are used routinely by television news networks to impose meaning on current events as well as to suggest potential future outcomes based on those of the past (37). Both Kitzinger and Hoskins are concerned with examining specific points of intersection between templates and events—incidents of suspected child abuse in Kitzinger's case and the Vietnam War and the two wars in Iraq in Hoskins'. They do not examine in any great detail how such templates might evolve over time or how or why they might travel across different media forms. The concepts of premediation and remediation offer insight into the temporal dimension of templates, as well as an explanation of how they flow across various media.

In Richard Grusin's (2004) original conceptualization of the term, "premediation" is identified as the consequence of an intense desire to avoid repeating the shock of the extreme immediacy produced in American media by the events of September 11, 2001. According to Grusin, the "logic" of premediation attempts to establish that the "future, like the past, is a reality that has always already been mediated" (2004, 29). From this perspective, premediation can be understood as a deliberate attempt to create media templates *before* they are needed, thereby creating reassuring frameworks that can be applied to future events, neutralizing their potential impact for social and cultural disruption. Astrid Erll, on the other hand, extends the notion of premediation to apply to all "existing media circulating in a given context [that] provide schemata for future experience" whether by design or not (2011, 141). While Grusin, Kitzinger, and Hoskins all concentrate on contemporary news media, Erll's interpretation of premediation is not limited to a specific time frame, nor is it restricted to one form of media.

Either as an attempt to forestall the shock of future events or as preexisting representations circulating across media, premediation, in the form of identifiable templates, is tangible evidence of the system of memory in operation, as well as a starting point for understanding that the past does not simply give way to the needs of the present.

Because representations of specific events are not restricted to one particular medium, there can be no premediation without remediation. If the former is useful in illuminating the temporal dimension of the system of memory, the latter brings out the significance of intermedial dynamics in the operation of the system. Bolter and Grusin's (2000) model of remediation refers not only to the appropriation of the characteristics of one medium by another but also to the repurposing of content across various media. Drawing on Pierre Nora's idea of *lieux de memoire*, Erll explains the significance of remediation to memory by suggesting that the persistent repurposing of events or narratives across a range of media contributes to the formulation of powerful "sites of memory" (2011, 141). In Erll's view, remediation stabilizes narratives and/or icons of the past and solidifies them within memory. Erll's example of one such site of memory is Richard Drew's photograph of the "Falling Man" from the events of September 11, 2001, an image remediated across print media, film, and television but also premediated, according to Erll, by Biblical associations with the fall of man and of the angels (141–142). Erll's idea of sites of memory bears some similarities, therefore, to the idea of media templates in that both refer to specific moments that resonate within memory and become recurring points of reference across various media. However, it seems to me that neither concept does quite enough to explain the dynamic development of larger structures of meaning or how sites of memory or media templates might be situated in relation to them. Erll identifies "9/11" as a "global site of memory" (141), for example, but does not explain how the "Falling Man" relates to this larger collection of narratives and icons. I propose that the distribution (or diffusion, to borrow a term from Hoskins [forthcoming]) and recategorization of content across media in the processes of premediation and remediation facilitate the formation of transmedia mnemonic structures that are significantly larger and both more volatile and more complex than media templates. Indeed, such structures may well contain templates but are not necessarily entirely comprised of them.

For example, World War II is far too large and complex a set of events to be considered a media template, yet representations of specific moments in the war coalesce within the larger framework to form media templates. Similar to the mathematical concept of the fractal, repeating patterns can be discerned at both the macro level of the structure but are also evident in the micro level of the templates. The Japanese attack on Pearl Harbor on December 7, 1941, for instance, operates as a powerful template for moments of crisis in American history, calling up a narrative of a righteous nation losing its innocence due to the devious and treacherous actions of others (a topic covered in more detail in the next chapter). Pearl Harbor proved a useful template in the rhetoric following September 11, 2001, as a means of generating support for political decisions by framing them within a familiar (and therefore reassuring) narrative of war as the only way to "defend freedom, secure civilization, and ensure the survival of our American way of life," as President George Bush put it in the National Pearl Harbor Remembrance Day Proclamation of December 7, 2001. Pearl Harbor functions very much as Kitzinger (2000) describes media templates by providing a shorthand for ideological perspectives used to frame present events. However, the use of this template also draws on the wider structure of World War II in order to suggest potential outcomes for the future, in this case by suggesting that the war can have no other result than unequivocal, total victory. Furthermore, concentrating only on its incarnation in news media ignores how the attack on Pearl Harbor has been remediated through films such as *Tora! Tora! Tora!* (Kinji Fukasaku, Toshio Masuda, Richard Fleischer, 1970) and the more recent *Pearl Harbor* (Michael Bay, 2001) and overlooks what each remediation might have contributed both to this specific template and to the broader structure of World War II. Furthermore, one of the most effective ways of relating templates to wider transmedia structures and of understanding the dynamism of their continual evolution is to examine not only the key texts that circulate within them but also the proliferation of paratextual networks that accrue around specific texts. Knowledge of the broader mnemonic structure of World War II is therefore essential in understanding how a template like Pearl Harbor accrues meaning and premediates future wars. Just as World War II premediates future wars, it is itself premediated by the structure of World War I, which in turn is premediated by the American Civil War and earlier wars. Transmedia mnemonic structures are thus intrinsically connected to other, similar structures. In mnemonic structures, each mediation is a remediation of past representations, as well as a potential premediation of future representations.

Elaborate intertextual and transmedial structures like that of World War II are, in effect, what Erll (2011) identifies as media of memory and memory of media. They are media of memory because individuals and institutions consider them as having a mnemonic function, in some cases—as will become clear in the chapters dealing with film and television in particular—operating as memorials in their own right. But they also make visible the memory *of* media through the ongoing reconstitution of elements of previous representations. To paraphrase Renate Lachmann (2008), the memory of a medium exists within the intertextuality of its references.[6] Mnemonic structures are constituted of networks of interrelated and repurposed material and therefore carry within them the memory of previous representations. The term "structure" should not, however, imply stability. Contrary to Erll's (2011) notion that the repeated repurposing of specific events "solidifies" them within memory, approaching memory as a procedural system reveals that mnemonic structures are extremely mutable and constantly evolving.

Nor should the term be taken as suggestive of deliberate design. Mnemonic structures such as World War II are generally embedded within the system to the extent that their underlying patterns become invisible because they are simply taken for granted. Part of the impetus for this book is to reveal the implications of repurposing the material of mediated memory and the meanings we take for granted in the configurations that emerge through remediation and premediation. One of the most effective ways of exploring the processes through which mnemonic structures are formed is through the concept of generational mediascapes. I move on now to a discussion of generations and to an explanation of how this concept is linked to both memory and media.

GENERATIONS

Like memory, "generation" is a slippery and multivalent term. Even at its most basic level, it has two applications. First, it may be used to differentiate between age groups within families, establishing the biological succession from grandparents to parents to children, and so on. But it is also applied to chronological population clusters determined by date of birth within set time frames, usually (but not always) arranged by decade. As Judith Burnett points out, these two vectors intersect, giving us a position in both the "kinship system and the cohort system, simultaneously" (2010, 2). Our position in both systems determines temporally defined stations within societal structures: whether we are required to attend school, for example, or the kind of health care we are entitled to receive. Some of the key analysis of generations therefore stems from sociological approaches, which cannot be discussed without some reference to Karl Mannheim. Mannheim's central contribution to the understanding of generations is that they are not determined through biological progression or even by copresence in the same historical location. In Mannheim's (1952) model, generations develop a distinct identity through their reactions to moments of social upheaval and transformation, especially if these occur during that generation's formative years, which Mannheim only vaguely identifies as the late teenage years or early adulthood. Uncoupled from biological time and from historical time, "subjectively experienceable time" becomes an ambiguous and potentially problematic indicator of contemporaneity for generations in Mannheim's approach (1952, 282). Mannheim's generations are thus defined and united by a rather mysterious "intuitive understanding" of coevality created by individual reactions to shared events and by "collective" memories of those experiences (282).

It is possibly due to the difficulties of identifying subjective time that subsequent approaches to generations in the social sciences and also in psychology tend toward either lifecourse or cohort analysis, as Judith Burnett points out (2010, 41–58), while the concept of generations remains largely in the popular sphere. Lifecourse analysis focuses on the family as a social unit and examines its connection to wider social systems as individuals move through different stages of life, but it is also an approach that draws on both sociology and psychology for an understanding of the development of the individual within social and cultural contexts (Burnett 2010, 42–43). Cohort analysis evolved from Mannheim's concept of generational "units"—smaller groups within generations that develop unique and self-conscious responses to shared historical challenges (1952, 307). The idea that groups developed shared identities in response to events occurring during their younger years presents the possibility of organizing research around easily classifiable populations at clearly identifiable and chronological points in time, as opposed to the difficulties involved in establishing group identities through perceptions of "subjective time." Cohort analysis is a pervasive approach that can be found in many spheres—from popular literature to the corporate world and commercial marketing.[7] Perhaps because of the different applications of cohort analysis, there is very little agreement in this particular field as to nomenclature or as to the dates that define population groups.[8] The identification of historical incidents regarded as key to that group's characteristics is similarly varied, although events on the scale of world wars are generally accepted as defining moments. Such discrepancies from study to study lend weight to Judith Burnett's description of the cohort as "a creature of the researcher" ultimately defined by the purpose of the study (2010, 47). Although most researchers in the field are aware of the dangers of homogenization in assigning blanket psychographic tendencies to a group, cohort analysis struggles to accommodate individual agency.[9] Cohort analysis also presents a rather narrow view of groups defined solely by their materially based historical situation and does not account for other factors that might lead to group individuation, including broader social and cultural influences. Although individual development is the focus of lifecourse studies, lifecourse in turn does not explain how generations gather momentum and self-awareness as massive population groups. Neither approach seems able to account for the persistence of the concept of generations in popular culture, where labels such as the Baby Boomers, the Greatest Generation, Millennials, and terms such as the "generation gap" circulate widely enough to be generally recognized.[10] Both lifecourse and cohort analysis thus struggle to account for the development of generational labels and also do not do enough to explain how generations become differentiated.

The perspective of generations as suggested by Mannheim emphasizes the significance of both individual agency and "cultural data" (1952, 294). Even if Mannheim is a little vague about the specifics of what constitutes "cultural data," he is clear that such material is essential not only to the formation of generations but also to perpetuating and communicating that generation's attitudes and ideas (305). The significance of cultural discourse surfaces again in the work of June Edmunds and Bryan Turner, who suggest that a generation gains momentum first by "constituting itself as a cultural identity" and second by successfully transmitting and maintaining a unique set of responses to historical events (2001, 7). Judith Burnett in turn distinguishes generations from cohorts at least in part because of the former's ability to produce large-scale "symbolic systems," such as "music, imagery, artefacts etc." (2010, 48, table 3.1). Like Edmunds and Turner, Burnett attributes a generation's ability to gain momentum and self-actualization to such "debris," her term for the cultural resources used and produced by a generation (48, table 3.1). However, neither Edmunds and Turner nor Burnett specify exactly how cultural material relates to generations or explain the processes through which "symbolic systems" express and transmit generational identity.

In contrast, Sofia Aboim and Pedro Vasconcelos suggest that the concept of generations *is itself a product* of the "dominant cultural narratives produced in a given time-space location" (2014, 175). Michel Foucault's (1969) identification of "discursive formations" is central to Aboim and Vasconcelos's approach to generations. Discursive formations are interconnected sets of "statements" concerned with the same topic or theme, which are frequently articulated through systems of knowledge and power and which shape the understanding and interpretation of information relating to that topic (Foucault 1969). Drawing on Foucault, Aboim and Vasconcelos describe generations as "more or less established systems of meaning designed to characterize specific historical locations and to interpret the voices of those living in particular times and spaces" (2014, 117). Whereas Foucault's approach emphasizes how meaning is generated through systems of discourse and is not concerned with interpretations at the level of the individual, Aboim and Vasconcelos consider the deployment of the cultural narratives that describe a generation's historical location as well as the ways in which individuals position themselves in response to those narratives as essential in the formulation of generations as a construct.

The conceptualization of generations as constructs articulated by and through cultural discourse avoids the difficulties involved in attempting to agree on fixed temporal boundaries for population groups, as well as the problems inherent in trying to reconcile historical time with "subjective time." Understanding generations as cultural structures allows for a far more dynamic perspective not only of the ways in which a generation's identity might be established but also of how that identity might shift over time. The ideas and narratives that feed into generational identity originate from a myriad of sources across social, political, and cultural institutions, extending, like memory, through time and across a range of media. Generations are therefore transmedia structures whose producers, according to Aboim and Vasconcelos, are multiple and who may or may not include members of the generation being labeled or identified (2014, 176). There is no doubt that moments of change or upheaval that occur as a generation's constructed identity is emerging are important, but approaches that focus on these moments alone do not explain instances where later formulations of generational identity prove so compelling that they challenge the ideations of youth. The generation for which World War II was a defining set of events, for example, has since been identified through labels such as the GI Generation (Howe and Strauss 1991, 32, figure 1–1) and the Vets (Zemke, Raines, and Filipczak 2000, 3). These labels demonstrate how the experiences of a minority, in this case of the soldiers who fought in World War II, are retrospectively identified as those who define the entire population. Regardless of whether or not individuals agree or identify with them, generational labels such as these are part of the discursive framework that describes a generation, and, as such, they reveal the ideological underpinnings of what Aboim and Vasconcelos refer to as the "apparatus of knowledge" that produces them (2014, 177). It is therefore vitally important to understand which concepts and narratives gain momentum in contributing to the construction of generational identity because these do not necessarily correspond to the entire spectrum of events or interpretations that could be selected from any given sociohistorical context (Aboim and Vasconcelos 2014, 177). The ideological implications of using the soldier to identify a generation will become clear as this book progresses, but it provides an indication here of how the system of memory might overlap with that of generations by illustrating how specific elements of historical events acquire significance in cultural discourse, while others do not. As will also become clear, the process by means of which some elements of the past endure and others do not is not quite as simple as remembering and forgetting but involves ongoing practices of selection and rejection.

Defining moments thus remain significant for the cultural construction of generational identity, but the individual's encounter with the discursive network that develops around those events is perhaps even more important because such networks mobilize a set of narratives and ideas that individuals negotiate in order to formulate an understanding of their location within history and of their place within the structure of generations. Contradictory and competing ideas of generational identity operating simultaneously within a culture may be selected or rejected on an individual level, but individuals cannot do otherwise than position themselves in relation to those discourses describing their particular historical location. As already established, the circulation and recategorization of narratives, images, and beliefs associated with historical events create transmedia mnemonic structures. Transmedia mnemonic structures are therefore a vital part of the discursive network that contributes to the cultural construction of generational ideologies and attitudes because the mediation and remediation of historical moments create a set of references that are subsequently accepted or rejected on an individual level. Generations are thus constituted both through cultural systems of knowledge and memory and through the individual's "selective and flexible" identification with them (Aboim and Vasconcelos 2014, 177). The generations examined within this book are therefore not considered as age cohorts, nor are they considered as communities united by an undefined yet implicit "collective" memory that shapes a common set of characteristics. Instead, each generation is understood as Aboim and Vasconcelos describe it: as a "relatively coherent corpus of meaning that immediately identifies a given era" (Aboim and Vasconcelos 2014, 177). Transmedia mnemonic structures are an integral part of the "corpus of meaning" that describes historical events and therefore operate at the intersection of the system of memory and the system of generations. The concept of generations in turn provides a useful framework through which to consider the evolution of transmedia mnemonic structures through different historical eras.

It is precisely because the generation shaped by World War II, the Baby Boomers, and the current generation are distinctly powerful structures articulated by cultural discourse and stretching across social, political, and economic spheres that I have selected these three generations as the focus of this book. This is not to suggest that other generations—my own generation, Generation X, for example—do not have a discursive presence. However, although it is difficult, if not impossible, to quantify exactly the amount of cultural material spread across all spheres in the wake of the World War II generation and the Baby Boomers, the accumulated weight of this "debris," to use Burnett's term, suggests that both generations are particularly impactful cultural constructs, and the current generation appears to be evolving in a similar fashion. As constructs of cultural systems, generations are intimately related to the media technologies, industries, and texts that produce the discourse defining them. Significant changes have occurred in the mediascape of each of these three generations, and these changes have in turn shaped the concept of generations as well as the evolution of transmedia mnemonic structures. I will explore some of these changes in more detail in the next chapter, but before we move on, I want to clarify my use of the term "mediascape."

Martijn de Waal argues that, whereas the idea of a mediated "landscape" is a "metaphor that conjures up a static image, ecology does justice to the notion of a system that is in a state of flux" (2007, 22). In this book, the term "mediascape" is intended not as a metaphor of landscape but as a concept that evokes a wide view of all media in operation at any temporal and physical location within the development of a generation's constructed identity. The concept of mediascape should not indicate stasis or stability, but neither does it quite call up the constant localized change that is the focus of media ecologies. The mediascape is subject to changes as a result of new technologies and practices—the introduction of television, for example, to the Baby Boomers' mediascape or of digital media to that of the current generation—and these may well be dramatic, but the term itself suggests that such changes must always be considered within a broader context in which older forms of media continue to operate. The introduction of new technologies does not in any way result in the segregation of the mediascape, which continues to function as a totality. Just as the mediascape contains both old and new forms of media, it also encompasses all the flotsam and jetsam that survive from past generations, as well as the output of the present. Old and new texts are in constant interaction, and as we have seen, sometimes accrue around specific historical events, such as wars or moments of social upheaval, to create complex and continually evolving intertextual and transmedial structures. The development of transmedia mnemonic structures is part of what identifies a generational mediascape, and the mediascape itself functions as the operational setting for the system of memory.

CONCLUSION

Understanding memory as a procedural system in which media are intrinsically involved allows us to move beyond the debates concerning the "loss" of the past through its mediation. Such an approach also avoids the problems involved in attempting to establish definitions for various "kinds" of memory—collective, cultural, social, individual, and so on—and the impossibilities of setting boundaries between them. Instead, this book focuses on the intermedial and diachronic dimensions of memory as a process. As both Marita Sturken (1997) and Alison Landsberg (2004) remind us, although it is important to consider the commercial imperatives of mass media industries, they are only one aspect of the significant role that mass media play in the processes of memory. More recently, advocates of media ecologies argue for a holistic approach to memory that moves away from focusing on individual mass media and that accounts for evolving relationships among culture, society, and individuals within an increasingly profligate network of media industries, technologies, and products. Approaches that draw on media ecologies are particularly useful in understanding the dynamic relationships between elements involved in the process of memory making, but systems theory in turn draws out the procedural nature of memory. Adopting one of the key principles of systems theory—namely, that memory is a procedural phenomenon in which data is not stored but continuously categorized and reformulated—facilitates a fluid understanding of how past, present, and future combine in the process of memory making. The remediation and premediation of representations of the past make visible the temporal and intermedial nature of the system of memory. The constant processing, reprocessing, and even preprocessing of cultural data related to specific events across media and through time give rise to intricate and continually evolving transmedia mnemonic structures. Because they are connected to specific historical events such as wars or moments of social turbulence, transmedia mnemonic structures have significance for the concept of generations. Understood as structures of meaning created through systems of cultural discourse, generations overlap with transmedia mnemonic structures because a generation, like memory, is in part shaped by the narratives, images, and belief systems that accrue around moments in history. Individuals encounter transmedia mnemonic structures as part of a constant negotiation with the discursive networks that feed into the perspective of the individual's historical location in both time and place, as well as relationships with members of both his/her generation and with other generations. Generations therefore offer an "integrative perspective," as Jürgen Ruelecke (2008, 121) calls it, of the system of memory and of all its constitutive elements.

This book considers World War II as a transmedia, transgenerational mnemonic structure. Its focus is on how World War II is configured within the current generation's mediascape, but to fully understand how the structure is organized today, it is necessary to examine its foundations in the media of previous generations. The next chapter identifies and outlines three features of the transmedia construct of World War II—the citizen soldier, the war as a visual construct, and the idea of the "good war"—and traces their development across the mediascape of the wartime generation and the Baby Boomers.

NOTES

1. For an excellent overview of the history of memory studies, see Erll (2011).
2. For an overview of some of the key approaches, see Burnett (2010).
3. Patrick Hutton (1987) provides a thorough analysis of the *ars memoriae*.
4. Both Hoskins (forthcoming) and Erll (2011) discuss the significance of metaphors to memory studies in more detail.
5. For a detailed analysis of Warburg's work, see Johnson (2012).
6. Original reads, "The memory of the text is formed by the intertextuality of its references" (Lachmann 2008, 304).
7. Neil Howe and William Strauss, for example, have produced a number of popular books claiming to predict trends in generational development by using cohort analysis. For a representative examples, see Howe and Strauss (1991 and 2000). For an example of the use of cohort analysis in the workplace, see Zemke, Raines, and Filipczak (2000). And for an exploration of cohorts and marketing, see Meredith, Schewe, and Karlovich (2002).
8. In only the three studies mentioned in note 7, for example, the generational cohort for whom World War II was a defining experience is referred to as the GI Generation and classified as those born between 1901 and 1924 (Howe and Strauss 1991, 32, figure1–1), the Vets, born between 1922 and 1942 (Zemke, Raines and Filipczak 2000, 3), and the World War II cohort, born between 1922 and 1927 (Meredith, Schewe and Karlovich 2002, 16, table 1.2).
9. For a good summary of the problem of homogenization and how key studies have dealt with it, see Reeves and Oh (2008).
10. Carolyn Kitch (2003) offers a useful overview on the development of some of these terms and of generations as a concept in one branch of the popular press, that is, American newsmagazines.

REFERENCES

Aboim, Sofia, and Pedro Vasconcelos. 2014. "From Political to Social Generations: A Critical Reappraisal of Mannheim's Classical Approach." *European Journal of Social Theory* 17, no. 2 (originally published online November 21, 2013): 165–183. DOI: 10.1177/1368431013509681

Assman, Jan. 1995. "Collective Memory and Cultural Identity." John Czaplicka, trans. *New German Critique* 65 (Spring–Summer): 125–133. www.jstor.org/stable/488538

Bartlett, Frederick. [1932] 1955. *Remembering: A Study in Experimental and Social Psychology*. Cambridge: Cambridge University Press.

Baudrillard, Jean. 1997. "Paroxysm: The End of the Millennium or the Countdown." *Economy and Society* 26 (November): 447–455. Accessed November 7, 2011. www.egs.edu/faculty/jean-baudrillard/articles/paroxysm-the-end-of-the-millennium-or-the-countdown/

Bolter, Jay David, and Richard Grusin. 2000. *Remediation: Understanding New Media*. Cambridge, MA: MIT Press.

Bowker, Geoffrey C. 2008. *Memory Practices in the Sciences (Inside Technology)*. Cambridge, MA: MIT Press.

Burnett, Judith. 2010. *Generations: The Time Machine in Theory and Practice*. Farnham, UK, and Burlington, VT: Ashgate.

Bush, George W. 2001. "National Pearl Harbor Remembrance Day Proclamation." Proclamation Archives, The White House, December 7. Accessed June 16, 2014. http://georgewbush-whitehouse.archives.gov/news/releases/2001/12/20011207-2.html

De Waal, Martijn. 2007. "From Media Landscape to Media Ecology: The Cultural Implications of Web 2.0." *Open 2007. The Rise of the Informal Media*, no. 13: 20–33. Accessed September 17, 2014. www.skor.nl/_files/Files/OPEN13_P20–33.pdf

Edmunds, June, and Bryan Turner. 2001. *Generations, Culture and Society*. Buckingham: Open University Press.

Erll, Astrid. 2011. *Memory in Culture*. Basingstoke: Palgrave MacMillan.

Esposito, Elena. 2008. "Social Forgetting: A Systems-Theory Approach." In *Cultural Memory Studies: An International and Interdisciplinary Handbook*, Astrid Erll and Ansgar Nünning, eds.: 180–189. Berlin: Walter de Gruyter.

Foucault, Michel. [1969] 1972. *The Archaeology of Knowledge and the Discourse on Language*. A. M. Sheridan Smith, trans. New York: Pantheon.

Fuller, Matthew. 2005. *Media Ecologies: Materialist Energies in Art and Technoculture*. Cambridge, MA: MIT Press.

Goddard, Michael. 2011. "Towards an Archaeology of Media Ecologies: 'Media Ecology', Political Subjectivation and Free Radios." *The Fibreculture Journal* 17. Accessed September 17, 2014. http://seventeen.fibreculturejournal.org/fcj-114-towards-an-archaeology-of-media-ecologies-%E2%80%98media-ecology%E2%80%99-political-subjectivation-and-free-radios/#1

Grusin, Richard. 2004. "Premediation." *Criticism* 46, no. 1 (Winter): 17–39. DOI: 10.1353/crt.2004.0030

Halbwachs, Maurice. [1952] 1992. *On Collective Memory*. Translated by Lewis A. Caser. Chicago: University of Chicago Press.

Hoskins, Andrew. 2004. *Televising War: From Vietnam to Iraq*. London and New York: Continuum International Publishing Group.

Hoskins, Andrew. 2011. "7/7 and Connective Memory: Interactional Trajectories of Remembering in Post-Scarcity Culture." *Memory Studies* 4, no. 3. (July): 269–280.

Hoskins, Andrew. Forthcoming. *iMemory: Why the Past Is All Over*. Cambridge, MA: MIT Press.

Howe, Neil, and William Strauss. 1991. *Generations: The History of America's Future, 1584 to 2069*. New York: William Morrow and Company.

Howe, Neil, and William Strauss. 2000. *Millennials Rising: The Next Great Generation*, New York: Vintage Books.

Hutton, Patrick. 1987. "The Art of Memory Reconceived: From Rhetoric to Psychoanalysis." *Journal of the History of Ideas* 48, no. 3 (July–September): 371–392. www.history.ucsb.edu/faculty/marcuse/classes/201/articles/87HuttonArtMemory ReconceivedJnlHistIdeas.pdf

Johnson, Christopher D. 2012. *Memory, Metaphor, and Aby Warburg's Atlas of Images.* Ithaca, NY: Cornell University Press.

Kitch, Carolyn. 2003. "Generational Identity and Memory in American Newsmagazines." *Journalism* 4, no. 2: 85–202. DOI: 10.1177/146488490342003

Kitzinger, Jenny. 2000. "Media Templates: Patterns of Association and the (Re)construction of Meaning over Time." *Media, Culture, & Society* 22: 61–84. DOI: 10.1177/016344300022001004

Lachmann, Renate. 2008. "Mnemonic and Intertextual Aspects of Literature." In *Cultural Memory Studies: An International and Interdisciplinary Handbook.* Astrid Erll and Ansgar Nünning, eds.: 301–310. Berlin: Walter de Gruyter.

Landsberg, Alison. 2004. *Prosthetic Memory.* New York: Columbia University Press.

Mannheim, Karl. 1952. "The Problem of Generations." In *Essays on the Sociology of Knowledge.* Paul Kecskemeti, ed.: 276–322. New York: Oxford University Press.

McLuhan, Marshal. 1964. *Understanding Media: The Extensions of Man.* New York: New American Library.

McQuire, Scott. 1998. *Visions of Modernity.* London: Sage.

Meredith, Geoffrey, Charles Schewe, and Janice Karlovich. 2002. *Defining Markets, Defining Moments: America's 7 Generational Cohorts, Their Shared Experiences, and Why Businesses Should Care.* New York: Hungry Minds.

Nora, Pierre. 1996. *Realms of Memory: Conflicts and Divisions.* Vol. 1. Lawrence D. Kritzman, ed. Arthur Goldhammer, trans. New York: Columbia University Press.

Olick, Jeffrey K. 1999. "Collective Memory. The Two Cultures." *Sociological Theory* 17, no. 3. (November): 333–348. www.jstor.org/stable/370189

Plato. 1938. *Phaedrus, Ion, Gorgias and Symposium, with Passages from the Republic and Laws.* Lane Cooper, trans. London: Oxford University Press.

Postman, Neil. 1970. "The Reformed English Curriculum." In *High School 1980: The Shape of the Future in American Secondary Education.* A. C. Eurich, ed.: 160–168. Quoted in "What Is Media Ecology?" Neil Postman. Media Ecology Association. Accessed September 17, 2014. www.media-ecology.org/media_ecol ogy/index.html

Reeves, Thomas, and Eunjung Oh. 2008. "Generational Differences." In *Handbook of Research on Educational Communications and Technology,* 3rd ed. J. Michael Spector, M. David Merrill, Jeroen van Merriënboer, and Marcy P. Driscoll, eds.: 295–303. New York: Taylor & Francis e-library.

Reulecke, Jürgen. 2008. "Generations/Generationality, Generativity, and Memory." In *Media and Cultural Memory: An International and Interdisciplinary Handbook,* Astrid Erll and Ansgar Nünning, eds.: 119–125. Berlin and New York: Walter de Gruyter.

Sturken, Marita. 1997. *Tangled Memories: The Vietnam War, the AIDS epidemic and the Politics of Remembering.* Berkeley: University of California Press.

Schwartz, Barry. 1990. "The Reconstruction of Abraham Lincoln." In *Collective Remembering,* David Middleton and Derek Edwards, eds.: 81–107. London: Sage.

Van Dijck, José. 2007. *Mediated Memories in the Digital Age.* Stanford, CA: Stanford University Press.

Zemke, Ron, Claire Raines, and Bob Filipczak. 2000. *Generations at Work: Managing the Clash of Veterans, Boomers, Xers, and Nexters in Your Workplace.* New York: Amacom.

2 World War II as a Transmedia Structure

INTRODUCTION: A CHARISMATIC EPOCH

According to Barry Schwartz, (1982, 390), a "charismatic epoch is not a fixed entity which imposes itself on the present; it is a continuously evolving product of social definition." As a series of events, World War II has obvious historical importance, but it is also a "charismatic epoch"—a set of circumstances and experiences that resonates across media and through time in a process of continual evaluation of past, present, and future. This chapter examines the formulation of World War II as a transmedia mnemonic structure that extends across the mediascape of two generations: the wartime generation and the Baby Boomers. As established in the previous chapter, transmedia mnemonic constructs are formed by the accumulation and subsequent reformulation of mediated material related to specific historical events. The material produced by one generation continues to circulate within such structures for each successive generation to encounter, preserve, challenge, reconstitute, or even ignore to serve the purposes and needs of their own times. As will become apparent, however, some of this material exerts pressures of its own as it is remediated in the present. This chapter is concerned with outlining three key features of the mnemonic structure of World War II—the citizen soldier, the "good war," and the visual construction of the war. Although the citizen soldier can be considered as a sign or symbolic structure, as established previously, focusing only on recurring symbols or topoi offers a limited understanding of the overall form and nature of transmedia structures. This chapter therefore also explores the ideological concept of the "good war" as a defining quality of the transmedia structure, as well as the visual construction of the conflict as an element that reveals how the structure responds to changes in media technologies and industries. All three elements demonstrate how the memory of World War II has evolved as a structure in the American mediascape of the last two decades and provide a basis for the case studies examined in this book.

Recent theories of media and memory emphasize the ubiquity of media in the current mediascape, but the media that shaped the memory of World War II, although perhaps not quite as pervasive, were part of a system that had complexities of its own. The qualities of the mediascape into which the construct of World War II first emerged contributed to the formation of the structure and are therefore worth examining briefly before moving on to the discussion of the three key elements. The conflict coincided with the burgeoning of various mass media technologies that became an integral part of the experience of the war itself. Throughout the war years, according to Philip Beidler (1998, 8), manufacturing the American experience of the war as "information and entertainment" involved all media from the start of the war to its end and was as crucial as any other facet of the industries mobilized for the war effort. The Roosevelt administration promoted the conflict as a fight for democratic inclusiveness and individual freedoms against the forces of fascism and imperialism. A unified national response was of paramount importance in achieving success in the war, and despite the fact that in reality American society was fractured by divisions of class, gender, race, and ethnicity and was even divided in its opinion of what the war was actually about, wartime media consistently positioned their audience as united in a common purpose throughout the conflict.[1] The diversity of American society was depicted in most wartime media as a source of strength rather than potential friction. This is not to suggest, however, that the media spoke with "one voice," as World War II veteran Paul Fussell later wrote (1990, 180) or that the impact of mediated messages was measurable and uniformly predictable. On the contrary, Vincent Casaregola (2009, 39) describes American wartime media as distinctly "polyphonic," particularly when contrasted with the strictly controlled media regimes of fascist Germany or imperialist Japan. There is no doubt, however, that the ways in which the American wartime generation encountered the war through media industries, technologies, and products shaped the ways in which the conflict was understood and eventually remembered.

Although diversity was an undeniable characteristic of the American public, audiences for radio and also for film cut across economic, cultural, and regional differences. Gerd Horten describes radio as the "primary medium" for a generation of Americans who "could not imagine their lives without their radio sets any more than later generations could imagine theirs without television" (2002, 2). Radio played a major role in generating that sense of national community so vital to the Roosevelt administration's war strategy, to the extent that Horten describes it as a "centrifugal force" (3). Half of the entire population of America tuned in together to Roosevelt's regular Fireside Chats (Schatz 2006, 148). Long before television, radio brought the sounds of war into living rooms around America, often with the unprecedented immediacy of live broadcasts, creating an intimate connection between the secure spaces of home and the spaces of war. Edward R. Murrow is perhaps the most well-known of the reporters who brought the war home to America, broadcasting live and at considerable risk from the rooftops of London during the Blitz before the US involvement in the war and reporting on the horrors of the Buchenwald camp toward the end of the conflict. Despite its undeniable importance as a source of news, radio also performed more functions than any other medium of the time, providing entertainment, advertising, special interest programming, sports, music, comedy, and drama (Horten 2002, 1–2). Partially due to the prominence of radio, Paul Fussell suggests that spoken language "mediated and authenticated" World War II to the extent that the war years are "a special moment in the history of human sensibility, for in those pre-television days the imagination was obliged to fill in the missing visual dimension" (1990, 180–181).

Those on the American home front who could not see the war live nevertheless did not have to rely solely on their imaginations to furnish images of the conflict. On the contrary, Susan Moeller (1989, xii) argues that, of all media, "it is photography that transports war into the safety and intimacy of our living rooms; it is photography that brings war home." Photojournalism grew alongside the war, and many of the photographs that contributed to the war's visual dimension became enduring iconic images that provide focal points for generational memory. One such image, Joe Rosenthal's photograph of the raising of the Stars and Stripes on the island of Iwo Jima on February 23, 1945, is explored in more detail in the next chapter. World War II also coincided with technological developments in both printing and photography, including the development of cheaper machine-coated paper and lightweight cameras, making it both possible and affordable to publish high-quality photographs weekly (Moeller 1989, 221). The year 1936 saw the launch of two magazines that would transform the way photographs were used in journalism: *Life*, by publisher Henry Luce, and *Look*, by Garner Cowles Jr. Whereas news magazines such as *Newsweek* and Luce's other publication, *Time*, used images to illustrate articles, *Life* and *Look* began to rely on photographs rather than on text to create "photo-essays." Having already claimed the twentieth century as the "American Century" (Luce 1941), it was almost inevitable that Luce would also claim World War II as "America's war" (Luce 1942). *Life* situated itself, in the words of publisher Roy Larson in his own letter to subscribers published in the "Letters to the Publisher" section in the magazine's January 26 edition (1942, 2), as responsible for "recording for the American people what may well prove to be the most crucial era in the history of the world." Reader responses to Larson's letter about *Life*'s expected role in World War II indicate an acceptance both of the magazine and of photography's supposed ability to record and preserve history. As one wrote in a letter to the publisher in the same issue, "we vision your magazine *Life* as a vast modern museum, far greater than any museum yet built" (January 26, 1942, 2). World War II certainly boosted *Life* magazine's circulation figures, transforming it into the "kind of journalistic *succès fou* that television was eventually to become" (Moeller 1989, 219).

Despite its mass circulation, *Life*'s readership did not, however, come close to the audience for film. More than ninety million Americans went to the cinema every week during the war years, increasing admissions by around 33 percent (Winkler 2000, 40). Perhaps even more importantly, cinema during these years offered what George Roeder (1993, 4) terms a "communal viewing experience," which he argues is unique to the World War II era because it attracted a larger and more diverse audience than either before or since the war. Both the diversity of the audience and exhibition practices made the experience of cinema distinctive for the wartime generation. For example, in acknowledgment of changes to working hours as a result of the mobilization of war production, many cinemas stayed open twenty-four hours (Birdwell 1999, 173). Thomas Schatz (2006, 148–149) points out that cinemas additionally served a number of different purposes: as venues for war bond drives, as community centers, as collection points for materials considered essential for the war effort, and some even as the venue for scheduled radio broadcasts of Roosevelt's Fireside Chats, facilitating a communal listening experience. In terms of the films themselves, if there had been some resistance on the part of the film industry to openly advocate interventionism in the years preceding America's involvement in the conflict, Hollywood committed itself wholeheartedly to the war after the Japanese attack on Pearl Harbor (December 7, 1941).

World War II was widely referred to as the people's war at the time, but Bernard Dick (1985, 173) argues that the impression gained from Hollywood films of the 1940s is that the "people who mattered—were women." Given that the majority of men between the ages of eighteen and thirty signed up to serve their country (Mettler 2005, 26), it is understandable that the percentage of women in home front cinema audiences increased. Hollywood may well have recognized this shift in demographics, but to suggest that films of this time catered predominantly to a female audience oversimplifies the situation. Working in cooperation with the government, the film industry set up distribution centers across the war's various fronts for servicemen and by 1945, ten million personnel per week attended film showings in makeshift theaters around the world (Schatz 2006, 149). The industry had to meet the requirements of not only home front and war front audiences but also of an increasingly profitable British market, while simultaneously navigating a variety of governmental and internal agencies all with their own agendas and occasionally conflicting demands on content. Furthermore, the industry's own commercial imperatives could not be overlooked. More than fourteen hundred feature films were produced by the major studios between 1941 and 1945, and although the presence of the war permeates almost all of these in some form, only around twenty-five to thirty depict armed forces actively engaged in combat, and most of these involve ground forces in the Pacific (Slocum 2006, 5). As will become evident, the representations of World War II in subsequent generations have not only shifted attention from the Pacific war to the war in Europe but also have also framed the two theaters differently. The relative scarcity of films dealing directly with combat is an indication of the diversity of experiences that make up a total war, yet the soldier's experience of battle proved to be the most enduring in subsequent representations of World War II. The ways in which the soldier's experiences of conflict have become privileged in subsequent representations of World War II will be explored in greater detail both later in this chapter and throughout the case studies.

Of all the wartime generation's media, film in particular has been the focus of a great deal of scholarship and is frequently privileged as playing a pivotal role in providing the metaphorical models that both reflected and shaped wartime national identity. Film was undeniably an essential part of the wartime generation's mediascape, but it is important to recognize that it was nevertheless one component of a complex and interrelated system of media that worked in combination to shape the memories of the conflict. As Philip Beidler (1998, 16) points out, World War II was the last war to generate a significant amount of combat art, cartoons, and posters, all of which augmented the war's visual dimension. Newsreels, while a normal part of the program in most theaters, also attracted enough interest to sustain their own dedicated cinemas, twenty-one of which were in operation across the US by late 1941 (Schatz 2006, 149). Although not quite as up-to-date as other news media, newsreels provided the wartime generation with moving images to supplement radio's live broadcasts and the print media's photographs. World War II was thus mediated through both words and images, and it also developed its own soundtrack through a burgeoning music industry largely supported by radio. Music reflects the emotional landscape of the war, from the optimism of *Boogie Woogie Bugle Boy* (1941, written by Don Raye and Hughie Price and sung by the Andrews Sisters) and *Ac-Cent-Tchu-Ate the Positive* (1944, written by Johnny Mercer), to the melancholy longing of *White Christmas* (1941, sung by Bing Crosby and written by Irving Berlin) and *Every Time We Say Goodbye* (1944, composed by Cole Porter). The ability of various media to "bring the war home" is of specific importance to the US because the vast majority of the wartime generation experienced the conflict indirectly. The experience and memory of the various forms of media at work in the wartime generation's mediascape is therefore integral to the experience and memory of the war itself.

The massive amount of mediated material generated by American media during the war constitutes a particularly imposing and complex transmedia structure. The initial manifestation of the transmedia structure of World War II in American media is an essential part of the identification of the conflict as a distinctive "epoch in history of which Americans could be proud for endless generations" (Luce 1942, 86). The following sections explore the three key components that emerge within the structure of World War II memory in the wartime generation's media and are reformulated in that of the Baby Boomers. Although for the sake of clarity I discuss each element individually, it will become apparent that they overlap in significant ways. Because transmedia mnemonic structures are in a constant state of flux, and their components are continually premediated and remediated, it will also become apparent that the citizen soldier, the visual composition of the war and the idea of the "good war" do not evolve neatly or in a linear fashion. These sections are concerned with outlining the shape of each component as it evolves and are therefore not in any way intended as an exhaustive survey of representations of World War II in either generation's media. It is, of course, impossible to give an account of every instance of premediation and/ or remediation, and it is important to bear in mind that contradictory and competing representations of all three elements are in circulation within the structure at any given time. As established in the previous chapter, the existence of transmedia mnemonic structures like that of World War II does not presuppose a uniform acceptance or understanding of the construct by individuals. Instead, transmedia structures should be understood as discursive networks that the individual negotiates as part of the process of memory making. With these caveats in mind, we begin with the citizen soldier.

THE CITIZEN SOLDIER

Of course, the symbol of the soldier is much older than World War II. The soldier has been remediated and recycled in epic poetry, painting, and sculpture. Industrial technologies of media shifted the perspective of the soldier, just as industrial technologies of warfare changed the role played by soldiers on the battlefield. Photographs and films of the American Civil War (1861–1865), the Spanish–American War (1898), and World War I (1914–1918) undermined notions of the glories of war for the soldier and instead shifted attention onto the suffering and devastation caused by mechanized warfare. World War II, however, as Leo Braudy (2005, 478) notes, was the conflict that profoundly altered the status and perception of the common soldier. In *The Story of G.I. Joe* (William Wellman, 1945), war correspondent Ernie Pyle (played by Burgess Meredith), in a voice-over, gives names and backstories to the otherwise anonymous soldiers trudging past him on a dusty road in Tunisia:

> Joe McClowski, who mixed sodas in a corner drug store. And Harry Fletcher, who just hung out his law shingle. Danny Goodman who checked your oil in the summer and studied medicine in the fall. And here they are, guns in their hands, facing a deadly enemy in a strange and faraway land. This was their baptism of fire.

Pyle's speech exposes the nature of a military comprised of "boys" who abandoned varied but ordinary lives in America to face a "baptism of fire" fighting a war far from home.

More Americans (around 12 percent of the total population) were involved in military service in World War II than in any other war in US history, either before or since.[2] The US military was comprised of citizens who became soldiers in the expectation that once the war was over, they would revert to their civilian status. In other words, this was a military mostly made up of average American "Joes," as much a product of the war industry as the equipment and weaponry stamped with the words "Government Issue" (GI). The term itself reflects a wry recognition of, and resistance to, the process of subsuming the citizen's individuality into the mass conformity of military life. Being a GI was therefore, according to Edgar Jones (1946), a "point of view, not a military classification." More than at any other time, either before or since, the military closely reflected the ethnic and racial makeup of American society, although the percentage of white Americans was slightly higher in proportion to that of whites in the general population (Mettler 2005, 29). More women served in the armed forces in World War II than in any previous conflict, but they constituted only 2 percent of the total (Mettler 2005, 144). The experiences of the GIs, or "boys" as they were commonly referred to at the time, became characterized as the ones that define the remaining 88 percent of their generation, and the citizen soldier persists as one of the central organizing principles within the mnemonic structure of World War II.

The citizen soldier is of central importance to the wartime structure of World War II primarily because of its use as a lynchpin around which notions of cooperation and sacrifice could be mobilized. Shaping the soldier into a figure of national unity was part of a deliberate strategy adopted by the Office of War Information (OWI) to reconcile the obvious inequalities of race and gender in American society with the Roosevelt administration's vision of a cohesive nation in which all had equal responsibilities in facing the challenges of war. Formed in June 1942, the OWI was tasked with the responsibility of making certain that all branches of the media produced a consistent response to the conflict and with ensuring that the American people be "truthfully informed about the common war," as the *New York Times* (June 14, 1942) reported. Although radio and print media were important, it was believed at the time that film could play a powerful but never clearly defined role in influencing the general public's perception of the war. The public, according to the *Government Information Manual for the Motion Picture Industry*, a manual produced by the OWI for the film industry, would take its cues on how to behave during wartime from "what they see on the screen" (quoted in Locke 2008, 12). It therefore fell to Hollywood to remodel the figure of the soldier to reflect the administration's emphasis on sacrifice and solidarity (Westwell 2006, 31).

The solitary hero of previous wars was replaced by the military unit, with members drawn from every ethnicity and class, all working together to achieve the same objective. The ethnically mixed military patrol, squad, or platoon is a motif repeated so frequently in films made about the conflict that Jeanine Basinger ([1986] 2003, 56) considers it one of the defining elements of what she identifies as the World War II combat genre. Cooperation between the military and the civilian population is a major theme in *Wake Island* (John Farrow, 1942), the first film to be based on an actual incident in the fighting and one of the earliest to show US citizens engaged in combat. The emphasis on cooperation and unity continues throughout the combat films made during the war, from *Guadalcanal Diary* (Lewis Sieler, 1943) and *Bataan* (Tay Garnett, 1943), to films made toward the end of the conflict like *The Story of G.I. Joe* and Lewis Milestone's *A Walk in the Sun* (1945), which reflect in greater detail the cost of the war on US soldiers. The soldier is transformed in these films from the lone maverick in search of adventure and derring-do, who featured in prewar films such as *A Yank in the R.A.F.* (Henry King, 1941), to a member of a group united by a common purpose strong enough to overcome but not eradicate individual differences and disagreements. The sacrifice made by the soldiers in these films, some of which end in death and defeat, was a poignant reminder to civilian citizens on the home front not only to work together but also to undergo such hardships as were necessary without complaint for the sake of the common good.

Despite the ethnic mix of the military unit, the fact remained that the US military considered only certain citizens worthy of fighting in active combat. The segregation of African Americans within the military and racial tension on the home front presented a challenge to the idea of a war being waged in the name of democracy and individual rights. This was a problem for the OWI, inasmuch as the Roosevelt administration showed little inclination to secure equal rights for African Americans (Locke 2008, 4). The OWI settled on a subtle approach to promoting different ethnicities and developed guidelines for the avoidance of racial stereotypes (Koppes 1995, 33). Racial minorities were consequently underrepresented in wartime media in general, although there are a few exceptions in Hollywood films. *Bataan* is the most notable of these. Despite the fact that African Americans were excluded from active combat, *Bataan* goes beyond OWI guidelines to show Epps (played by Kenneth Spencer), fighting alongside members of his squad. Producer Dore Schary received a number of critical letters from the public because of Epps's participation in fighting the Japanese in the film, suggesting that for some members of the wartime generation at least, there were limits to the ideas of cooperation and unity (Suid 2002, 69). Despite the occasional acknowledgment of the involvement of different races in the conflict, the citizen soldier of the wartime generation's transmedia structure of World War II is most definitely white.

As a representative of the general population, the citizen soldier was the average boy next door, but he was called on to do extraordinary things. The transition from everyday life to fighting on the front lines reflected broader concerns involved in the nation's transition from peace to war and was consequently the focus of many wartime films. Robert Taylor, for example, as Sergeant Bill Dane in *Bataan*, questions whether his squad can make the transition from "jerking sodas, or selling shoes, or punching adding machines" to soldiers. The Marines of *Guadalcanal Diary* were once "high school athletes, grocers, clerks, taxi-drivers," and *The Story of G.I. Joe* connects the soldiers trudging through the dust of a "strange and faraway land" to the boys who may once have poured sodas or checked the oil for the civilian audience watching the film. As Leo Braudy puts it, the very ordinariness of the citizen soldier connected the "local world to the national effort—the uncommon common man called from his home to fight for his country" (2005, 478). The contradiction of the "uncommon common man" is perfectly illustrated by the representation of the soldier in wartime films. With the Hollywood star system still a powerful factor in the film industry, well-known actors played soldiers in war films and, along with the trappings of military life, gave the boys next door a glamour they could not aspire to as ordinary citizens. Despite, or perhaps because of his ordinariness, the citizen soldier retained an element of heroism.

One member of the wartime generation provides some idea of the persuasive power of the citizen soldier as an element of the transmedia structure of World War II in an admission that she married a man despite numerous warnings that he was an unsavory character because, as a soldier, "He could not be anything but a marvelous, magnificent human being" (interview in Terkel 1985, 118). Unfortunately, her trust was misplaced, and the marriage ended in disaster, but her story attests to the compelling nature of the construct of the citizen soldier in wartime cultural discourse. As we shall see later, the transformation from average American to warrior mirrors the national narrative of the US as an essentially peaceful and honorable country forced into conflict by the violent and treacherous actions of others (Casaregola 2009, 33).

The wartime citizen soldier was an emblem of national unity, sacrifice, and heroism but was also representative of American idiosyncrasy. The armies of the Japanese and Germans were similarly drawn from ordinary civilians, and wartime media therefore had to distinguish between the US soldier and the citizen soldiers of other armies. Pauline Kael observes that in wartime films the enemy could "never be people, who were just caught in the army the same way Americans were and told what to do" (interview in Terkel 1985, 123). In a process Marianna Torgovnick describes as "othering," the enemy soldier in wartime representations was a "stereotype, a mass, an abstraction" characterized by mindless fanaticism on the part of the Japanese or by fascist elitism on the part of the Germans (2005, 9). In contrast, as the term "GI" itself suggests, US soldiers demonstrated resistance to the military system and were "fertile with insult and cynicism," according to veteran Paul Fussell (1989). These are, after all, the same soldiers who came up with acronyms like SNAFU (situation normal, all f****d up) and FUBAR (f****d up beyond all recognition) to describe their circumstances. The Production Code prohibited profanities of this kind in Hollywood, but the quirky, occasionally dark humor of the GI in juxtaposition with the rigid hierarchies of military life and the stresses of war nevertheless became an established method of establishing the individuality of the citizen soldier in wartime films.

Although film is undoubtedly an important medium in the construction of the citizen soldier, the tension between the individuality of the GI and the restrictions of military life is most evident in the work of cartoonists. Perhaps the most well-known of these is Bill Mauldin's *Willie and Joe* series. Mauldin, who served in the army, is sharply critical of its commanding officers in his satirical depictions of two disgruntled and frequently disheveled GIs. *Willie and Joe* was immensely popular with both the soldiers and the public, and by 1945 *Time* magazine (June 18) reported that the strip was appearing in 138 newspapers, as well as in the army's *Stars and Stripes*. Mauldin's work (for which he won two Pulitzers) challenged the optimistic tone of newsreels and newspapers to show Willie and Joe struggling with the elements and the unrealistic expectations of both the home front and commanding officers, as much as with the war itself (Huebner 2008, 39). *Willie and Joe* provides an example of how the necessity for self-abnegation in the citizen soldier was balanced against the celebration of individualism as a core principle of American national identity in the wartime construct of World War II. Yet despite their dislike of orders and military hierarchy, the citizen soldier continued to wage war honorably, and there are almost no suggestions of atrocities or even misdemeanors being committed in any wartime media, an omission that takes on particular significance in the construction of the concept of World War II as a "good war."

The citizen soldier represents members of all branches of the military, but the troops on the ground, like Mauldin's Willie and Joe, seemed to capture what war correspondent Ernie Pyle ([1943] 2004, 246) referred to as the "worm's eye view" of the conflict. In the final years of World War II, citizen soldiers in films such as *The Story of G.I. Joe* and in Pyle's own dispatches were represented as "tired and dirty soldiers who are alive and don't want to die" but who retained the ability to laugh at themselves and at their situation (Pyle [1943] 2004, 246–247). Despite the persistence of self-deprecating humor and cynicism in the overall structure, the impact of the war on the soldier surfaced as an increasing concern in media in general. Pyle, for example, wrote that "[o]ur men can't make this change from normal civilians into warriors and remain the same people," but the changes he outlines include a tendency toward obscene language and a possible anathema to foreign travel in the future, not to severe difficulties in adjusting to civilian life (241). Pyle's outlook is consistent with OWI directives to reassure the civilian population that their soldiers could make the transition back to practicing law or checking oil with very little trouble once the war was over. Yet Pyle's dispatches, cartoons such as *Willie and Joe*, and the films made toward the end of the war contain traces of an aspect of the citizen soldier that would become much more pronounced as the structure developed within the next generation's media—the idea of the surviving soldier as a victim of war.

As an essential component of the transmedia structure of World War II, the citizen soldier is present in some form or another across wartime media and is a complex and multifaceted cultural construct. However, the central qualities that define the citizen soldier as the structure of World War II circulates into the next generation's media can be summarized as follows. The citizen soldier of the wartime transmedia construct of World War II is a symbol of both national unity and individualism. He is white and male. Self-sacrifice is integral to the citizen soldier, but so too is humor, often of a dark and cynical kind. Despite a resistance to authority, the wartime citizen soldier wages war honorably, no matter what his background or wartime experience, and is a defender of freedom and a liberator of the oppressed. Changing ideas of warfare, along with shifts in attitudes toward citizenship, government, and the military that surface in the transmedia structures of Cold War conflicts, affected the construct of the World War II citizen soldier and remediated it in a disjointed process that reflects the conflicted attitudes to warfare in the general discourse that defines the Baby Boomer generation. One of the most vital alterations to the fundamental makeup of the citizen soldier evident throughout the process of reformulation, however, is a shift away from the idea of war as a necessary collective enterprise to that of war as a damaging and individual masculine endeavor.

The roots of an increasing focus on the soldier as the primary victim of war can be traced back to the aftermath of World War II. As Andrew Huebner (2008, 276) notes, the novels and films of the postwar years "increasingly took the suffering of the individual . . . as their primary narrative focus." As the US struggled with the largest demobilization in its history, popular novels, films, and the press indicate that the transitions from citizen to soldier and back again were, at times, fraught with complications. The memoirs and novels of veterans such as Norman Mailer's *The Naked and the Dead* (1948) and James Jones's *From Here to Eternity* ([1951] 1998) portrayed GIs who bore little resemblance to the optimistic and righteous citizen soldier in the media of the war years. Films such as William Wyler's *Best Years of Our Lives* (1946) show the challenges faced by returning veterans, including alcoholism and disability, but Wyler's film ends optimistically and implies that veterans can eventually become productive citizens once again. There are hints of darker concerns regarding the impact of the war on the male psyche in the stylized crime dramas of postwar *film noir*. As Richard Maltby (1984, 67) points out, a narrative feature common to the *noir* films of the immediate postwar period is one in which the protagonist, frequently a veteran with an undisclosed and murky past, has to account for his actions and follows a "trajectory either towards recuperation or death." Described by Maltby as "the unstable occupant of a paranoid world," the disturbed psyche of the individual becomes the "controlling perception" of *noir* and draws the viewer in to the viewpoint of the damaged veteran looking out at a broken life (67–68).

In an example of how transmedia mnemonic structures intersect and overlap, representations of the Korean War and later of the conflict in Vietnam considerably reinforced the idea of the soldier as the damaged victim of conflict and resulted in a retrospective remodeling of the mediated construct of the World War II citizen soldier to reflect this perspective. Partially as a result of the influence of the transmedia structures of both Korea and Vietnam, the World War II citizen soldier in the mediascape of the Baby Boomers is an unsettled construct rife with contradiction. In the transmedia mnemonic structure of the Korean War, the connections between the soldier and the ideologies of the political and military institutions that produced him are severed (Huebner 2008, 134). As Lieutenant Benson (Robert Ryan) says in *Men in War* (Anthony Mann, 1957), "Battalion doesn't exist. Regiment doesn't exist. Command HQ doesn't exist. The USA doesn't exist. We're the only ones left to fight this war." The photographs of the Korean War reflect similar themes of isolation and despair. According to George Roeder, photographs or depictions of soldiers crying during World War II were extremely rare, kept out of sight by both "censorship and customary practice" (1993, 124). Yet one of the most iconic photographs to emerge from the Korean conflict is that taken by photographer David Douglas Duncan of corporal machine gunner Leonard Hayworth, who had lost all but two of his squad and was out of ammunition, with tears streaming down his face. The photo-essay in *Life* magazine (1950, September 18) in which Hayworth's photograph appears emphasizes the struggle of the US Marines against not just the enemy but also against the elements, failing equipment, and a lack of logistical support. While films of World War II show squads that are in desperate situations, as in *Bataan*, they generally work together despite internal differences. In contrast, the military units in films of the Korean conflict are fractured by violent disagreements. *Men in War* and Sam Fuller's *The Steel Helmet* (1951) demonstrate a breakdown in military discipline that also results in atrocities. A prisoner is used as bait in *Men in War*, while in *The Steel Helmet*, another is ruthlessly murdered. The soldiers of the Korean transmedia mnemonic construct are characterized as brutalized by war and abandoned by the systems meant to support them.

Partially due to the influence of representations of Korea but also due to the impact of the memories of World War II veterans as they were translated into memoires, novels, and films, the association in the World War II mnemonic structure between the citizen soldier and ideas of national solidarity began to unravel. For the first time, the possibility that the US citizen soldier might not always have behaved in an exemplary fashion crept into the transmedia structure of World War II. The film adaptation of James Jones's novel, *From Here to Eternity* (Fred Zinnemann, 1953), for example, features sadistic commanding officers and internal conflict that ends in death for a number of the soldiers before the war even begins. The theme of the breakdown of military unity is also evident in *Attack!* (Robert Aldrich, 1956). The theatrical trailer for *Attack!* declares that the film tells the story "every soldier knew, but none would dare tell." *Attack!* deals with the controversial subject of how soldiers occasionally dealt with incompetent superior officers in the field, long before the term or the concept of "fragging" became familiar from the Vietnam war.[3] *From Here to Eternity* and *Attack!* complicate the idea of the World War II citizen soldier as a heroic figure, and representations of the war in Korea, as well as the recollections of World War II veterans themselves, cast doubt on the military's support of the soldier in World War II. However, one film produced shortly after World War II ended left an imprint on the citizen soldier influential enough to resist challenges to heroism in the structure, at least until the Vietnam War made this film's particular brand of military heroism difficult to sustain.

Alan Dwan's *The Sands of Iwo Jima* (1949), revisits the theme of transformation from citizen to soldier and unites it with the idea of war as a testing ground for individual masculinity. Despite the claim made in an interview for the *New York Times* by the film's associate producer Edward Grainger that there are "no heroics" in the film and that it "show[s] the heroism of the average American as he readjusted from civilian life to the war" (interview in Goodman 1949), Sergeant Bill Stryker (John Wayne) is the undisputed hero of the film. Most well-known for playing rugged frontiersmen and lawmen operating on the edges of civilization, Wayne's star persona introduces a new layer of intertextuality to the citizen soldier. Wayne's portrayal of Stryker knits the qualities of the resolutely unyielding Western individualist, for whom violence is second nature, to those of the citizen soldier. The tension evident in wartime depictions of the citizen soldier as the uncommon common man is eradicated in the figure of Stryker, a larger-than-life hero whose primary identity is that of a forceful but troubled warrior most at home on the battlefield. As the title implies, the battle for the island of Iwo Jima is pivotal in the film, but the moment for which this battle was renowned in the US—Joe Rosenthal's iconic photograph of a group of Marines raising the Stars and Stripes on Mt. Suribachi—plays out in the background and is not as significant as Stryker's death. René Gagnon, Ira Hayes, and John Bradley, the three flag raisers who survived the war, make an appearance in the film, but their presence as actual citizen soldiers and veterans of the conflict is effectively overwhelmed by Wayne's persona. According to Vincent Casaregola, Wayne's portrayal of Stryker similarly replaced the "everyday faces of fathers and uncles who had actually fought in the war" to become the "face" of the World War II soldier for the next generation (2009, 5).

A large body of evidence supports Casaregola's claim and suggests that Wayne's impact on the cultural construct of World War II should not be underestimated. Wayne figures prominently and repeatedly in the accounts of the soldiers who fought in Vietnam.[4] Many attest to buying into what one soldier refers to as the promotion of the Vietnam conflict as "a John Wayne test of manhood," while another admits to being "seduced by World War II and John Wayne movies" (quoted in Baker 2002, 24 and 12). The confluence between national and martial identities in the citizen soldier has an ideal representative in Wayne, who became an enduring "symbol of the American fighting man, the defender of the nation" (Suid 2002, 129). Although the depiction of heroism in *Sands of Iwo Jima* is more complex than the accounts of the Vietnam veterans imply—Stryker is a troubled veteran who takes risks only when he absolutely has to and who tells his recruits to "[l] et the other guy die for his country. You'll live for yours"—more important for the memory of the citizen soldier is the shift in emphasis away from the ideological reasons for America's involvement in World War II and onto the portrayal of war as a proving ground for masculinity—a schism between soldier and war in the transmedia structure of World War II that would be widened even further as a result of the influence of the discourse related to the Vietnam war.

If World War II entered American living rooms via radio and news magazines, the Vietnam conflict is irrevocably associated with the new medium in the mediascape of the Baby Boomers: television. The prominence of the Vietnam War on television screens is one potential reason why Hollywood avoided making films about the conflict while it was in progress, although the public dissent associated with the US involvement in Vietnam potentially provides another.[5] Yet the same medium that carried nightly news of the war in Vietnam was also responsible for the ongoing circulation of World War II films made during previous decades, including *The Sands of Iwo Jima*, which had a positive impact on recruitment to the US Marine Corps every time it aired (Suid 2002, 123). Television thus facilitated the flow of cultural material from the wartime generation's mediascape into that of the Baby Boomers, but at the same time, the new medium also remediated the construct of World War II and the citizen soldier in drama series like *Combat!* (ABC, 1962–1967), *The Gallant Men* (ABC, 1962–1963), and *Twelve O'Clock High* (ABC, 1964–1967). *Combat!* is the longest running World War II drama in television history. The series maintains the basic framework of the citizen soldier as established in the mediascape of World War II, but the soldier is also retrospectively remodeled according to the affordances of the medium to reflect some of the concerns and issues arising as a result of the Vietnam War.

Combat! follows a single infantry squad on its missions through Europe after D-Day. The series shows the same worm's-eye perspective of the war as Ernie Pyle's dispatches or Mauldin's *Willie and Joe*, but the expanded nature of televisual narratives (*Combat!* ran for five seasons for a total of 152 hours of television) allows for the inclusion of an array of characters such as resistance fighters, orphaned children, and deserters from both sides in situations that demonstrate how the cost of total war is borne not only by soldiers but also by civilians. The series covers a wide range of complex and controversial issues more usually associated with the Cold War conflicts of Korea and Vietnam than with World War II, such as the fragging of superior officers ("Beneath the Ashes," series 3:2), the difficulties and ambiguities of dealing with civilians who may be enemy informants ("The Little Jewel," series 2:9), and pointless military orders ("Hills Are for Heroes," series 4:25 and 26). The squad meets these situations with a mix of desperation and dark humor familiar from the wartime transmedia construct of the conflict. Whereas the central unit works together and demonstrates the necessities and benefits of cooperation among individuals in order to achieve patriotic goals, *Combat!* departs from the previous generation's representation of World War II soldiers in that it also includes individuals who are cowardly, disorganized, ineffective, and recalcitrant.

The uncomfortable possibility that US soldiers could be less than heroic and, more disturbingly, capable of committing atrocities was a truth that had been already acknowledged in the literature and films of the Korean War but that proved impossible to ignore in Vietnam. Andrew Huebner (2008) argues, however, that the recognition of the terrible damage that soldiers could inflict on civilians, in events such as the massacre of villagers at My Lai, was tempered by the portrayal of the perpetrators as victims of the institutions that sent them there.[6] John Wayne's stamp of recalcitrant individualism on the citizen soldier is therefore challenged by the perspective of the soldier as a helpless cog in the machine of war, brutalized not only by the conflict itself but also by the government and military institutions that trained him to fight and gave him his orders. The idea of the citizen soldier as an anonymous and insignificant component of war is, of course, not restricted to the discourse surrounding Vietnam and can also be seen in the worm's-eye view of the media of World War II. However, the discourse surrounding the Vietnam War intensified the notion of the soldier as the primary victim of conflict.

A series of big-budget, large-scale, epic films set in World War II produced during the 1960s and 1970s abandoned the worm's-eye view completely in favor of a bigger picture of war on an industrial scale but reinforced the notion of the citizen soldier as a mere cog in the machine of war. In sharp contrast to the intimate, detailed portraits of soldiers drawn in *Combat!*, the epic World War II films such as *The Longest Day* (Ken Annakin, Andrew Marton, and Bernhard Wicki, 1960), which features John Wayne as just one member of an extremely large cast of stars, *The Battle of the Bulge* (Ken Annakin, 1965), and *Tora! Tora! Tora!* (Richard Fleischer, 1970) show the citizen soldier as one of a range of resources to be used up on the industrial battlefield. According to James Jones (1963), who worked on the script of *The Longest Day*, the scale of the film is precisely the point in that it demonstrates how industrialized warfare renders "basic human character" extraneous. I will explore the transition in focus in these films from the experiences of the soldier onto the spectacle of war in more detail in the section on the war as a visual construct, but the individualism of the citizen soldier ultimately resisted erasure in the transmedia structure of World War II, although it is recalibrated in the wake of the conflicts in Korea and Vietnam into something more cynical and overtly antagonistic in the group Jeanine Basinger calls the "war-is-hell-but-dammed-exciting" films ([1986] 2003, 183).

Two of these, *The Dirty Dozen* (Robert Aldrich,1967) and *Kelly's Heroes* (Brian G. Hutton, 1970) foreshadow the way in which World War II will be treated in the computer and video games of the next generation in that war is the setting for excitement and adventure rather than trauma. In these films, the uncomfortable relationship between the individuality of the US citizen and the restrictions of military life, once a source of humor in the wartime construct of World War II, develops into outright aggression and resistance, a reflection of the solider as victim not only of war but also of the institutions that perpetrate conflict. Fighting dirty in these films is a strategic necessity, and the soldier battles the military system as much as he battles the enemy. The cooperation of the military unit, a prominent feature of the wartime transmedia construct of World War II, becomes transformed into what Basinger refers to as "unholy teamwork" ([1986] 2003, 183). *The Dirty Dozen* subverts the process of transition from citizens to soldiers by featuring instead the transformation of criminals into soldiers and anti-heroes. In *Kelly's Heroes*, the war is chaotic and disorganized, and soldiers are at risk as much from their own forces as from the enemy. Friendly fire, a subject almost untouched within the wartime transmedia structure of the conflict, features prominently in *Kelly's Heroes*. In sharp contrast to the moral certainty evident throughout wartime media, Telly Savalas (as Master Sergeant Big Joe) could be talking for the soldiers in the Vietnam conflict when he remarks in *Kelly's Heroes* that "We're just soldiers, right? We don't even know what this war's all about. We fight and we die and we get nothing out of it."

As it cycles through the mediascape of the Baby Boomers, the citizen soldier is an unstable figure in transition. Self-sacrifice and cooperation, so central to the citizen soldier's makeup in the World War II generation's media, are abandoned in favor of an increased focus on the individual and his response to war. The citizen soldier of the Baby Boomers' transmedia structure of World War II is often involved in violent disagreements with members of the same squad and in subversive acts that undermine the authority of officers and of the military itself. In the Baby Boomer's mediascape, the citizen soldier is brutalized not only by war but also by the forces that send him out to fight. As a result, although the Baby Boomer's construct of the citizen soldier acknowledges, albeit fleetingly, the possibility of atrocities committed by GIs in World War II, the soldier is presented as both the perpetrator *and* victim of these atrocities. The citizen soldier in the Baby Boomer's mediascape is therefore simultaneously a cog in a machine *and* a heroic figure battling forces beyond his control. Through all the contradictions, however, the citizen soldier of the Baby Boomer's transmedia construct of World War II remains war's primary victim.

In the 1990s, however, as part of the wave of commemoration to mark the fiftieth anniversaries of various events in World War II, a change developed in the discourse relating to the citizen soldier. Popular histories began to reimagine the citizen soldier as part of the Greatest Generation engaged in a "good war." Journalist Tom Brokaw, who popularized the moniker in a book entitled *The Greatest Generation*, writes of a "life-changing experience" during a trip to Normandy for the fortieth anniversary of D-Day in

1984 (1998, xviii). As he looked around at the US veterans, Brokaw realized that, despite the presence of their generation in his life as he grew to adulthood, he had "failed to appreciate what they had been through and what they had accomplished" (xviii–xix). Although Brokaw's book includes interviews with a cross-section of the wartime population, he concludes by referring to the experiences of the veterans as the "essence of the American experience" of World War II (389). Brokaw describes that experience in terms that will be familiar after the examination of the citizen soldier in the wartime structure of World War II: as men going off to "fight war in distant places" before returning to the "familiar surroundings of their youth" with their ordinary lives "enriched by the values they had defended" (389). Implicit in Brokaw's work is an unfavorable comparison between subsequent generations and the Greatest Generation, and the popularity of the book provides one example of how one generation may be defined by the cultural discourse of another.

The work of historian Stephen Ambrose similarly fed into the identification of the citizen soldier as the embodiment of an entire generation. Ambrose ([1992] 2001, 312) admits that, like "many other American men my age, I have always admired—nay, stood in awe of—the GIs." Both Brokaw and Ambrose uncover facets of the structure of the citizen soldier that were temporarily obscured in the intervening decades and restore the GI to his configuration as a "marvelous" and "magnificent" human being. In the case studies, I will explore in more detail how representations of World War II toward the end of the 1990s and into the next decade continue to represent combat as the essence of the American experience of World War II and the citizen soldier as the quintessential representative of the wartime generation. As the epitome of the Greatest Generation, the citizen soldier is an intrinsic part of an ideological feature of the transmedia structure of World War II—the idea of the conflict as a "good war."

THE "GOOD WAR"

In a note to his book *The Good War*, Studs Terkel (1985) explains that this phrase came into use to distinguish World War II from "other wars." The designation of World War II as "good" could therefore occur only after the "bad" Cold War conflicts in Korea and Vietnam (Terkel 1985). Terkel gestures to the incongruity of the juxtaposition of the two words by framing them in quotation marks. Although the war was not described at the time as "good," the term reflects what Terkel refers to as a "kind of crazy truth" (15) that the conflict was enthusiastically supported by a large portion of the American population, who regarded World War II not only as a necessary war but also as a virtuous one. If World War II was a war fought by magnificent and marvelous soldiers, much of the wartime media also suggested that it was a righteous war in which good and evil were easily distinguishable and the US was on the side of the former. In the immediate aftermath of the war, veteran Edgar L. Jones (1946), vexed by the pervasiveness of the idea of honorable war, asked "what kind of war do civilians suppose we fought, anyway?" In answer to his question, the transmedia mnemonic structure of the conflict presents World War II as a "good war."

There is no question that the media in operation in the US during World War II reflected and supported the views of the Roosevelt administration. As a result, much of the material that feeds into the mediated construction of the war qualifies as "propaganda." But despite an unprecedented and unrepeated level of governmental control over media industries, propaganda in the US did not operate in the same way as that of the totalitarian regimes it opposed in the war. In contrast to the rigid control exerted on the media by Nazi Germany and Imperial Japan, in the US regulation of the media operated through an intricate combination of negotiation and cooperation among various organizations and industries, generally facilitated by voluntary compliance. For the most part, government propaganda in the US during World War II is distinguished from that of Nazi Germany or Imperial Japan by its emphasis on encouraging a positive perspective of the war.

Vincent Caseregola suggests that much of the mediated material produced during the war years consists not so much of propaganda as of the "consistent 'propagating'" of American values, virtues, and ideals drawn from preexisting cultural frameworks (2009, 38). Even before the United States' entry into the hostilities, Henry Luce (1941, 65) identified the love of freedom, the desire for equality, and the need for independence despite recognizing the necessity of cooperation as "especially American" ideals, which he argued should be incorporated into America's role as an emergent power on the world stage. Once the US entered the war, these ideals were translated into the qualities of the citizen soldier, as the symbolic representative of a united nation. President Roosevelt also envisaged extending American values to the world. In an address to Congress on January 6, 1941, Roosevelt identified four freedoms—freedom of speech, of worship, from want, and from fear—which he argued could be maintained everywhere in the world through the "moral order" of a "good society." In the wartime transmedia structure of World War II, the US is imagined as a moral and good society defending these four freedoms, which in turn are positioned as distinctly American values. Promoting a positive view of the war is thus inextricably linked to a positive view of the US.

Frank Capra's *Why We Fight* series (1942–1945) is a prime illustration of how American values were connected to the ideology of waging a righteous war. *Why We Fight* was originally conceived as a series of induction and training films for the military. In an example that demonstrates the dialectic nature of the US system of propaganda, the OWI felt that the *Why We Fight* series was one-dimensional and biased, but following President Roosevelt's enthusiastic declaration after a White House screening that "every man, woman and child" in the US should see the films, they were released to the general public (quoted in Dick 1985, 2–4). In *Why We Fight*, Capra appropriates Axis propaganda—in particular Leni Riefenstahl's techniques in *Triumph of the Will* (1935)—and subverts it. Capra undercuts the visual techniques used in *Triumph of the Will* by contrasting them with American values. Long shots of massed, synchronized armies, for example, are juxtaposed with images and a narrative that celebrates American individualism. The *Why We Fight* series draws on the American Declaration of Independence and invokes aspects of the US origin myth to imply that belief in freedom and democracy are uniquely American traits. *Why We Fight* thus implies that American national identity itself is at stake in the war.

The prevalence of a positive view of US national identity and of the war within the wartime transmedia structure does not, however, preclude the existence of contradictory positions and perspectives. Part of what distinguishes American war propaganda from that of the Axis countries was the possibility, even if rarely executed, of expressing opposition to the dominant perspective. George Roeder identifies Preston Sturges's *Hail the Conquering Hero* (1944) and Alfred Hitchcock's *Shadow of a Doubt* (1943) as films that challenged the prevailing mode of propagating the "good" side of both the war and of American culture but notes that such films were the exception rather than the rule (1993, 100). Roeder also points out that *Casablanca* (Michael Curtiz, 1942) includes sympathetic portrayals of characters who are highly mistrustful of propaganda and argues that such films "reflected public opinion as much as they shaped it" (1993, 101). *Casablanca* is therefore a reminder that the ideology evident in the transmedia structure of World War II was not universally accepted. Indeed, evidence suggests that US soldiers and the public were not only aware but also thoroughly suspicious of attempts to manipulate their point of view. Vincent Caseregola, for example, points out that historical evidence as to the effect of the *Why We Fight* series on military morale is ambiguous at best (2009, 47). From a civilian perspective of the series, Bernard Dick remembers that his own childhood reaction to the first installment in the *Why We Fight* series, *Prelude to War* (1943), was, quite simply, "ugh!," and he notes that the adult audience appeared similarly unimpressed and bored by the film (1985, 4). The same person who wholeheartedly embraced the mediated construct of the citizen soldier, as mentioned in the previous section, nevertheless goes on to observe in her interview with Studs Terkel that wartime audiences "recognized a lot of crap" in the films and advertisements of the time (1985, 120).

Because of the ability of the wartime audience to recognize "crap," what was omitted from wartime media had a greater impact than what was included. The role played by the Office of Censorship, established on December 19, 1941 just after the attack on Pearl Harbor, was therefore of equal importance to the role played by the OWI in determining how the war was constructed in wartime media. What was left out of wartime mediations of the conflict facilitated the development of what George Roeder (1995) refers to as America's "master war narrative"—the conceptualization of

America as an essentially peaceful country roused into the virtuous defense of democracy and liberty through the reprehensible actions of others. The idea of American virtue in the war could be sustained only through the omission of any mention of American transgressions. The elisions of wartime representations eventually came to define the "good war" concept as the gaps form a design feature that is relatively consistent throughout the transmedia mnemonic structure of World War II. In other words, it is primarily the absences in the mediated memory of World War II that lead to the perception that it is possible for a war to be "good."

The first set of omissions concern those actually involved in fighting the war. As mentioned in the previous section, the perception of the wartime soldier as a paradigm of US citizenship was partially maintained by avoiding the subject of atrocities. Although films such as *Guadalcanal Diary* show Marines bayoneting wounded Japanese soldiers, such behavior is rationalized through the characterization of the enemy as treacherous and dirty fighters, not only in the film itself but also throughout the media in general. In contrast, the widespread practice peculiar to GIs in the Pacific of collecting body parts as trophies scarcely features in any print media or in the films set in this theater.[7] But not only atrocities were omitted from narratives about the "boys." Any indication of GIs acting less than honorably is extremely rare. Looting, which was endemic among US soldiers in Europe, is mentioned by Ernie Pyle but in euphemistic and almost indulgent terms as a cavalier and opportunistic "disregard" for personal property ([1943] 2004, 242). Photographic evidence of more serious crimes committed by GIs, such as rapes, murders, and beatings, was routinely censored, as George Roeder (1995) notes in his extensive study of declassified images from the war. In fictional combat films, mention of GIs committing crimes was similarly uncommon. For instance, although *Bataan* includes a soldier with a dubious background, he fights alongside the others and performs his duty, albeit with an unusual measure of cynicism for a film made so early in the war. In the absence of substantial evidence to the contrary, America's citizen soldiers were represented as a disciplined and unified force in the service of a righteous and organized war.

One of the greatest challenges to the overarching narrative of America's boys engaged in the noble pursuit of a Great Crusade, as General Eisenhower referred to the war in his D-Day statement to the Allied forces in June 1944, was the fundamental ignobility of the industrialized battlefield. It is, of course, debatable whether any kind of warfare can ever be described as a noble undertaking, but mechanized warfare in particular nullifies the potential value of individual endeavor on the battlefield. An unprecedented array of weaponry deployed in World War II subjected the human body to innumerable forms of injuries and caused death on a scale unparalleled in any war that had gone before. Despite being commonly described as radio's war, World War II was more comprehensively covered by photographers and filmmakers than any previous conflict. The resulting struggles of the visual media and the US government to reconcile the brutal realities of combat footage within the country's narrative of a just war created another set of omissions that contributed to the development of what Paul Fussell would later refer to as "military romanticism"—the idea that war contains certain "desirable elements," including "the consciousness of virtue enforced by deadly weapons" (2004, xv).

The US entry into the war was marked by a series of defeats in the Pacific, including the battles for Wake Island (December 7–23, 1941) and Bataan (January–April, 1942). The government feared that if made public, details of casualties from these battles would undermine confidence in the war. Consequently, in the first year following the US involvement in the conflict, no images of dead GIs appeared in print media. Death in battle was a rarity even in the Hollywood films of this period. A study conducted by the OWI from May to November in 1942 found that only five out of sixty-one films released in that time showed Americans dying in combat (quoted in Roeder 1993, 21). One of these films, *Wake Island*, remediates the national myth of the "last stand," as exemplified by the battle of the Alamo, to reframe the defeat of its citizen soldiers through grand narratives of doomed sacrifice in American history.[8] *Wake Island* elevates the death of the citizen soldier to the level of noble and meaningful sacrifice, an inflection that recurs throughout the media's depiction of America's dead soldiers.

As the war progressed, however, the absence of death in the media proved to be one omission that was conspicuous enough to provoke the civilian population, many of whom had lost loved ones in the fighting and were all too aware of the cost of war. Elmer Davis, the director of the OWI, had from the outset declared that the American public wanted news of the war to be "brutally frank" (quoted in Roeder 1993, 10). A survey conducted by the OWI in the first year of the war appeared to vindicate Davis's perspective. The American public resented being treated "like babies," according to a report on the survey, and wanted the Censor to discard his "rose-tinted glasses" (ibid., 101). Additionally, although the difficulties of the first year of the war led to fears of public disillusionment, a series of Allied victories in 1943 paradoxically created concern that the public would grow over-confident and therefore reluctant to support the war effort (ibid., 15). The OWI warned of the possibility of strikes and dissent on the home front and advocated the release of tougher imagery (ibid., 24–25).

As a result, images of dead soldiers began to appear in media, beginning with George Strock's photograph of three Marines killed on Buna Beach in New Guinea, published in *Life* magazine on September 20, 1943. Henry Luce's editorial describes the Marines as "three units of freedom" and goes on to reassure readers that despite their deaths, freedom lives on in other American soldiers (1943, 34–35). The shift to tougher imagery was mirrored in film. After initial reluctance due to its explicit footage of dead Marines, President Roosevelt agreed to the public release of the documentary short *With the Marines at Tarawa* (US Marine Corps) early in 1944.

Featuring footage more graphic than any seen in film theaters before, *With the Marines at Tarawa* includes a series of shots of dead soldiers scattered on the beaches of Tarawa. In turn, Hollywood responded to public demand for less rosy representations as well as the OWI's call for hard-hitting narratives by producing films that increasingly reflected the cost of war on America's soldiers. *Guadalcanal Diary*, for example, includes actual combat footage of dead Marines in the surf. Despite such grim imagery, death was never presented as senseless and was always linked to the wider narrative of the war. Like *Life*'s editorial, both films mentioned here end on a note of hope, illustrating the necessity, if not the nobility, of the ultimate sacrifice made by the GIs. Thus, despite the government's initial reluctance to incorporate the cost in American lives into the administration's war narrative, by the final stages of the conflict, death had become an essential component of the story of the war and was used to galvanize the home front and to demonstrate American commitment to the war for the Allies (Roeder 1993, 25). The Roosevelt administration even inflated casualty figures in the final years of the war to this end (Giangreco 2004).

Despite Davis's assertion that the public wanted the "brutal" truth about war, at no point during the conflict did any imagery fully acknowledge the terrible violence of mechanized warfare. Restricted by the Production Code, Hollywood could do no more than suggest the extremes of brutality of the battlefield. This should be placed in context, however; Stephen Prince notes that the violence found in World War II films is more graphic than any found in any other genre of that period (Prince 2003, 154). The final combat sequence in *Bataan*, which involves garroting, beheading, and bayoneting as the squad battles a Japanese onslaught, provides a good example and is described by both Prince (2003, 161) and Jeanine Basinger (2003, 54) as one of the most vivid depictions of brutality of all Hollywood films up to the late 1960s. Yet even with an increase in the level of permissible violence, death in wartime films is neat, with the soldier's body preserved whole. Similarly, in newsreels and in print media, images of dead GIs do not reveal the faces of the soldiers, and their bodies are intact. The avoidance of grisly depictions of the dismemberment, disembowelment, and disfigurement of soldiers in wartime media is justifiable according to the parameters of what is considered culturally and morally acceptable in mediated representations of war. It is also understandable as a consequence of consideration for the families of the soldiers and because of fears that such imagery could undermine the morale of the civilian population and threaten the ongoing viability of the draft. However, there is a deeper consequence to the absence of such imagery, particularly in the US, one of the few countries in the world able to maintain a distinct division between home front and war front during the conflict. The lack of substantial evidence of the deadly effects of World War II weaponry on all but enemy soldiers in wartime media perpetuated the notion that war could be virtuous and that the US was waging an organized and disciplined war (Roeder 1995). The violent impact of weapons of war on the citizen soldier is a critical elision in the wartime transmedia construct of World War II, but the absence of any real indication of the war's impact on civilians is perhaps an even more serious and persistent omission.

That the defense of democracy and upholding the four freedoms across Europe went hand in hand with violence and chaos is a fact rarely acknowledged in the transmedia construct of World War II. Photographs and films of happy crowds of civilians, many with flowers and flags, welcoming US forces were commonplace in wartime media, but less so were images or stories of civilian deaths, particularly those of women and children, as a result of American and Allied actions. William Hitchcock examines the impact of the Allied campaign in Europe on civilians and points out that the wholesale annihilation of towns and cities in the course of the effort to oust the occupying Germans was a "consciously accepted dimension of the war of liberation" for the Allied commanders (2009, 3). Although there was some acknowledgment in wartime media of the destruction of enemy cities as a result of the controversial Allied strategy of "strategic" bombing, overall, the devastation of Europe was not a particularly well covered aspect in US media during the war. Furthermore, the profound complexities of the process of liberation, including the social and political implications of one of the largest mass displacements of populations in history across Europe and their interactions with the armies of various nations, were consistently understated throughout wartime media. The same holds true for the firebombing of Japanese cities and, more critically, for the two atomic bombs dropped on Hiroshima and Nagasaki. Photographs and dispatches detailing the damage done by the two atom bombs were suppressed in both the US and Japan. As a result, the cost of the restoration of liberty and democracy to the rest of the world never registered in any compelling way in the wartime transmedia structure of World War II, and the destructive power of World War II's weaponry lay beyond the experience of the majority of Americans.

The wartime transmedia construct of World War II consequently creates a starkly polarized perspective of war in which "good" and "evil" are clearly distinguishable. Of course, there is no question that Hitler had to be opposed and Japan's aggressive expansionism halted. That the war ended in victory and that the worst fears about the dangers of Nazi Germany's fascist regime and Japanese imperialism were confirmed in the stories of the liberation of concentration camps and the brutality of the Pacific theater served only to validate the righteousness of the victors. But it is exactly the moral certitude of World War II that also, according to Paul Fussell (1989), causes a reluctance to "probe very deeply into its murderous requirements." Many of the films and novels emerging from the postwar period suggested that war was hell for the citizen soldier, but for others in the US, the war was "a hell of a good time" as one of Terkel's interviewees describes it (1985, 573). In contrast to the large swathes of Europe and Asia that were devastated by the war, the conflict led to the recovery of the US economy and created a time of prosperity, which enhanced the perception of World War II as a war that was constructive rather than destructive. The massive amount of mediated material supporting the Great Crusade, even if punctured by crucial omissions, accumulated a momentum of its own within the transmedia construct of World War II and rolled the notion of the "good war" into the next generation's mediascape.

Vincent Casaregola suggests that for the next generation of Americans, memories of World War II were shaped not by what actually happened in the conflict but by "how it played out on screen" (2009, 106). Similarly, Jeanine Basinger points out that after the war, for both the generation that fought it and for the Baby Boomers, "the war was now war movies" ([1986] 2003, 141). An extremely cursory examination of films released during the 1950s reveals at least one hundred films, including dramas, comedies, and combat films, released during this decade with some connection to World War II, providing some credence to Casaregola and Basinger's point. These numbers decline steadily, however, through the 1960s (to around seventy) and 1970s (about twenty-five), until eventually dwindling to below ten in the 1980s.[9] But in addition to the new postwar films, wartime films continued to circulate into the next generation's media via the new medium of television. In addition, through the regular release of popular compendiums right into the 1980s, journals such as *Life* and *Time* ensured that the photographs that had helped shaped the home front's perceptions of the war continued to shape how the next generation would come to perceive it. Philip Beidler describes *Life's Picture History* (1950) as a text that is "almost invariably" cited by Baby Boomers as one of "the most prominent sources of their remembering" (1998, 66). The visual media of the wartime generation, with its blind spots intact, thus provided a compelling source of material for remediation in the next generation's media.

There are complex industrial reasons for the persistence of wartime mediated material in the Baby Boomers' mediascape, including the evolving relationship between the film and television industries that facilitated the circulation of wartime films onto television screens, as mentioned. However, there is also a political dimension to the preservation of the so-called master war narrative of World War II—the story of the US involvement in the war as both righteous and honorable—in the Baby Boomer's transmedia structure of World War II. According to William Hitchcock, the "tragedies and paradoxes" of World War II were too volatile to be sustained during the Cold War (2009, 369). Vincent Caseregola goes even further to suggest that the US master war narrative was simply folded into the Cold War argument for constant martial readiness (2009, 112). The elisions within the wartime structure of the conflict sustained the perception of the US as the honorable champion of freedom and democracy during World War II. When the war ended, those same elisions persisted because of a need to maintain the idea of the US as a country that had liberated the rest of the world from tyranny and oppression and that could therefore take its rightful place as the most powerful defender of democracy against the evils of communism.

According to Vincent Casaregola, the World War II films produced from 1949 through to the mid-1960s convey a dual message that not only celebrates the victory of World War II but also advocates military preparedness for future conflicts (2009, 134). William Wellman's *Battleground* (1949), for example, touches on some of the issues that wartime films did not engage with, such as the difficulties faced by civilians in the course of liberation, but these are couched within an overall narrative that reasserts the central tenets of the US war narrative and links these to future conflicts. In a multifaith service, the chaplain (played by Leon Ames) reassures the soldiers that the war has been "worth it" and provides a clear Cold War message for martial readiness: "[W]e must never again let any force dedicated to a super-race, or a super-idea, or super-anything, become strong enough to impose itself upon a free world. We must be smart enough and tough enough in the beginning to put out the fire before it starts spreading." A decade later, Darryl Zanuck made *The Longest Day* as a way of remembering "when our way of life is threatened" that the Allies, who once "defeated an evil because they stood together, can do so again"—a clear indication of the extension of the polarized perspective of World War II into Cold War narratives (interview in Scheuer 1962).

The Longest Day humanizes the Germans, who had become US allies in the Cold War, by implying that many of the soldiers are honorable men who are simply caught up in the machinery of war, much like the citizen soldiers of the US. Zanuck's film is part of a general trend in the transmedia structure of World War II during the Cold War to attempt to rehabilitate the Germans and the Japanese (as in *Tora! Tora! Tora!*, which depicts the Japanese military as generally orderly and honorable, with a few exceptions) and to downplay or completely ignore the role played by both the Soviet Union and the Chinese. Philip Beidler points out that the excision of Russia and China from the mediated structure of World War II continues in compendiums such as *Life's Picture History* (1950), which not only commemorate World War II but also provide a "new Cold War lens on Good War events" by omitting any photographs of Stalin or Chiang Kai-shek (1998, 74). The Baby Boomers' transmedia construct of World War II gradually obscures the Russian contribution to the war and correspondingly amplifies the role played by the US—a feature that persists in the current structure of the war and that the upcoming chapters explore in more detail.

The transformation of World War II into the "good war" in the Baby Boomers' transmedia construct of the conflict is not without challenges and contradictions. The Cold War conflicts of Korea and Vietnam caused a shift in the perception of war itself, which in turn influenced representations of World War II. Vincent Casaregola identifies *Kelly's Heroes, The Dirty Dozen*, and Cornell Wilde's *Beach Red* (1967) as examples of films that counter the "good war" narrative (2009, 182). Philip Beidler, in turn, borrows an acronym from the GIs to describe films and novels that present World War II as the "Great SNAFU" rather than the "good war" (1998,

150). Kurt Vonnegut's novel *Slaughterhouse Five* (1969), for example, features the controversial Allied firebombing of Dresden and a protagonist so disturbed by his experiences that he is literally unmoored in time and space. Mike Nichols' film *Catch 22* (1970) and Joseph Heller's (1962) novel of the same name, both capture the incomprehensible logic of military life and of war. War in *Catch 22* (both film and novel) is so chaotic and frenzied that it borders on the surreal. The dissolution of the Production Code in the film industry in 1968 paved the way for the inclusion of graphic depictions of violence in war films and thereby contributed to the portrayal of World War II as the Great SNAFU rather than the "good war." For instance, *Catch 22* includes a particularly bloody death scene as a pivotal moment in the film, during which Yossarian (Alan Arkin) inadvertently pulls open a massive wound in the side of Snowden (Jon Korkes), causing his intestines to spill out. *The Dirty Dozen* provides another example. The squad's mission ends when they trap German officers and civilian women together in a shelter and then burn them alive. As a result of the increasing cynicism evident in such films, Vincent Casaregola (2009) argues that the "good war" narrative collapsed completely during the 1970s. However, this line of reasoning does not take into account the fact that within the transmedia construct of World War II, the "good war," in the form of wartime films and imagery, existed side by side with the Great SNAFU. The "good war" ultimately proved more resilient, at least in part because of the sheer weight and continued circulation of material supporting the notion of World War II as a righteous conflict through the transmedia structure of the war.

A study conducted by Howard Schuman and Jacqueline Scott (1989) gives some indication of the endurance of the notion of World War II as a "good war." The study, conducted on eleven hundred and forty Americans eighteen years or older, tests the hypothesis that events occurring during a generation's formative years are key to structuring memories that create "cohort effects" (Schuman and Scott 1989, 379). Although the findings support the premise that such defining moments are significant, the study also raises questions it does not fully explore regarding the ways individuals process memories of events they have not directly experienced. Respondents born before and after 1945 all identify World War II as a significant event but demonstrate such major differences in their understanding of the conflict that Schuman and Scott question whether they are referring to the same war (371). Members of the wartime generation recalled World War II via autobiographical detail, whereas the majority of Baby Boomers recalled the conflict through the prism of the "good war" construct—as a polarized battle between good and evil in which the freedom of the entire world was at stake. Respondents who were Boomers thus attribute an ideological value to World War II and contrast it unfavorably with the Vietnam War (374). A large number of Baby Boomers cite loss of life as a reason for their identification of the Vietnam conflict as a noteworthy event, whereas very few Boomers give the same reason for World War II, despite its significantly higher mortality rate. The cause of the discrepancy in the evaluation of the significance of casualty figures for both wars may be explained by differences in personal experiences of loss, but it is possible that the relative scarcity of images of death of both soldiers and civilians in the wartime visual media of World War II is another contributory factor.

Schuman and Scott (1989) repeatedly attribute the source of the Boomers' perspective of World War II as a "good war" to what they might have "heard or read," and the study therefore only hints at the complex relationship between individuals and the range of media, including film, that forms the transmedia mnemonic structure of World War II. The pervasiveness of the ideological perspective of World War II as a "good war" for the Baby Boomers demonstrates that despite the undeniable presence of Great SNAFU narratives in the transmedia construct of the conflict, "good war" narratives prevail. The identification by Baby Boomer respondents of the wartime generation's world as filled with moral certainty and common purpose reflects the resilience of material within the transmedia structure that characterizes the conflict as a clear struggle between good and evil, fought by a united nation. According to the study, Baby Boomers in the study are so convinced by the unfavorable contrast between the Vietnam War, which Boomers view as divisive and morally ambiguous, and the "good war," that they yearn for the world and wars of the wartime generation. Schuman and Scott call this longing "vicarious nostalgia" (374).

Vicarious nostalgia is an increasingly evident quality in mediations of World War II of the last two decades and is particularly obvious in the work of popular historian Stephen Ambrose. Ambrose is a controversial figure who was accused of plagiarism in the final years of his career, but his work exerts a significant influence on the current transmedia construct of World War II and is particularly influential in perpetuating the notion of the "good war." One commentator describes Ambrose as "the most widely read and most identifiable historian in America" (Confessore 2001), and another acknowledges that he "has come to define [World War II] in the American mind" (Schwarz, 2001). Throughout the 1990s and into the next decade, Ambrose produced a series of best-selling books honoring the contribution of the American soldier during World War II, including *Band of Brothers* (1992), *D-Day: June 6, 1944* ([1994] 2002), *Citizen Soldiers* (1997), and *The Good Fight* (2001), a history of the conflict specifically aimed at the younger generation. Ambrose's work recalls aspects of the wartime transmedia structure of World War II but reframes it through the lens of vicarious nostalgia as the "good war."

In the prologue to *D-Day: June 6, 1944* ([1994] 2002), for example, Ambrose echoes the master war narrative's construction of the US as a nation of innocents called to war. He describes a generation of young men who "wanted to be throwing baseballs, not hand grenades" but who became the "soldiers of democracy" and the men to whom "we owe our freedom" ([1994] 2002, 26). Because most of Ambrose's work relies on interviews with veterans, it is understandable that his books focus on the experiences of US soldiers. However, by concentrating only on the soldiers' experience of war, Ambrose maintains the elisions that allow the "good war" structure to persist. While he admits to the presence of "jerks, Sad Sacks, profiteers and Jim Crow" in the US military, for the most part the GIs in Ambrose's histories are honorable defenders of freedom and democracy ([1997] 2002, 331). His books consequently underplay the difficulties endured by civilians in the process of liberation and ignore the sometimes combative relationship between US military forces and civilians during World War II (a topic explored in far more detail by Hitchcock 2009). In *Citizen Soldiers*, for example, Ambrose uncritically accepts and endorses an unnamed soldier's assertion that the sight of a squad of American GIs brought "the biggest smiles you ever saw to people's lips, and joy to their hearts" ([1997] 2002, 485). Ambrose honors the bravery and unimaginable sacrifices made by individual soldiers, but his work does not take into account the complexities of behavior during military operations and largely ignores the impact of a total war on civilians.

Ambrose's work also inflates the role played by the US as a whole in World War II. In *D-Day: June 6, 1944*, he argues for the Allied landings in Normandy as the "decisive battle" of World War II ([1994] 2002, 29). By consistently emphasizing June 6, 1944, as the pivotal battle of the war and charting an unbroken line from Normandy to Germany's surrender throughout his work, Ambrose ignores the pivotal battles of Stalingrad and Kursk and consequently maintains the blind spot in the transmedia mnemonic construct of World War II created during the Cold War that overlooks the part played by the Soviets in Hitler's eventual defeat. As one review of *The Good Fight* points out, the US was the "junior partner" in the war in comparison to the losses suffered by the USSR and the damage they inflicted on the German forces (Schwarz 2001). Ambrose's work overstates the role played by the US in overturning an undeniably reprehensible regime and consequently implies that the nation is entitled to a certain measure of moral superiority. His work reflects and sustains the memory of World War II as America's "good fight."

According to George Roeder, World War II continues to hold a "revered place" in American memory because it is one of the few "widely agreed-upon moral reference points" in times of change and diversity (1993, 3). It is the weight of material identifying World War II as a "good war" within the transmedia mnemonic construct of the war that ensures the conflict functions as a consistent moral reference point across the mediascape of the wartime generation, and that of the Baby Boomers. The gaps in the transmedia structure that make the "good war" possible are not aspects of the memory of the war which have been erased or forgotten. They are more accurately described through Marianna Torgovnick's notion of "active absences" (2005, 3). The war's devastating impact on soldiers, the numbers of civilian casualties, the damage inflicted by the Allied firebombings and by the two atomic bombs, and the role played by the Soviet Union are all examples of facts that are demonstrably accessible in the writings of veterans such as Paul Fussell and Howard Zinn and of historians such as John Erikson and Anthony Beevor, to name only a few. Information that contradicts the "good war" is thus freely available but has never significantly countered the idea of World War II as a good fight. As a good fight, World War II provides a point of comparison for subsequent conflicts. The "active absences" in the transmedia construct of World War II thus define its shape and safeguard its continuation because they ensure that the "past will have a place to loop back into the present" (Torgovnick 2005, 4). The next section explores how the development of a visual esthetic of warfare in the transmedia construct of World War II determines how the conflict is understood and recognized every time it loops back into the present.

WORLD WAR II AS A VISUAL CONSTRUCT

On November 30, 1942, *Life* magazine ran a two-page self-promotion piece entitled "There are Two Ways to Learn About War" (130–131). According to the advertisement, those who "live where the war breathes hotly in their faces have an intimate knowledge of what war means," but for the majority of Americans, World War II would be accessible only through "facts we read and hear." The American wartime generation, according to *Life*, therefore faced the difficult task of remaining resolute in the absence of enemy attacks on home soil. But in order to gain an understanding of war, they only had to turn to the magazine, which pledged to deliver in "vivid picture-story form what this war *looks* like, *feels* like, and *does to people*" (*Life* November 1942, emphasis in original). Just under two years later, in response to a photograph of the shrouded bodies of American soldiers awaiting burial in Normandy in the magazine's July 17, 1944, issue, a letter to the editor states that "pictures like this do more to wake us than bombs dropped on our cities" (6). Perhaps such a statement can be made only by someone who has never experienced an actual bombing, but it testifies to a widespread perception that visual media gave Americans on the home front powerful access to what war feels like, based on an impression of what war looks like.

Despite *Life*'s claim to a prime position in offering the US public access to the conflict, a variety of sources across visual media created what George Roeder regards as "the most intense collective visual experience in the nation's history" (1993, 62). John Chambers and David Culbert (1996, 10), in turn, argue that World War II should be understood as primarily a "visual construct" because of the pervasiveness of its visual representations. The way in which World War II was constructed visually for the wartime generation was the result of a complicated interaction of a series of factors, not least among these the guidelines established by the OWI and systems of censorship. Practices of visual representation during wartime, in turn, formed esthetic and ideological building blocks for the construction of World War II as a visual concept in the media of future generations. This section will unpack some of the elements that went into creating the look of World War II as it unfolded, before turning to the question of how wartime imagery shaped the evolution of the war as a visual construct for subsequent generations.

Practices of visual representation during the war begin with the filmmakers and photographers who documented the conflict. World War II was covered by official and unofficial civilian correspondents, photographers, and filmmakers, as well as by the combat photographers and cameramen of the specific branches of the military (Moeller 1989, 183). Nonmilitary organizations such as the American Red Cross and the Coast Guard also had photographers and filmmakers in the field. Individual cameramen and -women (Margaret Bourke-White was the first female photographer allowed on the front lines during World War II) had their agendas set by the agencies they represented. Although moments in the war were photographed or filmed for various reasons, ranging from the specific needs of intelligence gathering to unspecified notions of newsworthiness, military photographers, particularly those associated with ground forces, were instructed to make combat their priority (Maslowski 1993, 19). Both officially credited civilian correspondents and military photographers had relative freedom of movement and access to the front lines. Government policy dictated that all photographs and films, whether captured by military or civilian personnel, were pooled and made available to all agencies. Photographs and film taken by civilian correspondents could therefore be used by the War Office, and the footage captured by military photographers could be used by the civilian media. Once photographs or films were released, those in control of the production of visual media framed them in ways that connected the images to American traditions, values, and history in order to render the vast scope of the war, with its potentially bewildering spectrum of people, cultures, and places, manageable for the US public. On a very basic level, therefore, *all* wartime imagery ultimately served the war effort, regardless of why events were photographed or filmed.

Access to combat zones did not, however, guarantee that photographers and filmmakers managed to capture what Walt Whitman many years earlier called "the seething hell and the black infernal background of countless minor scenes and interiors" of mechanized warfare ([1892] 1949, 668–669). Despite advances in technologies that allowed photographers and motion picture cameramen far more mobility than their predecessors who attempted to record the American Civil War (1860s), the Spanish–American War (1898), and World War I (1914–1918), combat on the industrialized battlefield remained notoriously difficult to photograph and film. Problems facing cameramen profoundly influenced the visual construction of the war even before images reached the pool on the home front. The challenges for correspondents and military personnel alike can be condensed into three main areas.[10] First, those covering the war faced a range of transportation difficulties that were more severe for civilian correspondents than for military camera units and that hampered their ability to reach key locations. It was only after 1943 that the US military began to organize transport for civilian photographers, occasionally assigning them jeeps (Moeller 1989, 184). Correspondents in the Pacific, where the terrain of the islands and the kind of battles fought in this theater made mobility an issue, were particularly disadvantaged by the lack of transportation. Second, the nature of the fighting itself posed problems. According to a bulletin published by the US Marines in June 1945, in the Pacific, Marine combat cameramen noted that the Japanese habit of attacking by night caused them "considerable annoyance" (quoted in Maslowski 1993, 69), but the enemy in both the European and Pacific theaters were frequently invisible. Photographers and filmmakers struggled to represent the spectacle of modern warfare, not least because it posed a deadly threat to their own lives. Once they had reached the war zone, cameramen faced the same risks of combat—capture, injury, or death—as the soldiers doing the fighting.[11] Finally, although military photographers had the capability to develop stills on or near the front lines, most civilian photographs and all motion pictures had to be sent back to the home front to be developed. Arrangements therefore had to be made to transport film, both moving and still, to where it could be processed safely. Organizing the dispatch of film in a war zone was a potentially hazardous procedure, as illustrated by the loss of almost all the film shot by the army's Signal Corps units on D-Day in Normandy. The officer entrusted with the rolls dropped them into the sea while attempting to board a ship off the coast. Transport difficulties, the nature of combat, and issues of logistics all impacted how war's "seething hell" was portrayed and determined which of its minor or major scenes made it back to the home front.

Over and above these issues, the sheer scope of World War II also shaped the way it was visually constructed. The war took place in deserts, jungles, forests, mountains, cities, and seas. Differences in conditions on various fronts, particularly in Europe and in the Pacific, created definitive contrasts in imagery. Susan Moeller notes how the photographs and films of the European theater are characterized in general by a "gray, gritty look," not only because of the nature of the landscapes but also because the fighting in Europe took place mostly at dusk or dawn (1989, 237). Despite the fact that color footage exists of the war in Europe, the conflict here is predominantly associated with shaded and desaturated monochromatic tones. The bright sunlight and tightly concentrated battles of the islands in the Pacific, as Moeller points out, favored the cameraman and was more conducive to shooting in color, but even the black-and-white photographs and films shot in the Pacific have deeper contrasts and sharper outlines than those of Europe (1989, 238). In general, however, whatever the theater, black-and-white images were the norm and color the exception due to a mix of both convention and technical expediency. Color motion picture cameras were expensive and bulky, and the film required careful processing, which restricted their use for combat cameramen, particularly during the early years of the war (Maslowski 1993, 57–58). Technicolor was available to the film industry since the 1920s, but color was associated largely with the fantastic and the frivolous. In the words of Jeanine Basinger ([1986] 2003, 178–179), "color seemed to add unreality," and partially as a result, most newsreels, documentaries, newspapers, and war films were in black and white.

Robert Capa's photographs of Omaha Beach on D-Day offer a useful illustration of how all these factors combined with strategies of representation on the home front to create a particular esthetic composition of the war. As one of the accredited civilian correspondents covering the conflict, Capa landed with the 116th infantry on Omaha beach at just after 6 a.m. on June 6, 1944. The weather was bad, and the light only just favorable for taking pictures. Almost overwhelmed by the heavy artillery fire, Capa started taking photographs under conditions that made it difficult to even lift his head above the sand. He managed to shoot for over an hour before leaving the beach and hitching a ride back to the naval armada on another landing craft. In his biography of Capa, Alex Kershaw (2004, 126–130) describes in some detail the complicated route subsequently taken by Capa's films from Normandy to *Life*'s London offices, where they were developed before being transported to New York in time for the next deadline. During the course of this process, the darkroom crew inadvertently ruined all but a few out of between seventy and a hundred images of the day in their hurry to develop them.

Life's framing of Capa's photographs almost two weeks later in their photo-essay feature of D-Day in Normandy reveals some of the strategies at work in the visual media's presentation of the war. The piece (published in the June 19 issue of 1944) describes the photographs as "acutely real," reflecting an uncritical belief in the immediacy generated by the hypermediated nature of the grainy and indistinct images (30). The smeared quality of a photograph of a soldier in the surf is incorrectly attributed to Capa's "immense excitement" rather than to the developing mishap (27). The emotive language of the captions frames the battle as a thrilling experience but also reassures readers of the control and proficiency of the Allied forces. Troops "race" through "boiling surf" (26) while a landing boat cruises "easily" (28) toward shore under cover of smoke generated by Allied shelling. Another caption describes soldiers as "quietly and effectively heroic" (29). In general, the photo-essay creates the impression of an exciting but organized and efficient operation. In Capa's own words, photographs like this could show "more of the real truth of the affair to someone who was not there than the whole scene" (Steinbeck and Capa 1948, xvii). The grainy, smeared photographs, the product of a confluence of factors, form a visual synecdoche for June 6, 1944, just as D-Day in Normandy eventually came to function as a synecdoche for the entire war; both points that are covered in more detail in the next chapter. Capa's photographs of D-Day and their subsequent iconic status in the transmedia mnemonic structure of the war illustrate a belief in visual media's ability to provide access to the "truth" of war, based on associations between hypermediation (defined by Bolter and Grusin [2000, 41] as a "logic" that creates an awareness of the processes of mediation but that also reminds us of a desire to reach that which lies beyond mediation), monochromatic tones, and verisimilitude.

News media, however, formed only part of the visual construction of World War II during the war years. There is a tendency in scholarship on World War II media to discuss wartime Hollywood and news media in terms that foreground the influence of one upon the other. Peter Maslowski, for example, highlights the difficulties faced by cameramen attempting to photograph combat "so that it looked like Hollywood war" (1993, 67), while Jeanine Basinger (2003, 113) discusses the general influence of combat footage on the Hollywood war film. In the visual construction of the war, however, the relationship between factual and fictional media was one of reciprocal influence. If they were to remain credible, fiction films made about the war had to have at least some resemblance to the "acutely real" photographs and combat footage of newsprint and newsreels. The massive amount of visual material generated by World War II photographers and combat cameramen provided a valuable resource for Hollywood filmmakers. It was cheaper to use existing combat footage than to recreate it, particularly when it came to scenes involving naval maneuvers or aerial battles.[12] Footage of the battle for Iwo Jima, for example, including an aerial shot of the naval armada preparing for attack, is recycled in newsreels, Milton Sperling's documentary *To the Shores of Iwo Jima* (1945), and Allan Dwan's *The Sands of Iwo Jima*. According to Vincent Casaregola, the incorporation of combat footage into wartime fiction films gives them "an unprecedented sense of authenticity" (2009, 105). The blending of fictional and factual visual footage has a more subtle implication, however, in that it also literally transforms life into movie and war into war movie, to paraphrase Vietnam correspondent Michael Herr (1982, 58).[13]

Nowhere is the merging of the war with Hollywood war movie more evident than in the documentaries produced by directors such as John Ford, Frank Capra, John Huston, and William Wyler, who were among those in the industry who volunteered their services to the war effort. Jeanine Basinger observes that films such as Ford's *The Battle of Midway* (1943) and *December 7th* (1943), Wyler's *Memphis Belle* (1944), and Huston's *The Battle of San Pietro* (1945) all contain "their own kind of passionate storytelling" ([1986] 2003, 114). The particular kind of storytelling in evidence in these documentaries is not only representative of each director's individual directorial style but one that is also reliant on Hollywood iconography and narrative conventions (Westwell 2006, 44). *The Battle of Midway* provides a good example. The footage of the Japanese attack on

Midway captured by Ford and his assistant Jack Mackenzie Jnr. is dramatic enough for Basinger to conclude that the film "showed Americans clearly what it looked like to be in the midst of combat" (2003, 113). As with Robert Capa's subsequent images of Omaha Beach, however, the "look" of combat is based on a set of assumptions regarding the relationship between hypermediacy and realism, as well as on specific practices of representation.

Filmed in color, *The Battle of Midway* includes moments when the camera shakes as a result of an explosion or when the film itself seems to come unmoored from its sprockets or appears damaged as a result of heat. Such moments are hypermediated in that they draw attention to the nature of the medium producing them and are consequently extremely unusual in the Hollywood tradition of classical realism, which minimizes any indication of the filmmaking process. Hypermediation became a standard of war documentaries, however, to the extent that when shooting recreations of the battle of San Pietro, John Huston deliberately jolted the camera in order to mimic the percussion of artillery fire and explosions (Maslowski 1993, 89). Although *The Battle of Midway*'s hypermediated imagery creates a sense of immediacy and reinforces the notion that film could bring the realities of combat home to US public, it also relies on familiar iconography in order to do so. In the most striking example, soldiers raise the American flag apparently in the middle of battle, against a dramatic backdrop of black smoke and startling blue skies while the voice-over reassures the audience that "yes, this really happened." *The Battle of Midway* embeds combat footage within a storyline that echoes the narrative arc of the citizen soldier's transformation from "ordinary" American boys to warriors at their posts during battle, doing what the voice-over describes as their "jobs," calmly and efficiently. Those who make it home from the "day's work," as the narrative describes the fighting, do so smiling. For those who are not so fortunate, there is a peaceful burial at sea to the accompaniment of a choir singing softly in the background. *The Battle of Midway* domesticates the chaos of combat and presents it through esthetic principles based on a visual language recognizable not only from Ford's other films but also from Hollywood war films in general.

Just as Hollywood drew on combat footage to create battlefield scenes that would seem authentic to audiences who had been given an idea of what combat should look like from news media, so photographers and combat cameramen were pressured to produce images resembling those of war movies. Major Herbert Freeland, reporting on the difficulties of filming in the mountains of Italy, despaired of obtaining footage that would be "adequate for consumption by a public that has been educated to expect and demand excitement of the 'studio war' variety" (quoted in Maslowski 1993, 74). Signal Corps photographer Joe Zinni in a letter home to his wife (quoted in Maslowski 1993, 74) speaks of the pressure exerted on combat photographers to deliver images that matched Hollywood depictions of warfare, such as direct mortar hits and US soldiers killing Germans by bayonet and machine guns. The esthetic combination of war and war movie is not unique to World War II, but it intensified during this war and continues to exert a significant pressure on representations of subsequent conflicts.[14] Both wartime Hollywood and the news media combined to create an iconography drawn from three ubiquitous building blocks: men, machinery, and spectacle.

The implications of the citizen soldier's central place in mediated representations of World War II are covered in more detail elsewhere in this chapter, but in terms of the visual construction of the war, the juxtaposition of the human face of the soldier and the violence of the industrialized battlefield creates what Bernd Hüppauf (2006, 60) argues is the root of a basic contradiction in the visual construction of war—the attempt to establish "a dichotomy between war and civilization," which in turn implies that the latter can be maintained by the former. The ongoing emphasis on the soldier in the war's visual construction throughout the mnemonic structure of World War II thus preserves an archaic perspective of combat, in which the actions of the individual still have meaning on the battlefield.

Although the soldier is an important figure, the significant place occupied by war matériel in the visual construction of World War II is one of the distinguishing features of the transmedia mnemonic structure of this conflict. The products of American industry were a potent symbol of the belief that US manufacturing would be what Henry Luce (1942, 88) called the "instrument of victory" in the war. From the "inspiring and humorous life story" of the jeep, a six-page photographic essay in *Life* (July 20, 1942), which featured photographs by war correspondents George Strock and Dmitri Kessel, to the PT boats that are so crucial to John Ford's film, *They Were Expendable* (1945), images of the machinery essential to warfare emphasize both American military might and idiosyncratic American ingenuity. The symbolic importance attached to US war machines is evident in the fact that just as images of dead American soldiers were carefully mediated and moderated, so too were those that revealed the impact of the war on hardware. Susan Moeller notes that the wartime generation of Americans "saw few pictures of the extensive destruction of US property" (1989, 247). Despite instructions to photographers and filmmakers such as those issued by former fashion photographer Edward Steichen, recruited as head of the naval aviation's photographic unit, who told his men to concentrate their cameras on soldiers because "ships and planes will become obsolete, but the men will always be there" ([1968] 1985, chap. 12, unpaginated; also in Moeller 1989, 192), images of the naval armadas, jeeps, tanks, and various weapons of World War II endure as intrinsic components of the transmedia mnemonic construct of the conflict, long after the machines themselves became obsolete.[15]

The visual construction of World War II in the wartime transmedia structure thus draws on older perspectives of conflict in which war is the province of the soldier, but it also introduces what World War II veteran and philosopher Glenn Gray calls the seductively "weird but genuine beauty" of the machinery of war and of the pyrotechnic effects of weapons the likes of which had never been seen before ([1959] 1998, 31). Like the figure of the soldier, spectacle is intrinsic to visual depictions of warfare in general. The vast range of weaponry available during World War II, however, took displays of destruction to another level. Despite the difficulties of shooting film in war zones, as listed earlier, combat cameramen and photographers nevertheless managed to produce images that capture the immense power of mechanized warfare. As Susan Moeller puts it, "fireballs and black smoke came to symbolize the war—especially the war in the Pacific" (1989, 235). The need to "see" what war is like, according to Gray, offers the "satisfaction of the astonishing" ([1959] 1998, 29). For those on the front lines, the experience of war was comprised of long swaths of monotony and boredom punctuated by moments of extreme intensity and danger, but for those on the home front, World War II was characterized by spectacular images of combat. The injection of spectacle transforms ordinary places into liminal spaces of the extraordinary, unlike anything that was to be seen on the US home front.

Soldiers, machinery, and spectacular displays of destruction were part of an esthetic of warfare that drew a clear distinction between the spaces of war and those of the home front in the wartime transmedia structure of World War II. From the blurred, dramatic backgrounds of Capa's D-Day photographs to the claustrophobic studio jungles of *Bataan* or the hills of *The Battle of San Pietro*, the spaces of war belonged primarily to the soldier and the machine. *The Battle of San Pietro*, for example, ends with images of women and children returning to the village, but they can do so only once war, with its machines and soldiers, has moved on, as the voice-over to the film makes clear. The stark divisions between war and peace in the transmedia mnemonic structure of World War II reflect a distinctly American perspective of the conflict, made possible through the status of the US as the only one of the Big Three Allied nations (US, Britain, and the USSR) to escape repeated major attacks on the home front after the attack on Pearl Harbor. Both fictional and factual media composed a picture of war that may have been patchy in places (soldiers were among the most bitter critics of the home front's visual impressions of warfare) but that nevertheless, through repetition across media, became normalized for the wartime generation to the extent that the way Americans saw the war became, as George Roeder argues, a "way of seeing" in itself (1993, 81).

The visual construction of the war strengthened ideological binaries within the transmedia construct of the war between war and peace, good and evil, us and them. For Roeder (1993, 104), the legacy of the polarized way of seeing created by the visual construction of World War II is one of major costs of the conflict because it reinforces the idea of war as an acceptable means of bringing peace. In the words of one member of the wartime generation, Admiral Gene Laroque of the US Navy, World War II "warped our view of how we look at things today. We see things in terms of that war . . . the twisted memory of it encourages the men of my generation to be willing, almost eager, to use military force anywhere in the world" (interview in Terkel 1985, 193). The esthetic qualities of World War II established within the wartime generation's media are some of the most persistent attributes of the transmedia mnemonic structure of the war. The building blocks that formed the basis of the war's visual construction—men, machinery, and spectacle—and their ideological implications, were in turn remediated and repurposed according to the principles of representation operating in the Baby Boomers' mediascape.

For Hollywood of the late 1950s and into the 1960s, spectacle in particular became increasingly important, due in part to changes that impacted strategies of representation in the film industry. Falling attendance in film theaters in the late 1940s and into the 1950s, the result of a complex mix of factors including the significant impact of the introduction of television into the mediascape, expedited technological developments that eventually altered the experience of cinemagoing.[16] These included Eastmancolor in 1954, which facilitated the transition of the majority of films produced over the next decade from black and white to color, as well as Cinemascope and Vistavision, all designed to provide a striking alternative to the small screen, black-and-white viewing experience of television (Grainge 2002, 71). Hollywood began producing fewer features with bigger budgets to showcase these technologies, providing one potential reason for the difference in the number of World War II films produced during the 1950s and the 1960s. As early as 1949, however, the theatrical trailer for *Sands of Iwo Jima* made reference to war as the "screen's greatest entertainment." The inherent spectacle of industrialized warfare made World War II an ideal subject for the big-budget, epic cycle of films produced during 1960s and into the early 1970s.

The first film to fully realize the potential of World War II as spectacle was Darryl Zanuck's *The Longest Day*. *The Longest Day* mimics actual footage of the operations on June 6, 1944 so precisely that both Lawrence Suid (2002, 168) and Robert Burgoyne (2008, 32) point out that it is almost impossible to tell the difference between stills from the film and photographs taken on the day. In its faithful remediation of the photographs and films of the Normandy landings, *The Longest Day* replicates some of the wartime strategies of representation. As in *Life*'s photo-essay of Capa's photographs, excitement and the visceral thrill of combat are foregrounded over the horrors of industrial warfare. *The Longest Day*'s massive forty-two-star cast ensures that individual characters are not completely overshadowed, but the spectacle of modern warfare and the awesome power of its machinery are central to the film. Consequently, regardless of what the filmmakers' intentions might have been, *The Longest Day* obviates the cost of war and instead feeds into the "satisfaction of the astonishing" in its sheer scale. *The Longest Day* was a financial success, with a gross (according to the

Internet Movie Database [IMDb]) of around $39 million from the domestic US market alone.

The success of *The Longest Day* spawned a number of World War II films on a similar scale, all of which privilege spectacle and machinery as key esthetic elements and many of which recycle and repurpose actual combat footage from World War II. These include *The Battle of the Bulge* (Ken Annakin, 1965), *Tora! Tora! Tora!* (Richard Fleischer, 1970), and *Midway* (Jack Smight, 1976). In addition to big-budget spectacles such as these, films such as *Where Eagles Dare* (Brian G. Hutton, 1968), *The Guns of Navarone* (J. Lee Thompson, 1961), and its follow-up, *Force 10 from Navarone* (Guy Hamilton, 1978) strip war of almost everything but the visceral excitement generated through combat and present World War II as a background for adventure. Even films that displayed increasing cynicism toward the causes of war, like *The Dirty Dozen* and *Kelly's Heroes*, revel in the spectacle of warfare, with explosions filmed from multiple angles or in slow motion to prolong the visual experience of destruction.

There are mediations of World War II that present an alternative to the war-as-spectacle films within the transmedia mnemonic structure of the Baby Boomers' mediascape, but these are almost overwhelmed by the scale and presence of the big-budget epic and adventure films. Changes to Hollywood from the late 1940s onward, such as the Paramount Decree (1948), which put an end to vertical integration in the film industry, and the rise of art cinemas in the 1960s and 1970s, dismantled the studio system and paved the way for the rise of smaller, independent productions. One such production company, Theodora Productions Inc., funded Cornell Wilde's *Beach Red* (1967). In contrast to the majority of the epic World War II films, *Beach Red* lacks both a massive budget and the assistance of the US military in providing men and matériel. Instead, *Beach Red* gives the interior world of the soldier precedence over the external visual trappings of war. In its focus on the impact of war on the male psyche, *Beach Red* premediates films about the Vietnam War more than it resembles the epic World War II films that are its contemporaries. Similarly, on television, series like *Combat!* explored the emotional lives of soldiers, rather than the spectacle of war, and situational comedy series *Hogan's Heroes* (CBS, 1965–1971) presents World War II as a battle of wits between irrepressible American POWs and their incompetent German captors, rather than as a spectacular clash of warriors, weapons, and machines.

Although most original programming concerned with World War II in the television of the Baby Boomers mediascape focused on emotional landscapes rather than on spectacular battles, the legacy of World War II's visual media proved useful for the medium in other ways. NBC was the first network to mine the potential inherent in the massive amount of archival material left in the wake of World War II. *Victory at Sea* (1952–1953) is a twenty-six-part series produced by Henry Salomon as part of NBC's industrial strategy of shifting its schedule from live television to recorded programming. The series draws on sixty million feet of archive footage to create a narrative that charts the actions of the US Navy and Marine Corps during the war. In his analysis of *Victory at Sea*, Peter Rollins (2001, 110) points out that it favors "the machines of war and the visual excitement of the scene" rather than "the less photogenic" images of the impact of war on the individual human body. An evocative soundtrack, composed by Richard Rogers, directs emotional investment in the spectacle of war, while the voice-over (Leonard Graves) reassures viewers of the endurance of the "spirit of freedom" regardless of casualties, echoing similar sentiments that accompanied images of death in wartime media. However, as Rollins notes, the series demonstrates the survival of war machines and industry rather than of the individual and therefore misdirects attention from the human cost of war (2001, 110). The series repurposes the esthetic building blocks of World War II's visual structure to reinforce the Cold War doctrine of conflict as a legitimate course of action in the pursuit of spreading democracy across the world. While spectacle is more usually associated with war films on the big screen, *Victory at Sea* is an early illustration of how impressive scenes of combat could have their uses on the small screen and demonstrate that, as the transmedia structure of the conflict developed in the postwar mediascape, World War II was much more than "war movies." The series was a lucrative property for NBC and paved the way for the development of documentary in general on television, as well as marking the starting point of a legacy of World War II documentaries that continue well into the present day.[17]

In fulfilling the "satisfaction of the astonishing," *Victory at Sea* and the epic and adventure war films preserve the divisions in the visual construction of World War II. The spaces of war in the visual construction of war are filled with emotional intensity, astonishment, and wonder—a sharp contrast to the everyday spaces of home. The delineation of war from the normal and the mundane, in turn, perpetuates a fascination with combat as an amplified version of reality. Geoffrey Klingsporn (2006, 40) connects "the urge to exalt war as somehow more real than normal, everyday existence" with a persistent tendency to view mediated images of war as transparent, despite the fact that the indexicality of the photographic or filmic image in general has been thoroughly investigated in scholarship on visual culture. Jeanine Basinger, herself a member of the wartime generation, provides a prime example of the tendency to ignore the complexities of mediation by consistently suggesting that wartime media, both fictional and factual, "helped teach audiences what *combat really looked like*" ([1986] 2003, 113, my emphasis). Yet the look of World War II was the result of a series of factors, ranging from the practicalities involved in shooting combat to the political and ideological motivations of those disseminating the images across wartime media. As a consequence of these factors, wartime media created a visual construction of World War based on three key features: soldiers, machinery, and spectacle. These three building blocks were remediated and repurposed in the Baby Boomers' mediascape, but their constant repetition and recycling wears a "hard groove," to borrow a term from Frank Wetta and Stephen Curley (1992, 2), into the transmedia mnemonic construct of World War II. The persistence of the wartime generation's way of seeing the war in the transmedia mnemonic structure of World War II thus also preserves the ideological filters that transform war into a way of seeing.

CONCLUSION

Transmedia structures are formed by the constant circulation and repurposing of mediated material and are therefore in a state of continual flux, but by tracking the transmedia structure of World War II through the mediascape of the wartime generation and into that of the Baby Boomers, continuities and changes within the three key features of the structure become apparent. The citizen soldier remains central to the transmedia structure of World War II but evolves from a symbol of national solidarity to become both the hero and the primary victim of war. There are gaps in the transmedia structure of the war, particularly when it comes to representing the complexities of the behaviors of soldiers during wartime, as well as the devastating impact of a total war on civilians. As a result of these gaps, the idea of World War II as a righteous war persists in the structure and feeds into the notion of the conflict as a "good war." The visual construction of the war is the product of an intricate set of interlocking situational, industrial, ideological, and political factors that resulted in a focus on three esthetic elements—the soldier, the machines of war, and the spectacle of industrialized warfare. Although changing practices of representation as the mediascape evolved resulted in a shift in emphasis onto spectacle as a key element in the esthetics of visual representations, all three elements persist as essential components of the visual construction of the war.

Having outlined the evolution of the transmedia construct of World War II as it cycles through the mediascape of two generations, the remaining chapters turn to the ongoing development of the structure within the more recent media milieu. The upcoming chapters continue to track the citizen soldier, the "good war," and the war as a visual construct into the current generation's media and to explore how and why the memory of the "charismatic epoch" of World War II is appropriated and redefined in the mediascape of the last two decades.

NOTES

1. According to a memorandum by William B. Lewis to the Radio Bureau Division in June 1942, weekly intelligence surveys indicated that at least half the population was unclear as to what the conflict was about. Quoted in Horten (2002, 43).
2. During World War II (1941–1945), 16,112,566 served in all branches of the military, as opposed to 5,720,000 in the Korean conflict (1950–1953),

8,744,000 in the Vietnam War (1964–1973), and 2,225,000 in the Persian Gulf War (1990–1991) (Leland and Oboroceanu, 2010).

3. "Fragging" is a slang term developed during the Vietnam conflict referring to the murder of officers by men under their command, usually by means of a fragmentation grenade.

4. See Lewis (1985, 19–64) for a comprehensive collection of Vietnam veteran accounts testifying to the power of the World War II combat film and to the appeal of Wayne in particular.

5. The only exception is *The Green Berets* (Ray Kellogg, 1968), which featured John Wayne in the lead role as Lieutenant Colonel Michael Kirby as a member of a special unit fighting the Vietcong. Wayne's brand of strident nationalism did not transfer well to the uncertain morality of the Vietnam War, and the film met with vicious criticism. Lawrence Suid, however, points out that *The Green Berets* was nevertheless a box office success (2002, 256).

6. Huebner offers a detailed discussion of the events at My Lai and the fate of William Calley, the soldier accused of the worst of the crimes (2008, 210–217).

7. Roeder (1995) provides one rare example of a published photograph of this practice in the form of an image published in *Life* (May 22, 1944) of a woman looking at a Japanese skull sent to her by her boyfriend.

8. The siege of the Alamo, part of the Texan Revolution (1935–1836), took place over 13 days (February 23–March 6) in 1836, as Mexican General Antonio López de Santa Anna and his army laid siege to a fortified mission known as the Alamo, which ended in defeat for the Texan rebels inside. The battle functions as a media template invoking ideas of ultimate sacrifice for American ideals of freedom and independence.

9. These numbers should not be taken as an accurate count but were formed by conducting and collating basic searches for films released in each decade in the US on the Internet Movie Database (IMDb) and on the World Wide Web in general.

10. For a more comprehensive breakdown of the challenges of war coverage, see Moeller (1989, 181–212).

11. Casualty rates for civilian correspondents were actually four time higher than for the military (Moeller 1989, 183).

12. Jeanine Basinger notes that a National Archives estimate of uncut combat footage alone puts it at over thirteen and a half million feet ([1986] 2003, 113).

13. Original reads: "Life-as-movie, war-as-(war) movie, war-as-life; a complete process if you got to complete it . . ." (Herr 1982, 58).

14. The history of industrialized warfare is inextricably entangled with the history of photography and motion pictures. Of the substantial body of work exploring this relationship, Paul Virilio makes perhaps the most provocative claim that there "is no war then, without representation" (Virilio 1989 6). See also Slocum (2006) for a series of essays examining the relationship between war and cinema.

15. In some cases, machinery now supplants the soldier as the primary focus of representations of World War II. *World of Tanks* (Wargaming, 2010–present), for example, is a massively multiplayer online game that, as the name suggests, focuses on tank battles and on the machines involved. Following the success of *World of Tanks*, Belarusian war-gaming developers brought out *World of Warplanes* (2013–present) and are currently developing *World of Warships*. World War II tanks, planes, and warships feature heavily in all three games. The History Channel and the Military History Channel also regularly feature series that focus solely on the weapons and technology used in World War II. *Greatest Tank Battles* (History Television, 2010–present) is one example.

16. For a detailed examination of the impact of television on the film industry, see Stuart (1982).
17. *Victory at Sea* remained in circulation in syndication and did well in foreign markets throughout the 1950s. The soundtrack proved particularly popular, grossing $4 million dollars in the same decade (according to the Museum of Broadcast Communications, www.museum.tv). The series was rebroadcast in the mid-1990s by PBS as part of the commemorative celebrations that marked this decade, and it has since had a new lease on life through home distribution.

REFERENCES

Ambrose, Stephen E. [1992] 2001. *Band of Brothers: E Company, 506th Regiment, 101st Airborne from Normandy to Hitler's Eagles' Nest*. London: Pocket Books.

Ambrose, Stephen E. [1994] 2002. *D-Day: June 6, 1944: The Climactic Battle of World War II*. London: Pocket Books.

Ambrose, Stephen E. [1997] 2002. *Citizen Soldiers: From the Beaches of Normandy to the Surrender of Germany*. London: Pocket Books.

Ambrose, Stephen E. 2001. *The Good Fight*. New York: Atheneum Books for Young Readers.

Baker, Mark. (2002) *Nam: The Vietnam War in the Words of the Men and Women Who Fought There*. London: Abacus Books.

Basinger, Jeanine. [1986] 2003. *The World War II Combat Film: Anatomy of a Genre*. Middletown, CT: Wesleyan University Press.

Beidler, Philip D. 1998. *The Good War's Greatest Hits: World War II and American Remembering*. Athens and London: University of Georgia Press.

Birdwell, Michael. 1999. *Celluloid Soldiers: Warner Bros Campaign Against Nazism*. New York: New York University Press.

Bolter, Jay David, and Richard Grusin. 2000. *Remediation: Understanding New Media*. Cambridge, MA: MIT Press.

Braudy, Leo. 2005. *From Chivalry to Terrorism: War and the Changing Nature of Masculinity*. New York: Vintage Books (Random House).

Brokaw, Tom. [1998] 2002. *The Greatest Generation*. London: Pimlico.

Burgoyne, Robert. 2008. *The Hollywood Historical Film*. Oxford: Blackwell Publishing.

Casaregola, Vincent. 2009. *Theatres of War: America's Perceptions of World War II*. New York: Palgrave Macmillan.

Chambers, John Whiteclay, and David Culbert. 1996. "Introduction." In *World War II, Film and History*. John Whiteclay Chambers and David Culbert, eds.: 3–12. New York: Oxford University Press.

Confessore, Nicholas. 2001. "Selling *Private Ryan*." *The American Prospect*. September 24. Accessed September 19, 2014. www.questia.com/read/1G1-79026801

Dick, Bernard F. 1985. *The Star Spangled Screen: The American World War II Film*. Lexington: University Press of Kentucky.

Eisenhower, Dwight D. 1944. "D-Day Statement to Soldiers, Sailor and Airmen of the Allied Expeditionary Force, 6/44." DDE-EPRE: Eisenhower, Dwight D: Papers, Pre- Presidential, 1916–1952, Dwight D. Eisenhower Library, National Archives and Records Administration. Accessed September 19, 2014. www.archives.gov/historical-docs/todays-doc/?dod-date=606

Fussell, Paul. 1989. "The Real War 1939–1945." *The Atlantic Monthly*, August. Accessed May 2, 2011. www.theatlantic.com/past/docs/unbound/bookauth/battle/fussell.htm

Fussell, Paul. 1990. *Wartime: Understanding and Behavior in the Second World War*. New York: Oxford University Press.

Fussell, Paul. 2004. *The Boys' Crusade. American GIs in Europe: Chaos and Fear in World War Two*. London: Weidenfeld & Nicolson.

Giangreco, D. M. 2004. " 'Spinning' the Casualties: Media Strategies During the Roosevelt Administration." *Passport: Society for Historians of American Foreign Relations* (newsletter), December. Accessed May 28, 2011. https://kb.osu.edu/dspace/bitstream/handle/1811/30065/Passport%20December%202004.pdf?sequence=2

Goodman, Ezra. 1949. "From the Halls of Montezuma to Hollywood." *New York Times*, August 7. Proquest Historical Newspapers: *New York Times* (1851–2008).

Grainge, Paul. 2002. *Monochrome Memory*. Westport, CT: Praeger.

Gray, J. Glenn. [1959] 1998. *The Warriors: Reflections of Men in Combat*. Lincoln: University of Nebraska Press.

Heller, Joseph. [1961] 2011. *Catch 22*. London: Vintage.

Herr, Michael. 1982. *Dispatches*. London: Picador.

Hitchcock, William I. 2009. *Liberation. The Bitter Road to Freedom: A New History of the Liberation of Europe*. New York: Free Press.

Horten, Gerd. 2002. *Radio Goes to War: The Cultural Politics of Propaganda During World War II*. Berkeley: University of California Press.

Huebner, Andrew. J. 2008. *The Warrior Image: Soldiers in American Culture from the Second World War to the Vietnam Era*. Chapel Hill: University of North Carolina Press.

Hüppauf, Bernd. 2006. "Experiences of Modern Warfare and the Crisis of Representation." In *Hollywood and War. The Film Reader*. David J. Slocum, ed.: 57–67. New York: Routledge.

Jones, Edgar L. 1946. "One War Is Enough." *The Atlantic Monthly*, February. Accessed May 15, 2011. www.theatlantic.com/past/docs/unbound/bookauth/battle/jones.htm

Jones, James. [1951] 1998. *From Here to Eternity*. New York: Dell Publishing.

Jones, James. 1963. "Phoney War Films." *The Saturday Evening Post*, March 30. Accessed September 18, 2014. www.unz.org/Pub/SatEveningPost-1963mar30

Kershaw, Alex. 2004. *Blood and Champagne: The Life and Times of Robert Capa*. Cambridge, MA: Da Capo Press.

Klingsporn, Geoffrey. 2006. "War, Film, History: American Images of 'Real War,' 1890–1920." In *Hollywood and War. The Film Reader*. David J. Slocum, ed.: 31–43. New York: Routledge.

Koppes, Clayton R. 1995. "Hollywood and the Politics of Representation: Women, Workers and African Americans in World War II Movies." In *The Home-Front War: World War II and American Society*. Kenneth Paul O'Brien and Lynn Hudson Parsons, eds.: 25–40. Westport, CT: Greenwood Press.

Leland, Anne, and Mari-Jana Oboroceanu. 2010. *American War and Military Operations Casualties: Lists and Statistics*. CRS Report RL32492. Washington, DC: Congressional Research Service, February 26. Accessed September 27, 2014. http://fas.org/sgp/crs/natsec/RL32492.pdf

Lewis, Lloyd B. 1985. *The Tainted War: Culture and Identity in Vietnam War Narratives*. Westport, CT: Greenwood Press.

Life. 1942. "The Jeep," July 20. Accessed September 18, 2014. http://books.google.co.uk/books/about/LIFE.html?id=R1cEAAAAMBAJ

Life. 1942. "There Are Two Ways to Learn About War," November 30. Accessed September 18, 2014. http://books.google.co.uk/books/about/LIFE.html?id=R1cEAAAAMBAJ

Life. 1944. "Beachheads of Normandy," June 19. Accessed September 18, 2014. http://books.google.co.uk/books/about/LIFE.html?id=R1cEAAAAMBAJ

Life. 1950. "This Is War," September 18. Accessed September 18, 2014. http://books.google.co.uk/books/about/LIFE.html?id=R1cEAAAAMBAJ

Locke, Brian. 2008. "Strange Fruit: White, Black and Asian in the WWII Combat Film *Bataan*." *Journal of Popular Film and Television* 36, no. 1 (Spring): 9–20. Accessed September 18, 2014. http://colorado.academia.edu/BrianLocke/Papers/390054/

Luce, Henry. 1941. "The American Century." *Life*, February 17. Accessed September 17, 2014. http://books.google.co.uk/books/about/LIFE.html?id=R1cEAAAAMBAJ

Luce, Henry. 1942. "America's War and America's Peace." *Life*, February 16. Accessed September 17, 2014. http://books.google.co.uk/books/about/LIFE.html?id=R1cEAAAAMBAJ

Luce, Henry. 1943. "Editorial: Three Americans. Where These Boys Fell, A Part of Freedom Fell: We Must Resurrect It in Their Name." *Life*, September 20. Accessed September 17, 2014) http://books.google.co.uk/books/about/LIFE.html?id=R1cEAAAAMBAJ

Mailer, Norman. 1948. *The Naked and the Dead*. New York: Picador.

Maltby, Richard. 1984 *"Film Noir*: The Politics of the Maladjusted Text." *Journal of American Studies* 18, no 1 (April): 49–71. www.jstor.org/stable/27554400

Maslowski, Peter. 1993. *Armed with Cameras*. New York: Free Press.

Mettler, Suzanne. 2005. *Soldiers to Citizens: The GI Bill and the Making of the Greatest Generation*. Oxford: Oxford University Press.

Moeller, Susan D. 1989. *Shooting War: Photography and the American Experience of Combat*. New York: Basic Books.

New York Times. 1942. "President Forms Top News Agency; Elmer Davis Chief," June 14. Proquest Historical Newspaper: *New York Times* (1851–2008).

Prince, Stephen. 2003. *Classical Film Violence: Designing and Regulating Brutality in Hollywood Cinema, 1930–1968*. New Brunswick, NJ: Rutgers University Press.

Pyle, Ernie. [1943] 2004. *Here Is Your War: The Story of G.I. Joe*. Lincoln: University of Nebraska Press.

Roeder, George. 1993. *The Censored War: American Visual Experience During World War II*. New Haven, CT, and London: Yale University Press.

Roeder, George. 1995. "Missing on the Home Front: Wartime Censorship and Postwar Ignorance." *National Forum* 75, no 4 (September): 25. Accessed September 19, 2014. www.questia.com/magazine/1P3–9089661/missing-on-the-home-front

Rollins, Peter C. 2001. *"Victory at Sea*: Cold War Epic." In *Television Histories: Shaping Collective Memory in the Media Age*. Gary R. Edgerton and Peter C. Rollins, eds.: 103–122. Lexington: University Press of Kentucky.

Roosevelt, Franklin D. 1941. "Annual Message to Congress on the State of the Union." Collection: Public Papers and Addresses of Franklin D Roosevelt, The American Presidency Project (January 6). Accessed September 19, 2014. www.presidency.ucsb.edu/ws/?pid=16092

Schatz, Thomas. 2006. "World War II and the Hollywood 'War Film.'" In *Hollywood and War. The Film Reader*. David J. Slocum, ed.: 147–155. New York: Routledge.

Scheuer, Philip K. 1962. "'Gen.' Darryl Zanuck Takes Normandy, Reviews Battle." *Los Angeles Times*, April 1. Pqasb.pqarchiver: *Los Angeles Times* (1923–current file). Accessed September 19, 2014. http://pqasb.pqarchiver.com/latimes

Schuman, Howard, and Jacqueline Scott. 1989. "Generations and Collective Memories." *American Sociological Review* 54, no. 3 (June): 359–381. www.jstor.org/stable/2095611

Schwarz, Benjamin. 2001. *"The Good Fight*: Stephen Ambrose's GIs Are Plaster Saints Engaged in a Sanctified Crusade." *The Atlantic Monthly*, June. Accessed

September 19, 2014. www.theatlantic.com/past/docs/issues/2001/06/schwarz.htm

Schwartz, Barry. 1982. "The Social Context of Commemoration: A Study in Collective Memory." *Social Forces* 61, no. 2 (December): 374–402. www.jstor.org/stable/2578232

Slocum, David J. 2006. "General Introduction: Seeing Through American War Cinema." In *Hollywood and War. The Film Reader*. David J. Slocum, ed.: 5–21. New York: Routledge.

Steichen, Edward. [1968] 1985. *A Life in Photography*. New York: Harmony Books.

Steinbeck, John, and Robert Capa. 1948. *A Russian Journal*. New York: Penguin.

Stuart, Fredric. 1982. "The Effects of Television on the Motion Picture Industry: 1948–1960." In *The American Movie Industry: The Business of Motion Pictures*. Gorham Anders Kindem, ed.: 257–307. Carbondale: Southern Illinois University Press.

Suid, Lawrence H. 2002. *Guts and Glory: The Making of the American Military Image in Film* Lexington: The University Press of Kentucky.

Terkel, Studs. 1985. *"The Good War."* London: Hamish Hamilton Ltd.

Time. 1945. "Army and Navy: Bill, *Willie and Joe*," June 18. Accessed May 8, 2011. www.time.com/time/magazine/article/0,9171,775894-4,00.html

Torgovnick, Marianna. 2005. *The War Complex: World War II in Our Time*. Chicago: University of Chicago Press.

Virilio, Paul. 1989. *War and Cinema: The Logistics of Perception*. Patrick Camiller, trans. London: Verso.

Vonnegut, Kurt. 1969. *Slaughterhouse Five, or The Children's Crusade, A Duty-Dance with Death*. New York: Dell.

Whitman, Walt. [1892] 1949. *The Poetry and Prose of Walt Whitman*. Louis Untermeyer, ed. New York: Simon & Schuster.

Westwell, Guy. 2006. *War Cinema: Hollywood on the Front Line*. London: Wallflower Press.

Wetta, Frank J., and Stephen J. Curley. 1992. *Celluloid Wars: A Guide to Film and the American Experience of War*. New York: Greenwood Press.

Winkler, Allan M. 2000. *Home Front U.S.A. America During World War II*. Wheeling, IL: Harlan Davidson.

Part II

3 Inspiring the World to Remember

INTRODUCTION

In 1986, Jeanine Basinger speculated whether Sam Fuller's intensely personal film about World War II, *The Big Red One* (1980), would be the "very last combat film" made about the conflict ([1986] 2003, 197). From the 1950s onward, the number of films set in World War II progressively dwindled, and in the 1980s, directors such as Francis Ford Coppola, Oliver Stone, and Stanley Kubrick turned to making films about the Vietnam War. It appeared as if World War II was indeed fading from cinema screens in the US.[1] The 1990s, however, marked the fiftieth anniversary of key events in World War II. The media coverage of commemorations around the world, and of the disagreements that accompanied some of them, ensured that World War II featured prominently in the US mediascape of the 1990s.[2] Before the close of the decade, World War II returned to cinema screens in Steven Spielberg's *Saving Private Ryan* (1998), a film that according to its print ads, "inspired the world to remember" the conflict. But what is the film asking the world to remember, and how does it fit into the transmedia construct of World War II?

The first part of this chapter establishes that *Saving Private Ryan* is part of a general tendency in the memorialization of World War II in the US that positions D-Day in Normandy as a pivotal battle in the war. This chapter identifies *Saving Private Ryan* as a master mediation in the transmedia construct of World War II. By "master mediation," I mean a representation in any medium that claims the status of a definitive account of the war and of the wartime generation's experiences and memories and that subsequently functions as a touchstone for ensuing representations of the conflict throughout the transmedia structure. This chapter demonstrates how *Saving Private Ryan* uses the transmedia mnemonic structure of the war to authorize its representation of World War II and to position itself as part of an iconic legacy of mediations of the conflict. *Saving Private Ryan* remediates the citizen soldier, recalibrates the visual construction of the war, and repurposes the notion of the "good war." The film's adoption and adaption of all three central elements resonates across the current configuration of the transmedia structure of World War II. As a master mediation, *Saving Private Ryan* generates discussions about the meaning and nature of history, memory, and film that "cascade" through other media, as Thomas Elsaesser (1996, 167) puts it, to create "discursive realities" that persist long after the film's cinematic release date. This chapter examines some of these discussions in the wake of *Saving Private Ryan* in order to establish the film's impact on the transmedia structure of World War II.

As this chapter makes clear, *Saving Private Ryan* is intrinsically connected to the wave of commemorations that characterized the 1990s and to the drive to memorialize World War II. As such, the film is part of a reworked national narrative concerning US involvement in the war. Laura Hein (1995, 3) describes the narrative of remembrance that emerged in the cultural discourse of the 1990s in the US as an "idealized narrative of US culture, emphasizing decisiveness, bravery, simplicity, and national unity." To investigate how the transmedia mnemonic structure absorbs the US narrative of remembrance and transforms it, the second half of this chapter turns to the Clint Eastwood diptych, *Flags of Our Fathers* and *Letters from Iwo Jima* (both released in 2006). Eastwood's two films demonstrate that the war in the Pacific theater does not fold itself easily into the idealization of World War II as a "good war." *Flags of Our Fathers* and *Letters from Iwo Jima* expand the symbol of the citizen soldier to include the enemy, attempt to unpick the visual construction of the war, and challenge the idea of the "good war."

Charting the development of the World War II combat film as a genre, Jeanine Basinger suggests, "A group of films with very similar characteristics emerge, blend, and become one film in memory. When later filmmakers create films of the same type . . . they make the memory of the accumulated film" ([1986] 2003, 17). Although I agree that genre memory is undeniably important, Basinger's approach is limited in that it does not consider film as part of an integrated network of media. In contrast, this chapter examines how materials drawn from a range of texts in the mnemonic structure of World War II premediate all three films, and it considers the implications of the remediation of the citizen soldier, the visual construction of the war, and the "good war" in each film.

SAVING PRIVATE RYAN

Despite widespread media attention devoted to the commemoration of World War II in the 1990s, the film industry was slow to recognize the potential of the conflict as a lucrative subject. Spielberg himself did not anticipate that *Saving Private Ryan* would be a financial success; he believed that the violence in the film would limit its audience appeal and turn it into a "one weekend wonder" at best (interview in *Spielberg on Spielberg* [Schickel 2007]). Both Spielberg and Tom Hanks, star of the film, accepted reduced payments in return for a percentage of the gross takings. Paramount appeared to harbor similar doubts and would agree to coproduce only along with DreamWorks SKG. As Nigel Morris suggests (2007, 270), it is possibly due only to Spielberg's status that the film was made at all. The director was willing to take the risk, however, because he wanted to make the film as a tribute to his father and his father's generation (interview in *Spielberg on Spielberg* [Schickel, 2007]). Yet, despite the fact that Spielberg's father served in Burma, *Saving Private Ryan* is set in the European theater and opens with the landings on Omaha Beach on June 6, 1944—a day Spielberg describes in "A Special Message from Steven Spielberg," an extra feature on the DVD of the film (*Saving Private Ryan* Special Limited Edition DVD, DreamWorks 1999), not just as the pivotal battle in the war but as the "pivotal point of the 20th Century."

The reasons behind the selection of D-Day in Normandy as a focal point in the American memory of World War II are complex enough to form the subject of an entirely separate book, but in order to understand *Saving Private Ryan*'s position in the transmedia structure of World War II, it is important to establish at least a very broad understanding of why this particular moment, out of all the significant events in World War II, resonates so powerfully in the mediated structure of World War II memory. All major campaigns in the war had a D-Day, but the association of the term with June 6, 1944, above all others is an indication of the increasing importance of this date in the memorialization of World War II in the US. The film industry reflects a general shift in focus from the Pacific campaign, which featured heavily in films of the 1940s and the 1950s, to the war in Europe, with the 1960s being the first decade in which more films were made about the European theater than the Pacific.[3] More specifically, Bernard Dick (1985, 135–137) traces the exponential interest in the film industry in the events of June 6 from "an allusion" in *The Master Race* (Herbert. J. Biberman, 1944), to the climax of *Fighter Squadron* (Raoul Walsh, 1948), a "pre-invasion maneuver" in *D-Day the Sixth of June* (Henry Koster, 1956), until D-Day finally becomes the focus of *The Longest Day* in 1962. Zanuck's film spawned its own "nostalgia culture," as Philip Beidler (1998, 161) puts it, through invariable repeats on television every June. As mentioned, Zanuck's film expressly reflects Cold War concerns, but D-Day continued to serve political requirements into the 1980s. The commemorations at Normandy provided Ronald Reagan with a useful platform from which to reassert the New Patriotism and pride in the American military in one of the defining speeches of his career.[4] However, Marianna Torgovnick (2005) suggests that the appeal of D-Day is only partially explained by political contingencies. According to Torgovnick, the ease with which the day's events can be folded into a neat narrative has an esthetic appeal lacking in the longer and messier process of liberation that followed (2005, 42–43). The events of D-Day are generally reconstituted in discourses of remembrance as a successful military action during which US forces embarked on a "great crusade," as Roosevelt put it in his D-Day address, to save the world for democracy. In the commemorations of June 6, 1944, or what David Greenberg (2004) refers to as the annual "barrage of World War II nostalgia," D-Day functions as a synecdoche of the entire war, and the veterans who took part in the landings symbolize the entire wartime generation.

In the "Production Notes" booklet that accompanies the special limited edition DVD of *Saving Private Ryan* (DreamWorks Home Entertainment, 1999), screenwriter Robert Rodat cites the fiftieth anniversary of D-Day as part of the inspiration for *Saving Private Ryan*, along with the birth of his second son. From its very inception, the film is thus colored by a sense of one generation attempting to honor, or come to terms with, the actions of another. Its foundation is in sons honoring their fathers or in fathers attempting to ensure that the actions of grandfathers are not forgotten. Despite its advertising strapline, *Saving Private Ryan* is part of a groundswell of remembrance running through US culture half a century after the war, and it draws on material from the transmedia construct of World War II to "inspire" the world.

Despite the fact that he was actually contracted only after the film was completed, Stephen Ambrose is named as historical consultant on *Saving Private Ryan* (DiGiacomo 1998). In various interviews, Spielberg, Rodat, and Hanks all refer to Ambrose's books as inspiration for the film. Spielberg refers to Ambrose as the "first writer that got into the DNA of the combat veteran" (interview for the American Film Institute [AFI, 2011]). Interviewed in a feature entitled "Miller and His Platoon" (Bouzereau 2004) for the "60th Anniversary Commemorative Edition" of *Saving Private Ryan* (DreamWorks, 2004), Tom Hanks observes that Ambrose's histories "really bring it down to guys named Steve and Chuck." In the words of Marvin Levy, a spokesperson for Spielberg, DreamWorks SKG "would have been crazy" not to enlist Ambrose's support, given his status as an "expert" (quoted in DiGiacomo 1998). Ambrose's "expert" endorsement of the film as an authentic visual representation of the verbal testimony of the veterans that he interviewed over the years feeds into the film's status as a definitive account of the war. Ambrose's work, along with its uncritical reverence for the GI and the ideological issues associated with its historical focus on the role of the US in World War II, thus provides the primary model for the citizen soldiers of *Saving Private Ryan*.

In contrast to *The Longest Day*'s all-star cast, the cast of *Saving Private Ryan* was mostly unknown when the film was first released. Hanks is the only exception, but Spielberg justifies his casting by pointing out that Hanks is "great at playing everyman" (interview in "Miller and His Platoon" [Bouzereau 2004]). Unlike John Wayne, Hanks embodies the everyday American rather than the all-American hero. He is therefore perfect for playing "guys named Steve and Chuck"—"ordinary" Americans. Geoff King (2006, 293) points out that Hanks is also old enough "to play paternalistic roles while maintaining a sufficiently glamorous movie-star aura to appeal to younger generations." Through Hanks, *Saving Private Ryan* remediates the citizen soldier and makes the figure appealing and accessible to a demographically mixed contemporary audience. In a similar way, the film also recalibrates the visual construction of the war.

An analysis of the theatrical trailer for *Saving Private Ryan* establishes the film's relationship to the transmedia structure of World War II from the outset and gives an early indication of the film's approach to the war as a visual construct. Jonathan Gray describes trailers as "concentrates" of a film's meaning (2010, 48). According to Gray (ibid.), trailers are instrumental in "initiating textuality, creating a genre, networking star intertexts and introducing us to a new storyworld." Trailers are therefore a significant part of transmedia structures, in that they distill some of the major issues at stake in a film and, perhaps more importantly in the case of *Saving Private Ryan*, indicate how the film is situated in a network of related World War II texts. The trailer begins with a somber male voice-over and the words, "Dear Mr. Brian Boyd, no doubt by now you have received the full information about the untimely death of your son, however, there are some personal details that. . . ." The voice-over fades out as the image of the letter of condolence that is being read aloud appears on the screen. A montage of grainy black-and-white photographs of scenes from World War II and images of more letters follows. The images are reminiscent of Robert Capa's D-Day sequence, but one photograph, of a GI's helmet lying upturned on the beach, specifically recalls a still used in some of the posters for *The Longest Day*. The monochromatic photographs and the old typeface used in the letters immediately situate *Saving Private Ryan* in the mediated past of World War II.

The first moving image to appear is Tom Hanks, playing Captain Miller. He is pictured in extreme close up and in color, although the tones are faded and desaturated. His face is dirty, and his eyes have a haunted expression. If all the images preceding the image of Hanks can be described as conjuring up a general impression of World War II, this is the first that is specific because Hanks' star status makes him instantly identifiable. He is an icon of the present, set in images that deliberately recall iconic images of the past. The trailer continues to blend still and moving images, ending with the picture of a solitary soldier whose face is obscured, in silhouette against the sky. The final still is a memorable (and potentially iconic) image and is repeated on the posters for *Saving Private Ryan*. In an example of film operating as both memory of media and media of memory, the trailer's remediation of iconic imagery from World War II and its attempt to create its own iconicity simultaneously engages with the transmedia structure of World War II and contributes to it. The juxtaposition of imagery acknowledges previous mediations of the war, both written and visual, but also suggests that the film tells a new story. The underlying suggestion is that the film exceeds both "official" versions of events and previous representations. The trailer thus positions *Saving Private Ryan* from the outset as a master mediation of World War II.

The film itself is anchored in the present by the opening and closing scenes that Spielberg refers to as the "bookends," and according to the director, they are intended to honor "all the dads who were part of the Greatest Generation" (interview in *Spielberg on Spielberg* [Schickel, 2007]). Both scenes are set in the US cemetery in Normandy and show a veteran and his family visiting the graves. Marita Sturken (1997, 254) describes survivors as inhabiting the "juncture of memory and history, tugging by their very presence at the boundaries of each." The figure of the grandfather thus forms an intersection of past and present and functions as a living embodiment of memory, in contrast to the memorial gardens to the dead through which the family walks. However, as Michael Hammond (2004, 164) observes, although the family are moved by the experience, they do not appear to be aware of the specific details of the old man's memories. The remainder of the film offers itself as an intervention in generational memory by providing a bridge from the grandfather to his children and grandchildren.

The notion that what follows the first cemetery scene is the grandfather's recollection of the war is supported by the cinematic convention of a camera movement into an extreme close-up of his eyes, which we assume are looking inward to his own memory (Figure 3.1).

Yet the first image that follows this is a documentary style, factual note, informing the audience that it is June 6, 1944, and that the desolate beach in the background is "Dog Green Sector, Omaha Beach" (Figure 3.2).

The use of factual titles immediately situates memory in history and implies that there is no distinction between the two. The next twenty-five minutes of film are shot in a style designed to mimic World War II combat footage. In the "Production Notes" booklet for the DVD of *Saving Private Ryan* (DreamWorks, 1999), Spielberg admits that he "grew up watching war movies" and acknowledges the "tremendous influence" they had on him, together with newsreel footage and documentaries of the war. More specifically, in an interview for the BBC with Mark Cousins (1998), Spielberg names *With the Marines at Tarawa* (U.S.M.C., 1944) and *The Battle of*

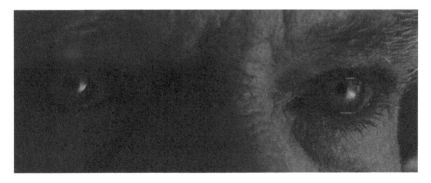

Figure 3.1   Close-up of the grandfather's eyes.

Figure 3.2 Documentary-style caption introducing the landing sequence.

San Pietro (John Huston, 1945) as particularly influential. In "Making *Saving Private Ryan*" (Bouzereau, 2004), Spielberg also refers to *The Battle of Midway* (John Ford, 1943) as providing a template for how combat scenes in general would be shot in *Saving Private Ryan* and to Robert Capa's photographs as a vital visual reference for the look of the landing sequence on D-Day. As a result, *Saving Private Ryan* preserves elements of the principles of representation at work in the wartime generation's media but recalibrates them through the use of contemporary filmmaking technologies.

Spielberg encouraged the camera crew to think of themselves as combat cameramen shooting newsreel footage in order to give the audience the impression that "[w]e were there, that we actually were there" (interview in "Making *Saving Private Ryan*" [Bouzereau, 2004]). To replicate the urgency of combat both in his crew and on the screen, Spielberg made the decision to shoot the Omaha landing scenes sequentially and without storyboarding (bearing in mind that the entire scene was nevertheless carefully choreographed to avoid injury to the cast or crew). He demanded that each shot be filled with bullet hits to create the "physical energy" of war (quoted in Magid 1998). The film was stripped of 40 percent of its color, and cinematographer Janusz Kaminski used the same 45- and 90-degree shutters used in the 1940s to replicate the look of color newsreel footage of the time (Magid 1998).[5] Spielberg and Kaminski additionally opted for techniques and technologies that deliberately destabilize the camera, eschewing the use of the steadicam in favor of what Geoff King refers to as "the radically 'unsteadicam'" as part of a "deliberate handicapping" of cinematic techniques (2006, 290). Their approach recalls and elaborates the shaky camera footage of films like *The Battle of Midway* and *The Battle of San Pietro*. The unstable camerawork, along with deliberately engineered camera flares, and the occasional "blood" and sand that splatters the camera lens, all contribute to a sense of hypermediated immediacy by drawing attention to the medium itself. By specifically referencing the work of World War II combat cameramen and the documentaries of filmmakers such as Ford and Huston, Spielberg replicates the assumptions and ideologies of the wartime media's visual construction of the war, including the assumed relationship between hypermediacy and a realist esthetic, as well as the same faith in visual media's ability to provide access to what war feels like. The remediation of the visual construction of the war anchors *Saving Private Ryan* firmly in the transmedia structure of the conflict and creates the sense that the film is very much part of the visual history of World War II. According to Geoff King (2006, 290) authenticity thus becomes a special effect in its own right—both a compelling recreation of a moment in the past and an impressive display of contemporary cinematic virtuosity.

Despite the fact that the lenses and shutters are designed to create the look of newsreel footage of the 1940s, a number of factors destabilize the recreation of a mediated past in *Saving Private Ryan*. Although John Ford established a powerful connection between unstable camerawork and the drama of combat in *The Battle of Midway*, in reality, as Toby Haggith (2002) points out, most combat cameramen did their utmost to hold the camera steady while filming in order to save film and to ensure that what they produced would be usable for newsreels or military intelligence. The extreme unsteadiness of the camera in *Saving Private Ryan* is therefore more the product of an esthetic established and perpetuated by Hollywood principles of representation than a replication of the production values of World War II combat cameramen. Unlike wartime media, *Saving Private Ryan* explicitly depicts the carnage of industrialized warfare. Men are torn apart by explosions, lose limbs, and are disemboweled. While many of these effects are done in camera, *Saving Private Ryan* was one of the first war films to employ computer-generated imagery (CGI)—most notably in the scene where an unfortunate GI has just removed his helmet to examine a bullet hole following a miraculous escape and is almost immediately shot in the head as he does so. The audience may well be unaware of the CGI involved here, but it would have been astonishing for a combat cameraman to capture the soldier's death as it appears in the film, given the random and unpredictable nature of the battlefield. Similarly, combat cameramen of the time could not have filmed the underwater scenes of soldiers struggling to survive in the surf because the water would have destroyed both camera and film. Although Spielberg's intention was to fill the scene with the sense of the "three-dimensional momentum" of combat through an almost constant barrage of bullet hits (Magid 1998), in reality bullet hits did not register on film at the time. In addition, throughout the sequence, colors are desaturated, but Spielberg wanted one in particular to retain its vividness—the color of blood. The effects team worked to create their own brand of stage blood in order to ensure that blood retained its intensity against all other colors. By highlighting this one color, the footage is infused with a subtle but powerful sense of propinquity. These factors combine to recalibrate the 1940s visual construction of World War II for consumption in the 1990s, using contemporary images of violence and current techniques of filmmaking.

The conflation between past and present and between history and memory is a result of not only the cinematography but also of the film's sound design. Sound designer Gary Rydstrom created a soundtrack that works alongside the visuals to create an immersive sensory experience for the spectator through three-dimensional, digital THX sound technology. Bill Nichols (2000, 10, also in Morris 2007, 275) therefore criticizes *Saving Private Ryan* for the seemingly "bogus" combination of a wartime visual esthetic with contemporary sound technologies, as if the soundtrack should somehow replicate that of the period (Morris 2007, 275). Recording synchronous sound in combat in the 1940s was, of course, impossible due to the restrictions of the equipment. The imagery of *Saving Private Ryan* replicates the mediated visual construction of the war as a marker of authenticity, but the soundtrack attempts to recreate the *actual* sounds of the battlefield. According to Rydstrom, Spielberg did not want the sound to "be Hollywood," by which Rydstrom understood that "[h]e didn't want the clichés . . . there might be a lot of cheating in the sound effects from the classic war movies that are wrong" (interviewed in "Music and Sound" [Bouzereau 2004]). Spielberg's position on "cheating" in Hollywood sound effects does not appear to extend to similar issues of "cheating" in visual effects (as with Ford's deliberately shaky camerawork during the recreation of the battle of San Pietro) and therefore implies a faith in the visual construction of the war as somehow unmediated. Rydstrom therefore drew on veteran's memories and on research into the sounds of various weapons rather than on mediations of World War II in order to create the soundtrack. The combination of digital sound (an anchor of the present) with the antique visual footage (recalling mediated memories of the past) creates a destabilizing and anachronistic effect that adds to the hypermediation of the landing scene.[6]

The goal of hypermediation, according to David Bolter and Richard Grusin, is to "get past the limits of representation and to achieve the real" (2000, 54). The "real" is not perceived in their definition as a philosophical abstract but is described in terms of spectator response: "It is that which would evoke an immediate (and therefore authentic) emotional response" (ibid.). In the landing sequence, wartime practices that fed into the visual construction of the conflict combine with contemporary techniques of filmmaking, both visual and auditory, to generate powerful emotional responses that approximate the experience of combat. But the landing scene is positioned in the film as a flashback, a memory so detailed and powerful that it erases all sense of the present and transports the individual back into a moment in the past.[7]

Despite the intertitles, therefore, and the duplication of the practices of combat footage, both of which feed into a documentary esthetic, the landing scene's structure mimics the impossible level of detail and the emotional impact associated with traumatic memory. Hanks is the first person shown in close-up after the cut from the old man's eyes to the intertitles on the beach, and his star persona facilitates the assumption that he is the younger incarnation of the old man in the cemetery. *Saving Private Ryan* might draw on the esthetic conventions of wartime films and documentaries, but it inverts their narrative structure. There are no scenes establishing the identity of the individual soldiers before they engage in combat, and as the only recognizable actor, Hanks is initially the focal point of the film. When the actual landing begins, however, changes in auditory and visual perspectives effectively inhibit the spectator's identification with Hanks, and eventually the unexpected and unconventional loss of the lead actor in the chaos is the source of some of the impact of the scene. *Saving Private Ryan* breaks the tradition of war films that feature lingering, slow motion, or multiangled shots of the spectacle of warfare and instead splinters the landing into multiple perspectives and experiences, far more than any one person could have experienced unless that individual were "dreaming or remembering traumatically," as Janet Walker argues (2003, 125). The hypermediated esthetic deployed in the landing scene consequently not only attempts to replicate the "real" experience of combat but also to reproduce a flashback memory of that experience.[8]

When the camera eventually closes in again on Hanks, the frenetic chaos of the soundtrack recedes into a ringing silence that imitates the tinnitus caused by close proximity to a loud explosion. In contrast to the free-floating perspective of the preceding moments, the sound facilitates a shift to an intensely subjective point of view and puts the spectator inside Miller's head, as Gary Rydstrom suggests (interview in "Music and Sound" [Bouzereau, 2004]). At the same time, the visual perspective also shifts to Miller's point of view, and what follows are some of the most explicit shots in the entire scene. Seen through Miller's eyes, the images include that of a soldier, seemingly oblivious to the explosions and gunshots around him, looking for something on the beach. It turns out to be his severed arm, which he casually retrieves and carries away. Ablaze but still walking, GIs stumble out of a Higgins boat. A soldier sits hunched against a comrade, weeping and attempting to draw every limb out of the line of fire. World War II veteran Glenn Gray ([1959] 1998, 28) writes of the "tyranny of the present"—a compression of space and time during combat into an internalized, singular moment of almost overwhelming emotions. Studies such as those conducted by Alexis Artwohl and Loren Christensen (1997) have shown that loss of sound is one of the most common sensory distortions experienced by combatants in battle situations, together with a sharpened visual acuity and distortions to time, all of which describes almost exactly what happens to Miller as he huddles on the beach. Paradoxically, the emotional intensity of combat can also generate a sense that the soldier is a spectator of, rather than a participant in, the moment. Referred to by trauma therapists as "dissociation," this is a response to an overwhelming situation that "distracts from the reality of the experience by allowing detachment" (Kreidler et al. 2000). Through the use of the soundtrack, the viewer is positioned inside Miller's head in a moment of concentrated identification that mimics the emotional and sensory dissociative affect of a soldier caught up in the "tyranny of the present." Yet at the same time, because of the landing sequence's position in the film and its hypermediated construction, the moment of identification with Miller also functions as the recreation of a vivid and affect-laden traumatic memory.

Although these few shots reestablish contact with Miller, perspectival shifts continue throughout the landing scene, and sound in particular cues moments of intense subjectivity—fading out when Miller discovers that the man he is attempting to drag to safety has had the lower half of his body blown off, for example, or receding as a sharpshooter (Barry Pepper) takes aim while muttering a prayer. The absence of recognizable characters apart from Hanks and the constant shifts in perspective are disorienting, generating an unfocused, generalized sense of empathy for all the soldiers involved in the landing. The landing scene thus meets Alison Landsberg's criteria for the creation of "prosthetic memories," in that it has the potential capacity to unsettle spectators and to put them in the position of seeing and hearing through someone else's eyes and ears, which for Landsberg suggests the possibility of transferring memory across experiential and temporal chasms. *Saving Private Ryan* therefore allows for the transference both of aspects of the experience of combat and of its traumatic memory from the World War II citizen soldier to the spectator.

At the close of the film, it becomes apparent that the flashback to the landing scene, along with the memories of the war in general that follow, cannot belong to the man in the graveyard, who is in fact the elderly Ryan. Nor do they belong to Captain Miller, whose grave is the one around which the family are clustered in the final scene. Because the memories belong to none of the soldiers in particular, they belong to all of them and, by extension, to everyone who witnesses them. *Saving Private Ryan* thus establishes its authority as a master mediation by "speaking for" the grandfather in the graveyard, as well as for the soldiers interred there, and by communicating their memories to subsequent generations. As Michael Hammond points out, the film preserves the silence of veterans who cannot verbalize their memories of the war because the grandfather does not actually talk about any of his experiences (2004, 164). *Saving Private Ryan* both explains and resolves the silence that trauma imposes on memory, not only for the family gathered around the grandfather in the graveyard but also for the audience. The film thus retrieves the traumatic memory of combat from the veteran and reconstitutes it in the public spaces of the transmedia mnemonic structure of the war.

But the film is more than just the opening twenty-five minutes, and after the landing at Omaha, *Saving Private Ryan* settles into a more conventional narrative following one squad on its mission behind enemy lines in occupied France. The squad contains a mix of ethnicities and personalities familiar from wartime films—including a Jew, an American Italian, a cheeky but tough soldier from Brooklyn, and an untried clerk who has little experience of combat—but any further resemblance to the squads of wartime cinema citizen soldiers ends there. The GIs of *Saving Private Ryan* question the validity of their mission, are occasionally insubordinate, curse extensively, and exhibit signs of combat fatigue. Miller and his squad reflect traits that manifested in the citizen soldiers of the Baby Boomer's mediascape; they are victims of conflict, in a situation beyond their control, and have no connection to the ideology of the war itself. However, *Saving Private Ryan* introduces a new element into the figure of the soldier. Whereas the citizen soldier of wartime representations fought for ideals such as democracy and freedom, and those in representations of World War II following the Korean and Vietnam conflicts were in the main depicted as being out for themselves, the soldiers of *Saving Private Ryan* fight for one another.

Miller's squad does not set out to liberate Europe or even to fight fascism but to save an American soldier. In *Saving Private Ryan*, civilians are almost nonexistent, intensifying the perception that the soldier's experience and subsequent memories of the battlefield are the quintessential memories of World War II. The squad's sole encounter with French civilians ends in disaster. Their attempt to rescue a child ends in the death of one of the squad and seems to endorse Miller's exhortation that "we're not here to do the decent thing. We're here to follow orders." Spielberg identifies the search for decency in the hell of war as the central theme of the film (interview in "Parting Thoughts" [Bouzereau, 2004]), but the "one decent thing" that the squad sees itself doing is saving Ryan. The film is quite simply about American soldiers saving American soldiers. The quest for decency in war therefore cannot be characterized as a universal moral theme in *Saving Private Ryan*, inasmuch as the film is very specifically "rooted in American perceptions of man, nature, society" (Hedetoft 2000, 294). The major issue in the crystallization of conflict around the experience of the American soldier in *Saving Private Ryan* is not that the film elides the reasons for the US involvement in the war (arguably the ideological and political background of the war is not the concern of Miller or his squad), nor that it excludes any mention of the Allied forces and civilians involved in the war, but that its recalibration of the figure of the citizen soldier and the structure of the "good war" constitutes a very specific narrative about America's armed forces and their involvement in conflict.

When the squad eventually finds Ryan, he refuses to leave, stating that he will stay and fight "for the only brothers I have left." This echoes the notion of soldiers as a "band of brothers," a theme introduced earlier in the film by the clerk Corporal Upham (Jeremy Davies), who intends to write a book on the subject of comradeship in combat. During the war itself, the notion of self-sacrifice was a vital component of the citizen soldier, consistently linked in visual media to the defense of democracy and freedom and utilized to encourage the civilian population to undergo war shortages and difficulties without complaint. Sacrifice remains an important part of the citizen soldiers of *Saving Private Ryan*, but it is reframed in the celebration of one of war's "secret attractions," as Glenn Gray refers to those aspects of war that make it appealing; in this case, the "delight in comradeship" ([1959] 1998, 28–29). The willingness to die for the man next to you rather than for a larger ideological purposes is a common theme throughout veterans' accounts of World War II, so much so that Gray identifies the impulse in soldiers to die for their comrades as "[a]n intrinsic element in the association of organized men in pursuit of a dangerous and difficult goal" (91). In *Saving Private Ryan*, the dangerous and difficult goal pursued by Miller and his squad involves saving one of their comrades, which preserves sacrifice as a central feature of the citizen soldier but which also effectively circumvents any question of the soldier's moral responsibility in war. The citizen soldier's "quest for decency" in war therefore sets him apart from the enemy in *Saving Private Ryan*. As Marilyn Young (2006, 316) argues, the soldier who fights for his life and for that of his brother in arms becomes the primary victim of war, but those he kills are the "perpetrators of violence" because their only goal is to take life, not preserve it.

Despite initial misgivings about the mission, the squad rallies together in the end to fight for Ryan in another extended battle scene set in the French village of Ramelle. In contrast to the landing scene, however, the final battle draws on two narrative standards of Hollywood representations of the conflict in Europe (King 2006). The first involves the defense of a tactically critical bridge, perhaps most familiar from *A Bridge Too Far* (Richard Attenborough, 1977). The second is the template of the "last stand," as Miller designates the squad's final fallback point near the bridge as the "Alamo." As Geoff King observes, the last stand narrative is more usually associated with the Pacific theater in wartime films (2006, 298–299). The previous chapter examined how the last stand was used in films such as *Wake Island* (John Farrow, 1942) and *Bataan* (Tay Garnett, 1943) to translate an unfamiliar and uncertain war into a comforting narrative in which the battle may be lost but the overall conflict is always won. King therefore questions its use in *Saving Private Ryan*, because five decades after the end of the war, World War II is itself part of a reassuring narrative about US victory over reprehensible enemies (299). King suggests that the defense of the bridge reconnects the squad to the broader story of World War II and that the last stand template has a symbolic resonance that links Miller, a member of the 2nd Ranger Battalion, to the memory of the Texas Rangers and the idea of heroic death (298). But perhaps more importantly, the defense of an essential bridge and the idea of the last stand focus the narrative into one episode of extreme intensity that accentuates the themes of brotherhood and self-sacrifice.

Throughout the final battle, which is in fact slightly longer than the Omaha landing scene, individual members of the squad fight to defend both Ryan and the bridge, with all but two giving their lives to do so. The characters are now familiar, and their deaths therefore have a different impact than the deaths of the soldiers on Omaha beach. The rhetorical frame of the last stand gives the graphic depiction of violence in the final battle a different resonance to that of the landing scene. Because the frontier functions in the last stand template as the front line in the fight to maintain American national identity, violence in the space is not only justified but expected. The deaths of members of the squad are not meaningless because they are reframed through the ideological shorthand of the last stand that connects self-sacrifice to the service of a worthy cause. In *Saving Private Ryan*, the worthy cause is a US soldier, and Miller urges him with his dying breath to "earn" the sacrifices Miller and the squad have made for him. As with *Schindler's List* (Spielberg 1993), *Saving Private Ryan* is predicated on a concept from the Talmud that "[w]hoever saves one life, saves the entire world" and in doing so, Spielberg "accepts the principle that the one can represent the many, that the part can stand for the whole" (Elsaesser 1996, 178). Returning to the final scene in the cemetery, the veteran the audience can finally identify as Ryan seeks vindication from his wife that he has earned the sacrifice of Miller and his men. She reassures him that he is indeed a "good man." As a survivor of D-Day and the war, Ryan represents his entire generation, and implicit in his wife's assurance is the notion that they are all good men. The final bookend thus reasserts World War II as a "good war" because it is a fight made "decent" and ennobled through the willingness of citizen soldiers to fight and die for one another and, by extension, for future generations of Americans.

By replicating the strategies of representation of wartime media, the film also reinforces the polarities inherent in the visual construction of World War II. Both battle scenes reconfigure spectacle into what Geoff King (2006, 292) terms the "spectacular-authentic"—an esthetic that depicts the battlefield as an extraordinary space of extremity and intense sensory impact that contrasts sharply not only with the scenes in the graveyard but also with the Norman Rockwell–style depiction of the Ryan homestead. The divisions between home and war are further accentuated by the absence of information on the civilian identity of Captain Miller. His civilian status as a teacher of English composition is revealed only partway through the film, after a particularly shocking incident that results in the death of the squad's medic. The incongruity of Miller's peacetime occupation and his role in the war deepens the divisions between home and war, between civilian and soldier. As Miller says, "Every man I kill, the farther away from home I feel"—a foreshadowing that for Miller at least, there will be no going home. Civilian identities and concerns have no place in the spaces of war in *Saving Private Ryan*. The relative absence of civilians in *Saving Private Ryan*, together with the strict divisions between home and war, feeds into a conceptualization of war as soldiers killing soldiers. By bracketing the film with the scenes in the graveyard, the film reinforces the notion that war can bring about peace. Moreover, because the film is about the rescue of an American soldier and demonstrates the ongoing survival of future generations in the form of Ryan's children and grandchildren, *Saving Private Ryan* not only suggests that peace is achievable through war but also implies that war is a force that can be legitimately deployed to save lives. Thus, despite vividly depicting the effect of mechanized warfare on the bodies and minds of its citizen soldiers, *Saving Private Ryan* nevertheless maintains the notion of World War II as a "good war."

After the death of the squad's medic, Miller says he does not know how he will tell his wife at home about "days like this." The film offers itself as the ultimate explanation. By representing "days like this" for Ryan and his entire generation, *Saving Private Ryan* offers closure and levels personal memory into history. In turn, the film itself has subsequently become incorporated into the history and memorialization of D-Day and World War II on both the public and private levels. Hanks and Spielberg both attended the sixtieth anniversary commemoration ceremony in Normandy in 2004, alongside veterans and then presidents George Bush and Jacques Chirac. A special edition of the film was also released as part of these commemorations, leveraging a space for the film in official acts of memorialization. *Saving Private Ryan* gained further status as an officially endorsed historical document when Spielberg was awarded the Department of Defense's (DOD) highest civilian award for what the DOD described in its transcript of the Award Ceremony (1999) as an "historic contribution to the national consciousness." In turn, due in part to his portrayal of Captain Miller, in 2006 Tom Hanks became the first actor to be inducted into the Army Ranger's Hall of Fame, an honor usually reserved for those who have served in the unit and an act that blurs the boundaries between history and film. Like *The Longest Day*, *Saving Private Ryan* has generated its own culture of nostalgia. First optioned by television network ABC, whose contract with Spielberg stipulated that the film would be aired uncut, *Saving Private Ryan* continues to be shown on US television on or around Veteran's Day (November 11). In a further example of the blurring of the film with history, as well as of the nostalgia industry that has built up around World War II, *Saving Private Ryan* has been appropriated by the industry offering commemorative tours for World War II. One such tour group, Specialty Tours (http://spec-tours. com/saving-private-ryan/) offers a special *Saving Private Ryan* tour visit to the grave of the Niland brothers (on whom the story is loosely based), while another, Battle of Normandy Tours, lists *Saving Private Ryan* under one of its Battle Sites/Sights on its website (www.battleofnormandytours.com/omaha-beach.html).

If World War II tours and the US military's support of Hanks and Spielberg validate the film's claim to history, the response of veterans to *Saving*

Private Ryan endorses its status as memory. Unsurprisingly, veterans feature prominently in the discursive events around *Saving Private Ryan*. In heavily publicized affairs, veterans attended special screenings, and their responses authenticate the film's ability to accurately recreate and recall combat. A veteran of the Vietnam War (quoted in Wallace, 1998) admits to being reduced to "a whimpering, sobbing pile of blubber" by the film's combat scenes, and a World War II veteran notes, "It makes you feel like you're there. And as I was, and this is how it happened, people should know it" (quoted in Hughes 1998). Even Paul Fussell, one of the most vocal critics of Hollywood's depictions of warfare, writes that "[t]he movie's treatment of D-Day is so unrelenting in its appalling honesty that few combat veterans will emerge from it without crying and trembling all over again" (1989). A dedicated telephone line was set up by the Department of Veterans Affairs in the US to offer counseling to veterans or their families traumatized by the viewing, lending credence to the idea of the film as a trigger for traumatic memories. *Saving Private Ryan* also features in accounts of veterans (see Wallace 1998 for one example) talking about their experiences as they had not done before, supporting the idea that the film offers itself as an intervention between generations and breaks the silence imposed by traumatic memory.

Saving Private Ryan may have saved the memories of veterans from the silence imposed by trauma, but it embeds those memories in an uncritical homage to the Greatest Generation. The influence of Stephen Ambrose's work is evident in the vicarious nostalgia that pervades *Saving Private Ryan* and in the implicit unfavorable comparison between the generation that fought the war and their progeny. Because *Saving Private Ryan* suggests that combat is the experience that defined and refined the wartime generation, the film's nostalgic view of the Greatest Generation cannot be separated from nostalgia for the war itself. Howard Zinn, a veteran of World War II, is uncomfortable with the term "Greatest Generation" and questions why it has been attributed to "participants in war" rather than to any other generation in America's history (Zinn 2001). Zinn points out that there are ideological and political consequences in commemorating the soldier and combat as the focal points of the Greatest Generation because it leads to the celebration of "[m]ilitary heroism [as] the noblest form of heroism, when it should be remembered only as the tragic accompaniment of horrendous policies driven by power and profit" (ibid.). According to another commentator, nostalgia for the Greatest Generation and for World War II is precisely what enables the conflict to function as a "touchstone for martial combat" and to be used to invest future wars with the same sense of righteous purpose (Hayes 2006).

Responses to the film provide evidence of the ideological and political impact of *Saving Private Ryan* and the spread of vicarious nostalgia. On the day that *Saving Private Ryan* opened in cinemas in the US (July 24, 1998), America Online (AOL) launched a special section on its website dedicated to the film, with links to reviews, historical accounts, and books about World War II, as well as a message board. After receiving around 30,000 posts on these forums, AOL, in partnership with DreamWorks, published a collection of responses edited by Jesse Kornbluth and Linda Sunshine in the form of a book called *Now You Know: Reactions After Seeing* Saving Private Ryan (1999). According to AOL chairman Steve Case, the book provides evidence that *Saving Private Ryan* is more than "just a film"; it is a "a profound and personal experience for millions of Americans" prompting a "national conversation" about the war (quoted in Confessore 2001). It should be remembered that despite the pledge from both AOL and DreamWorks that all royalties and earnings from the book would go to the National D-Day Museum in New Orleans (founded by Ambrose), the publication of *Now You Know* is not altogether altruistic. The collection provides a platform to advertise AOL, as well as an additional source of publicity endorsing the film (no negative responses are included). Nevertheless, the collection is useful in providing insight into aspects of the discursive activity around the film close to its cinematic release.

In *Saving Private Ryan*, the bookish and untried clerk, Corporal Upham (Jeremy Davis), quotes Ralph Waldo Emerson, describing war as bringing "men into such swift and close collision in critical moments that man measures man." There is a distinct sense throughout *Now You Know* that *Saving Private Ryan* acts as a similar catalyst but positions World War II as a critical point of comparison for generation to measure generation. From the "survivor's guilt" of the viewer who felt after seeing the film that "my career, home, and all things I hold dear appear underserved, as I have not earned them" (Kornbluth and Sunshine 1999, 104) to the two active servicemen who question their own preparedness for war (32 and 74) and the sixteen-year-old chastising his generation for ignorance and indifference and asking whether they have "earned" their freedom (94), the responses indicate that Miller's exhortation to Ryan to "earn" the sacrifice made by his men is read as a directive to subsequent generations of Americans, who feel themselves wanting in comparison to the Greatest Generation. The elevation of military heroism above all other kinds of heroism is implicit in such responses, although one AOL member states this explicitly, exhorting the members of the X Generation to reevaluate the meaning of heroism "next time your 'heroes' sing in concert or do a dance in the end zone" (81).

There is an entire section of responses, titled "I Understand My Father Now" (38–49), devoted to accounts indicating that *Saving Private Ryan* not only breaks the silence surrounding traumatic memory but also allows for its preservation. Significant in these responses is the empathy apparent not only for the veterans of World War II but for all American combat soldiers. In the words of one respondent, "After seeing *Saving Private Ryan* I finally have a much better understanding of why my husband will not talk about his experiences in Vietnam and why my father will also not talk about his experiences during WWII" (41). *Saving Private Ryan* consequently does more than rescue traumatic memory. The film also effectively restores the memory of *all* American soldiers to something approaching the "magnificent, marvelous human beings" they were once regarded as before Cold War conflicts tainted them with moral and ethical uncertainties (interview in Terkel 1985, 118). A common thread running through all the comments recorded in the section on "understanding" the previous generation is a veneration of all US soldiers in all wars, including Vietnam and the more recent Gulf War. In recalibrating the memory of the citizen soldier, *Saving Private Ryan* thus has the potential to influence attitudes toward future wars. "After all," writes the twenty-one-year-old son of a veteran, "we are the age of people who will be the flesh of the Armed Forces, or the people who may vote to use those forces" (43).

The conversation about *Saving Private Ryan* extends far beyond AOL and America's borders and continues as of this writing. Published just before the seventieth anniversary of D-Day, an article by John Biguenet (2014) debating the "profound contradiction" of *Saving Private Ryan* and ending with an exhortation that echoes Miller's last words to Ryan—that subsequent generations need to "earn" the sacrifices made by the generation who fought in World War II—prompted an online debate about the film's ideological message. The Internet Movie Database's (IMDb) user comments and reviews on its page for *Saving Private Ryan* are another example of the ongoing discursive activity engendered by the film.[9] A thread entitled "Is This Film US Propaganda?" (started February 17, 2013), for example, initiated heated discussions not only regarding the nature of the German army but also the present state of security in the US. The user reviews in turn reveal that the film instigates more complex responses than those suggested by *Now You Know*. Although most reviews are positive—as of this writing, 1,026 reviews "loved" the film, while 616 "hated" it according to IMDb's points rating—some negative reviews stem from a dislike of a perceived moral superiority of the US soldiers in the film or in response to the omission of the Allies and civilians.[10] In both positive and negative responses, however, the Omaha Beach sequence is frequently regarded as a direct line to the past created through emotional responses to the hypermediated depiction of combat, which are unproblematically incorporated into personal experience and memory. In the words of one such review (posted July 31, 1998): "[F]rom the opening frame, I was 'there'. I wasn't watching a moving tribute, I was being shot at, watching comrades die horribly, and running for my life."

Saving Private Ryan returned a worldwide gross of over $481 million (according to thenumbers.com), vindicating the risk that Spielberg and Hanks took with the film, but as the ongoing interest in the film suggests, its theatrical release represents only part of the film's life cycle and cascading impact on other media. In 1999, the film made the most successful debut onto rental at the time, with the video alone earning $44 million in the sell-through market (Graser 1999), even before the release of the film onto DVD and Blu-ray. While *Saving Private Ryan* focuses on D-Day as the pivotal moment in the war, its financial success restored World War II in general as a viable subject for the entertainment industry, directly and indirectly influencing subsequent productions across a range of media. These include television series *Band of Brothers* and *The Pacific* (HBO, 2001 and 2010, respectively) and the *Medal of Honor* games franchise (EA Games, 1999–present), which will be discussed in more detail in the remaining chapters. The success of the film also indirectly resulted in a spate of World War II films, including *U-571* (Jonathan Mostow, 2000), *Pearl Harbor* (Michael Bay, 2001), *Windtalkers* (John Woo, 2002), and the Eastwood diptych in 2006. *Saving Private Ryan* not only inspired the world to remember a particular version of World War II but also restored the history of conflict as a source of lucrative cultural capital for the media industry in general.

As the nexus point for both public and private memory as well as a catalyst for other mediations of the conflict, *Saving Private Ryan* is a master mediation of World War II. As such, the film significantly impacted the architecture of the citizen soldier, the "good war," and the esthetic depiction of warfare. In its redeployment of spectacle through the esthetic of the "spectacular-authentic," *Saving Private Ryan*'s hypermediated battle sequences left an indelible mark on the visual construction of World War II and set a benchmark for all future representations of industrialized warfare. If the citizen soldier of the Baby Boomers' mediascape was an unstable figure in transition, *Saving Private Ryan* marks the end of that transitional period. Severed from the ideological and political framework of the wider conflict, the citizen soldier of *Saving Private Ryan* fights instead for his brothers in arms and emerges clearly as the primary victim of war. The emphasis on sacrifice for the "man next to you" in *Saving Private Ryan* marks a profound shift in the architecture of the citizen soldier. It is a shift implying that men can be brought into a recognition of their "true nature and their essential relationships" only in the crucible of warfare (Gray [1959] 1998, 48). By making the soldier's willingness to die for his comrades central to the identity of the citizen soldier, *Saving Private Ryan* perpetuates the association between the soldier and sacrifice. The film's focus on self-sacrifice masks the fact that, as Joanna Bourke points out, the fundamental action of men in war "is not dying, it is killing" (1999, xiii). The notion of self-sacrifice elevates suffering and death on the battlefield to the level of nobility and allows for the persistence of the idea of World War II as a "good war." I will continue to explore the rehabilitation of the citizen soldier and the consolidation of the structure around the notion of brotherly love and sacrifice in the remainder of this book, but it is important to note that the shifts in the citizen soldier have spread outward into the transmedia structures of other wars. For example, toward the end of *Black Hawk Down* (Ridley Scott, 2001), a film based on

a disastrous incident involving US Army Rangers and Delta Force opera-
tives in Mogadishu in 1993, one of the Delta Force soldiers remarks that
civilians do not understand that war is "[a]bout the men next to you. And
that's it. That's all it is." The reduction of war to an exclusive, liminal
space of masculine endeavor and relationships not only perpetuates its
appeal but also obviates the necessity of questioning the morality or suitability of a military response to a given situation, an issue that takes on
particular significance in the light of US involvement in more recent conflicts in Iraq and Afghanistan.

Although the events of June 6, 1944, are particularly well suited to
narratives emphasizing pride in the US involvement in World War II, the
unprecedented ferocity of the fighting in the Pacific theater is more difficult to accommodate in neat narratives of unambiguous military success,
perhaps accounting for the shift in interest in the two theaters in films
of the 1960s. In the absence of the racial stereotyping that once served
as justification for the savage nature of the war waged by both sides in
the Pacific theater, it has become increasingly tricky for Hollywood to
reconcile the constructs of the citizen soldier and the "good war" with
the extreme behaviors that characterized the war in this arena. Marilyn
Young suggests that a resemblance between many of the Pacific islands
and the terrain of Vietnam provides an additional explanation for why
the Pacific theater gradually proved to be a "less popular location in
which to revisit World War II" (2006, 317). This is not to suggest, however, that the Pacific disappeared from cinema screens. On the contrary,
a few months after *Saving Private Ryan*, an adaptation of James Jones's
novel about the battle for Guadalcanal, *The Thin Red Line* (Terence
Malick), was released in January 1999. With philosophical voice-overs
in which characters meditate on man's role in combat and in life, as well
as shadowy enemy forces who blend with the tropical vegetation and
remain an enigma, *The Thin Red Line* is closer in both theme and visual
structure to films about Vietnam than to representations of World War II,
validating Young's point. In contrast, *Flags of Our Fathers* and *Letters
from Iwo Jima* revolve around an iconic image from the war in the Pacific
that serves as an enduring symbol of American national identity: Joe
Rosenthal's photograph of the flag raising on Iwo Jima. Whereas *Saving Private Ryan* uncritically incorporates aspects of the wartime visual
structure of World War II, Eastwood's two films attempt to interrogate
the principles of representation in operation during the war, questioning
the constructed nature of images of conflict. *Flags of Our Fathers* and
Letters from Iwo Jima reveal the processes through which subsequent
generations encounter and challenge the meanings that have accrued in
the transmedia structure of World War II. The next section examines the
reconfiguration of the citizen soldier, the "good war," and the visual construction of the war in a theater of operations widely regarded as more
brutal than the war in Europe.

FLAGS OF OUR FATHERS AND LETTERS FROM IWO JIMA

Shortly after the release of *Saving Private Ryan*, Spielberg secured the film rights to James Bradley's book, *Flags of Our Fathers* (2000), a book written about his father, John Bradley, and his father's involvement in Joe Rosenthal's photograph of the flag raising on Iwo Jima. Feeling that he had already completed his "tour of duty" with *Saving Private Ryan* (interview in Daly 2006), Spielberg acted as producer on what would eventually became two films, both directed by Clint Eastwood, *Flags of Our Fathers* and *Letters from Iwo Jima*. The films promised to deliver a dual perspective of the history of the battle for the island, one of the most ferocious fights of the Pacific campaign. According to Karal Marling and John Wetenhall (2002), Iwo Jima represents a "holy place in [American] civil religion, where emotions gather and linger—for generations." At least two iconic iterations of the citizen soldier associated with Iwo Jima provide evidence of the ongoing emotional resonances of the battle in US media. The first is Rosenthal's photograph, which the editors of *US Camera Magazine* described at the time as depicting the "soul of the nation," according to *The Chicago Times* (2006). The second is John Wayne's portrayal of Sergeant Stryker in *The Sands of Iwo Jima* (Allan Dwan, 1949). In 1971, the Marine Corps League named John Wayne as the man who best epitomized what it means to be American (Bourke 1999, 14). Both Rosenthal's photograph and Dwan's film are indicative of inextricable connections between US national identity and martial traits in the transmedia structure of the war. Like *The Sands of Iwo Jima*, *Flags of our Fathers* and *Letters from Iwo Jima* are part of ongoing iterations and remediations of Rosenthal's photograph, and they also demonstrate how the citizen soldier, the notion of the "good war," and the visual construction of the war developed in the wake of *Saving Private Ryan*.

Joe Rosenthal's photograph meets the criteria of what Andrew Hoskins calls a "flashframe," in that it is "instantly and widely recognizable as representing a particular event or moment in history" (2004, 6). The circumstances surrounding Rosenthal's photograph reveal the significance of flashframe images in the mediated construct of the war and indicate some of the processes through which meaning accrues around them. It is therefore worth briefly examining the conditions under which the photograph was taken and came to prominence, before turning to an analysis of *Flags of Our Fathers* and *Letters from Iwo Jima*. The raising of the flag on Mt. Suribachi was a kind of "presentational spectacle" in itself, as Philip Beidler puts it, because it was deliberately intended to boost the morale of the US forces after four days of vicious fighting on the island (1998, 57). Colonel Chandler Johnson, commander of the 2nd Battalion of the US Marines, ordered a unit from the 28th Regiment to plant the flag on Mt. Suribachi, the highest point on the island, "if" they made it to the summit (Bradley and Powers 2006, 202). Expecting at any moment to be attacked by the Japanese, who were still embedded in the underground network of tunnels and bunkers honeycombing the entire island, the unit made it to the top of the mountain with relatively minor opposition and raised the first US flag to be planted on Japanese soil. At the sight of the flag, Marines all over the island cheered and shouted, while vessels offshore blew their horns. Shortly afterward, a smaller group of men was sent up with a larger flag to replace the first one, which the regiment's colonel wished to secure as a souvenir for the unit. The raising of the replacement flag was photographed by Associated Press photographer Joe Rosenthal, who also arranged a few posed pictures of the soldiers on the summit around the flag. The second flag raising received little attention from the forces massed on the beaches and anchored offshore. Like most civilian photographers in the field, there were no facilities available for Rosenthal to develop his own film, and he was consequently unaware that he had produced an extraordinary photograph.

Joe Rosenthal's photograph captured the essence of the citizen soldier's emblematic significance for wartime America. The flag raisers are engaged in a collective endeavor that suggests that the labor of war is constructive rather than destructive and that symbolically unites the martial and the civilian aspect of the anonymous GI.[11] Upon its publication in the US press on February 25, 1945, the photograph was presented according to wartime principles of representation. Reports that carried the photograph emphasized the resilience of the Marines and the fierceness of the fighting for the island. In the *Los Angeles Times* (1945a), for example, the text accompanying the photograph describes how "United States Marines hoist American Flag atop Suribachi . . . after battling Japs to rim of crater." Rosenthal's photograph was framed by US media as a moment of triumph for US forces, and the flag raisers were presented as daring heroes who captured the mountain, when in fact the fighting for the island, including Mt. Suribachi, was far from over. Newspapers were inundated with requests for reprints following the photograph's publication, and the image became "one of the most talked-about pictures of the war," according to an article on the photograph a month later in *Life* (1945a, 17). A few days later, when congratulated on the success of his photograph by another war correspondent, it did not occur to Rosenthal that any picture of the second flag raising would be considered significant. Consequently, in the belief that the correspondent was referring to one of the staged photographs, he replied in the affirmative when asked if the picture had been posed. As a result of a convoluted amalgamation of Rosenthal's misunderstanding, confusion around the two separate flag raisings, difficulties in correctly identifying the men involved (some of whom had been killed in the fighting), and the subsequent adoption of both the picture and the surviving flag raisers in the massive public relations exercise that was the Seventh War Bond Drive, the photograph and its history became, in Beidler's words, a "classic instance of the interpenetration of American myth and American reality, of imaginative fiat and actualized event" (1998, 57).

Eastwood's *Flags of Our Fathers* investigates the fissures between American myth and reality and exposes the tension between the mediated construction of the citizen soldier and the public perception of the symbol with the actual experiences and memories of individual soldiers. Cowritten with journalist Ron Powers, the book on which *Flags of Our Fathers* is based is the product of James Bradley's need to understand why his father, John Bradley, never spoke about what happened on the island. As with much of the writings of Stephen Ambrose, who endorsed the book, *Flags of Our Fathers* is drawn from a collection of interviews conducted with survivors and their families. Like *Saving Private Ryan, Flags of Our Fathers* is thus part of one generation's drive to come to terms with the actions of their forebears. According to Clint Eastwood in "An Introduction by Clint Eastwood" (Rowen 2007), an extra feature on the 2007 DVD release of the films (Warner Home Video), it is "important" that subsequent generations come to know the wartime generation because that generation "had a spirit; they believed." Both *Flags of Our Fathers* and *Letters from Iwo Jima* situate the figures of the American and the Japanese citizen soldier as representative of their respective wartime generations.

The film adaptation of *Flags of Our Fathers* juxtaposes the memories and experiences of the three surviving flag raisers—Ira Hayes (played by Adam Beach), Rene Gagnon (Jesse Bradford), and John "Doc" Bradley (Ryan Phillippe)—of the battle for Iwo Jima with the celebrations and public events they are subject to on home ground, illustrating the chasm between home front perceptions of the war and the soldiers' firsthand knowledge of combat. Once correctly identified by the US military, Ira, Rene, and "Doc" Bradley were labeled the "heroes of Iwo Jima" and were drafted into becoming figureheads and feted celebrities for the Seventh Bond Drive. Throughout the film, the three Marines are forced not only to reencounter the photograph in various forms but also to reenact the circumstances that led to the flag raising. One of these reenactments takes place at Soldier Field in Chicago, where they are asked to climb a papier-mâché mountain to reenact the flag raising while "pretending" that their dead brothers in arms are with them. "Hey," says one of the promoters when the men are incredulous at the request, "that's showbiz!"

The film returns to the scene at Soldier Field at various points throughout the narrative, literally breaking the moment apart and highlighting the artifice of reenactment and the cost it exacts from the three survivors. The traumatic memories harbored by Ira, Rene, and Doc are thus set at odds with the national story being constructed around the photograph. Early in the film, the men are shown struggling uphill in the dark, the sky lit by explosions and flares, in a scene that creates the impression that they are engaged in battle (Figure 3.3). But as they reach the top of the "mountain," the stadium and the cheering crowds of Soldier Field are revealed, and it becomes apparent that the sky is lit by fireworks, not firepower (Figure 3.4).

Figure 3.3 Two of the flag raisers in what appears to be combat on Iwo.

Figure 3.4 Their view from the "summit" as Soldier's Field is revealed.

This scene does more than subvert the spectator's expectations; it demonstrates how traumatic memory overrides the present and transforms it into the past. Later, when the film returns to the papier-mâché Mt. Suribachi, the scene of the recreation is intercut with flashbacks to the conflict on the island during which each man witnesses the death of the other flag raisers. *Flags of Our Fathers* thus brings the "showbiz" recreations of the battle for the island into sharp contrast with the individual traumatic memories of the soldier.

In exposing the chasm between public perceptions of combat and the experiences of the soldiers who do the fighting, the film also explores the tension between the wartime mediated image of the citizen soldier and the soldiers themselves. For the character of Pima Indian Ira Hayes, the gap between the conceptualization of the citizen soldier as a hero and the brutal realities of the battlefield proves impossible to negotiate. As he puts it, "I can't take them calling me a hero. All I did was try not to get shot. Some of the things I saw done, things I did, they weren't things to be proud of, you know?" Despite the sense of common purpose suggested by the photograph and the motto "Now All Together" emblazoning the posters for the Seventh Bond Drive, Ira is expelled from a bar that refuses to serve Native Americans in an incident that suggests that the idea of national unity so vital to the war effort is as much a façade as the papier-mâché construction of Mt. Suribachi. All three men are positioned as victims not only of war but also of a ruthless administration willing to exploit them in order to achieve its goals and of a civilian population with no understanding of the realities of warfare. Despite their attempts to deny their status as heroes and to stress the banal reality of the circumstances of the flag raising, a member of the Treasury Department sums up their situation when he tells the three that "you're in the picture, you raised the flag, that's the story we're selling, boys."

In contrast to the story being "sold" by wartime media and the US military, the three GIs of *Flags of Our Fathers* are depicted in the film as "ordinary boys" caught up in circumstances beyond their control. Unlike *Sands of Iwo Jima* and John Wayne's depiction of Sergeant Stryker, there is no major star persona in *Flags of Our Fathers* to distinguish the soldiers. Similar to Spielberg in *Saving Private Ryan*, Eastwood deliberately cast relatively unknown actors in an attempt to underscore the ordinariness of the flag raisers. The film's final scene returns to Iwo Jima, as the men who raised the second flag strip off their uniforms to swim in the ocean. According to the character of James Bradley (played by Thomas McCarthy), who speaks the final lines of *Flags of Our Fathers* in the voice-over of this scene, "If we wish to truly honor these men we should remember them the way they really were." Implicit in Bradley's words is the idea that *Flags of Our Fathers* is not merely another showbiz recreation of the events around Joe Rosenthal's photograph. Instead, the film supposedly reveals the ordinary boys beneath their uniforms as "they really were."

Flags of Our Fathers deconstructs the wartime citizen soldier and counters the notion of individual heroism as represented by John Wayne's Sergeant Stryker, but despite claiming to present the soldiers as "they really were," the film reaffirms the structural design of the citizen soldier in more recent representations of World War II. The citizen soldiers of *Flags of Our Fathers* may fight for their country, but they die "for their friends," as James Bradley's character puts it in the final lines of the film. Rather than rejecting the concept of heroism, *Flags of Our Fathers* rearticulates it through the citizen soldier's willingness to sacrifice himself for "the man in front, for the man beside him," in the words of the voice-over that ends the film. Self-sacrifice consequently emerges once again as a mainstay in the construction of the citizen soldier, creating a morally inviolate category of heroism in which the soldier may be celebrated even if the war is not. According to one of the taglines for the film on its posters and DVD releases, "every soldier stands beside a hero"—a statement presumably intended to reflect the self-effacing character of the citizen soldiers who fought in World War II but one that inadvertently implies that *all* soldiers are heroes simply by virtue of being soldiers, regardless of the ideological and political circumstances of war itself. In keeping with this line of reasoning, the enemy faced by America's citizen soldiers on Iwo Jima receives the same designation.

Letters from Iwo Jima presents the battle from the perspective of the Japanese and challenges one of the central tenets in the wartime media's representations of the war: the extreme dehumanization of the Japanese. During the war itself, the Japanese were routinely depicted in American media through exaggerated racial stereotypes; at best, they were caricatured and, at worst, divested of humanity through representations as animals, insects, or monsters. In the Pacific, racial hatred on both sides created a war so extreme that anthropologist Simon Harrison (2012) considers it as verging on a fight between species. John Dower (1986, 92) reminds us that Marines on Iwo Jima went into battle with the legend "Rodent Exterminator" on their helmets in an example of the "fear, fury, and protective black jokes" characteristic of the GI, as well as of the racial hatred that pervaded the Pacific theater. The furious cynicism of the citizen soldier is dying out in current representations, and there is no trace of it to be found in either *Saving Private Ryan* or *Flags of Our Fathers*, but the extreme manifestations of the GI's dark humor that characterized the Pacific war were justified at the time through the process of othering. The othering of the enemy can perhaps be understood as an inevitable consequence of war's twisted logic because rendering the enemy so radically different that they are scarcely human is necessary in order to enable acts of destruction and killing (Torgovnick 2005, 9). Yet, although US media made ideological distinctions between Germans and Nazis, as Dower points out, there was no Japanese equivalent to the "good German" in the wartime transmedia structure of the conflict (1986, 8).

Hollywood's denigration of the Japanese, which Bernard Dick (1985, 230) describes as "unparalleled in movie history," supported idioms in the national war narrative of American national superiority and therefore reflected the general principles of representation at work across wartime media. After the war, however, as the image of the Japanese underwent a gradual rehabilitation due to their repositioning as a Cold War ally against Communist China, the ferocity of the fighting in the Pacific could no longer be "justified" through the othering of the enemy as it had been in films such as *Bataan* and *Guadalcanal Diary* (Lewis Sieler, 1943). Instead, films like *None but the Brave* (Frank Sinatra, 1965) and *Beach Red* (Cornell Wilde, 1967) turned to the Pacific theater to portray the damage that war inflicts on soldiers of both sides and to reflect contemporary concerns about the moral implications of armed conflict during the Vietnam War. Although it is unusual to have two separate films present opposing perspectives of the same battle, *Flags of Our Fathers* and *Letters from Iwo Jima* are thus not entirely unprecedented in their portrayal of soldiers on both sides of the Pacific war. *None but the Brave* and *Beach Red* similarly explore the brutalizing impact of battle on the "countless varieties of ordinary men blown together by a wind called war," as the Japanese commander in *None but the Brave* describes his soldiers.

Similar to the flag raisers in *Flags of Our Fathers*, the soldiers of *Letters from Iwo Jima* are at the mercy not only of war but of the governing body that sent them out to fight. The Imperial Regime, according to General Kuribayashi (Ken Watanabe), is "deceiving not just the people, but us as well." The casting of Ken Watanabe in the role of Kuribayashi serves a similar purpose to that of Tom Hanks in *Saving Private Ryan*, in this case providing a perfect bridge not just between generations but also between cultures; Watanabe is well-known both in Japan and America. Although a career soldier, Kuribayashi does not fanatically embrace the tenets of Japanese Imperialist aggression and instead struggles against a traditional military mind-set that threatens to undermine and overthrow his strategies for the defense of the island. While Kuribayashi represents the military elite, the character of Saigo, played by Kazunari Ninomiya, is the Japanese version of the citizen soldier as an "ordinary man." The casting of Ninomiya, a member of a popular boy band and a well-known figure in Japan, provides an entry point for a younger audience that otherwise might not have formed part of the film's demographic. However, like Kuribayashi, Saigo also provides a familiar point of reference for American audiences. While Kuribayashi evokes the archetypal figure of the refined and educated Japanese commander familiar from films such as *Three Came Home* (Jean Negulesco, 1950) and *None but the Brave*, Saigo is the one soldier who most resembles the grumbling, humorous GI Joe of American wartime films and cartoons, particularly George Baker's *Sad Sack* comic strip, which featured a hapless and clumsy GI. "Damn this island," he says at the start of the film, "the Americans can have it." In contrast to wartime depictions of fanatical and single-minded Japanese soldiers, Saigo does not want to fight. More than anything, Saigo wants to return home to his wife and child and, crucially, he does not embrace the idea of honor through self-sacrifice.

While Americans were drawing on narrative traditions celebrating those who fought to the last man in films like *Wake Island* and *Bataan*, the unwillingness of the Japanese to surrender was portrayed in American media as evidence of their inhumanity (Dower 1986, 12). An officer in *Guadalcanal Diary*, for example, describes the determination of the Marines as "bulldog tenacity," but the film depicts the refusal of the Japanese to capitulate as evidence of blind fanaticism. Just as *Flags of Our Fathers* deconstructs ideas of wartime heroism, *Letters from Iwo Jima* dismantles the wartime myth of Japanese fanaticism. Interviewed in "Red Sun, Black Sand: The Making of *Letters from Iwo Jima*" (Rowen 2007), Clint Eastwood observes that American soldiers landed on Iwo Jima hoping to survive, whereas Japanese soldiers knew they had been sent there to die. Consequently, *Letters from Iwo Jima* is a last stand narrative in which Japanese soldiers fight on an isolated outpost to protect their homeland. However, in contrast to the tradition in the US last stand template that depicts soldiers as heroic defenders of freedom (as in *Wake Island* and *Bataan*), the Japanese soldiers of *Letters from Iwo Jima* are sacrificial victims of the very ideology they are fighting to defend. As Robert Burgoyne (2012, 178) points out, the key moments in *Letters from Iwo Jima* are not those in which the beleaguered soldiers of the island engage with the enemy but those that represent internal battles for survival.

Letters from Iwo Jima shows how, in order to prolong the Japanese defense of the island, Gen. Kuribayashi struggles to overcome a military philosophy that values the death of soldiers more than their lives. Emiko Ohnuki-Tierney (2007) points out that "[w]hile the Nazis told their soldiers to kill the enemy, the Japanese military told their soldiers to kill themselves." The standing order in the Japanese military that soldiers commit suicide rather than surrender to the enemy dates back to the first Sino-Japanese War of the late 1800s. By World War II, as Uki Tanaka (1996, 9) explains, the belief in honorable self-sacrifice had been incorporated into a concept known as *gyokusai* (literally meaning "shattered jade" but that also translates as "glorious self-annihilation"), in which soldiers were expected to display their loyalty to the emperor by dying in his service. Suicidal attacks are not unique to the Japanese, but what differentiates the concept of *gyokusai* is that in the final years of the war, special units specifically designed for suicidal attacks were incorporated into official military strategy, reflecting what Tanaka identifies as a wider tendency in the Japanese military to "undervalue the strategic importance of minimizing casualties" (1996, 198). Kuribayashi orders his men to fight rather than to die needlessly but nevertheless acknowledges that the defense of the island is doomed from the start. As a result, every soldier is forced into a personal confrontation with the concept of *gyokusai*.

Some, like Lieutenant Ito (Shidou Nakamura), seek out self-sacrifice willingly, while others, like Saigo, resist it. In the film's most graphic scene of self-sacrifice in which a group of soldiers commit suicide by blowing themselves up with grenades, Robert Burgoyne describes how "each character seems to wage combat, a battle of wills, against an opponent who forces their arms and moves them according to its own desires" (2010, 180). The primary struggle for these Japanese soldiers is thus not about killing their enemies in combat but a confrontation between their own drive for self-preservation and a cultural mind-set that demands their annihilation. The other two scenes of suicide in the film, of Baron Nishi (Tsuyoshi Ihara) and of Kuribayashi himself, are more serene. In contrast to the men in the cave, both Nishi and Kuribayashi have already been severely wounded and their deaths consequently take on a different resonance. In Robert Burgoyne's reading of the film, Nishi's suicide echoes the gestures of Western heroes, expressing the "history of a nation—of national ideology—in ruins" (2012, 359), while that of Kuribayashi merges "the samurai sword and the Colt .45, the landscapes of island and Western desert" (2012, 362). In both cases, however, the last stand template and its associations with the extreme spaces of the frontier (the island of Iwo Jima really does mark the edge of Japanese national territory) ennobles the act of suicide and makes it accessible, if not acceptable. *Letters from Iwo Jima* therefore inverts the usual application of the last stand template in war films like *Bataan* and even in *Saving Private Ryan*, where the desperation of the situation justifies the extreme violence of combat. Instead, the violence of the Japanese soldier in *Letters from Iwo Jima* is primarily directed inward at annihilation of the self rather than of the enemy.

Letters from Iwo Jima consequently preserves the perspective that the primary role of soldiers in war is to die, not to kill. Crucially, none of the suicidal acts causes any damage to American soldiers. The only Japanese soldier who attempts a suicide bombing is a pathetic figure, lying for two days in various ditches waiting in vain for an American tank to roll over him. It is therefore possible to argue, as Robert Burgoyne does, that the film humanizes an act that continues to register as "deeply other" in American perception—namely, the act of self-annihilation made "glorious" through its service to a powerful belief system (2010, 175). However, it is important to bear in mind that *Letters from Iwo Jima* manages to render self-annihilation accessible only by avoiding any indication of damage to American soldiers and by representing the Japanese soldiers as the sacrificial victims of their belief system and of the culture that created it. The soldiers in *Letters from Iwo Jima* are victims of the ideology of their times.

Yuki Tanaka points to a tendency in recent scholarship on Japan to reinforce a distance between the current generation and the wartime generation, allowing the latter to be perceived as "other," with whom the former "share nothing, including responsibility" (1996, 6). *Letters from Iwo Jima* reclaims the humanity of the Japanese from the enemy "other" of American wartime media by resurrecting aspects of the US citizen soldier almost lost in the transmedia structure of the war in the figure of Saigo—a bumbling sad sack who always draws the worst duties and who never actually fires his weapon. But by representing the Japanese soldiers as victims of a brutal regime and of an ideology that adopts suicide as an acceptable military strategy, *Letters from Iwo Jima* also reconstitutes the soldier of the wartime generation as an accessible figure for the current generation in Japan.[12] However, by situating the soldiers as sacrificial victims, *Letters from Iwo Jima* elides the extremely problematic and complex issue of the Japanese soldier's complicity with the aggressive militaristic ideology that fueled the country's territorial expansion across Asia.[13] Just as *Flags of Our Fathers* never quite resolves the tension between citizen soldiers as ordinary men and their designation as heroes, *Letters from Iwo Jima* does not address the contradictions inherent in the soldier who is not simply the victim of belligerent militarism but also a willing participant in an ideology that preached its own brand of racial superiority as justification for war.

By showing the damage inflicted on soldiers on both sides of the war, *Flags of Our Fathers* and *Letters from Iwo Jima* avoid the comfortable assumptions about good versus evil that characterize the "good war" strand running through the transmedia construct of World War II. Nevertheless, both films perpetuate the binaries inherent in the wartime visual construction of the conflict that characterize American mediated memories of World War II—most significantly, those between war and peace and between chaos and order. The persistence of the wartime way of seeing conflict is due in part to an ongoing reliance on the wartime visual media still circulating in the transmedia construct of the war to provide a visual template for the "authentic" representation of combat scenes. Tom Stern, director of photography on both films, explains how a collection of photo annuals of all the "finest photographs" taken during each year of the war influenced not only his own approach to filming the battle scenes but also other areas of the production, including editing (interview in Williams 2006). Informed by these annuals, the combat sequences of *Flags of Our Fathers* and *Letters from Iwo Jima* adopt a visual style that resembles war correspondent footage. Michael Owens, visual effects supervisor, in an interview on the "Visual Effects" segment of the 2007 DVD (Rowen 2007), describes the style used in the films as a "photorealism-type" of esthetic. The esthetic of "photorealism" is therefore drawn from a perception that, as Julian Levi (visual effects producer) notes, "everyone" knows what World War II looks like because of the "hundreds and hundreds and hundreds of pictures" they have seen of the war (ibid.). *Flags of Our Fathers* and *Letters from Iwo Jima* are both concerned with the fissures between the visual construction of the war, as represented by one of those hundreds of photographs, and the individual experiences of soldiers on the island, yet the two films paradoxically rely on wartime images in order to reconstruct their own visual representation of the fighting on Iwo Jima.

Despite the attempts of cinematographer and visual effects team to cultivate a resemblance to combat footage and develop a realist esthetic, in both films Iwo Jima is constituted as a space so different from any other that it borders on the otherworldly. In *Flags of Our Fathers*, the island is the setting for dreams and traumatic flashbacks. In *Letters from Iwo Jima*, it is the habitation of ghosts, whose stories are released with the discovery of the letters at the beginning of the film.[14] The island itself provides some explanation for the films' depiction of the battle as unearthly. Iwo Jima was in actuality a unique environment. Extended shelling and the aerial bombardment ahead of the landing exposed a bizarre volcanic landscape of black sand and barren rock. In the words of one veteran, it was "one of the strangest battlefields in history" (quoted in Wheeler 1980, 188). Although much of the actual footage of the battle, including Milton Sperling's documentary, *To the Shores of Iwo Jima* (1945), is in color due to the conversion to 16-mm color film by Marine combat camera units at this stage of the war, Tom Stern opted for a black-and-white color palette for the scenes on the island in order to create a "[m]onochromatic world, a kind of über hell on earth" (interview in Williams 2006). Stern's choice reflects the persistence of monochromatic tones as the dominant color palette for the visual construction of World War II. As in *Saving Private Ryan*, however, certain colors, such the colors of the US flag and of blood, are accentuated in order to generate an emotional impact on the present. The result is a distinctive esthetic that separates Iwo Jima from other temporal and spatial locations in both films. As an *unheimlich* space that isolates the soldiers both literally and figuratively, the island is the perfect setting for what Glenn Gray refers to as "the strange" ([1959] 1998, 15)—events in war that are so far beyond the familiar experiences of home that they create an extreme discontinuity in the soldier's life, fitting with nothing that has gone before and proving impossible to assimilate once the soldier returns home. The two films reinforce the perception of war as an exclusive arena for the staging of extreme masculine emotions and the exploration of intense masculine relationships that have no equivalent in the spaces of the everyday. In both films, women are associated with the home front and with peace. Soldiers therefore are the primary victims of World War II in *Letters from Iwo Jima* and *Flags of Our Fathers*, and their experiences on the battlefield are the defining ones of the war.

In both films, spectacle and machinery play a crucial role in further delineating the spaces of war from those of the home front and in contributing to the sense of "the strange." Although the two films draw attention to the continuities in the experiences of the soldiers on both sides, the spectacle of mechanized warfare has a distinctly different emphasis in each film. *Flags of our Fathers* replicates much of the footage available from the invasion of Iwo Jima, including iconic scenes from *To the Shores of Iwo Jima*, such as aerial shots of the massive naval armada steaming toward the island and the numerous Higgins boats circling in holding patterns before landing on the beaches. As in *Saving Private Ryan*, stitched into the combat scenes are moments that would have been impossible to capture at the time, such as a sequence shot from the point of view of the cockpit of an American plane strafing the island or the moment in which Ira Hayes is hit by the severed head of a fellow Marine following a mortar blast. Digital effects combine with wartime imagery to create a spectacular-authentic visual construction of the war, based on similar principles of representation as in *Saving Private Ryan*. Through replicating wartime footage, *Flags of Our Fathers* reproduces the function of spectacle and machinery in the wartime media's visual construction of the war, as visual references of American military might. *Letters from Iwo Jima*, however, demonstrates the impact of American martial power and consequently casts a shadow of doubt on its moral application.

In *Flags of Our Fathers*, the bombardment of the island is part of the awe-inspiring spectacle of American war machinery at work. In *Letters from Iwo Jima*, spectacle is absent inasmuch as the bombs inflict little physical damage on the soldiers deep in the tunnels; instead, the bombardment is a form of psychological torture, gradually wearing down the morale of the troops. Similarly, the arrival of the US armada, which in *Flags of Our Fathers* is a symbol of relentless and ruthless power, becomes, in *Letters from Iwo Jima*, an intensely personal moment of discomfort for Saigo, and the scene in which he first sees the ships emphasizes the vulnerability of the Japanese forces in the face of superior technology. One weapon in particular illustrates the inversion of the perspective of machinery in the visual construction of World War II in *Letters from Iwo Jima*: the flamethrower. The flamethrower, either carried by infantry or mounted on tanks, is an iconic weapon of the Pacific war. Although the flamethrower was used by the US military in Europe, the weapon's effectiveness at neutralizing entrenched enemy positions otherwise impervious to attack made it particularly suitable for deployment against Japanese tunnels and bunkers in the Pacific theater. One of the most explicit sequences of photographs to come out of the Pacific depicts the death throes of a "Jap" in Borneo following a flamethrower assault, published in *Life* magazine toward the end of the war (1945b). Although *Life* describes the flamethrower as "[t]he most cruel, the most terrifying weapon ever developed," the article regards its deployment as inevitable "[s]o long as the Jap refuses to come out of his holes and keeps killing" (1945b, 34). Similarly, in *With the Marines at Tarawa* and *To the Shores of Iwo Jima*, the terrible spectacle of the flamethrower provides a dramatic visual demonstration of American weaponry at work while reassuring voice-overs imply that it is only due to the obdurate fanaticism of the enemy that such weapons are necessary (foreshadowing similar arguments used to justify the dropping of the two atomic bombs). In *Flags of Our Fathers*, the Marines deploy the flamethrower when all other measures have failed to clear a Japanese bunker, echoing its use in the photographic sequence in *Life*. Seen from the perspective of the Japanese soldier in *Letters from Iwo Jima*, however, the flamethrower is a hellish instrument of terror that unexpectedly shoots fire down into the black tunnels of the island. The deployment of the flamethrower, as well as the relentless bombing of Iwo

Jima, serves as explanation, if not justification, for the violence inflicted on an American soldier by a group of Japanese who have just witnessed one of their fellow soldiers burn to death. *Letters from Iwo Jima* therefore opens up the possibility of considering the consequences of the deployment of American weaponry and disrupts the delight in the spectacle and machinery of warfare that pervades the transmedia structure of the war.

Flags of Our Fathers points to the unreliability of official appropriations and interpretations of events in a conflict, but the film nevertheless relies on the wartime visual construction of the war as a measure of its own authenticity and consequently preserves some of the key polarities of the wartime visual construction of conflict—most importantly, the division between the spaces of war and those of the home front. Similarly, despite disrupting the visual construction of war by demonstrating the impact of American weapons on Japanese soldiers, the war in *Letters from Iwo Jima* is restricted to the island, and the impact of US weapons on civilians remains invisible. Of course, the concentration of warfare into a single space is due to the nature of the fighting on Iwo Jima (civilians were removed from the island ahead of the battle), but *Letters from Iwo Jima* represents the Japanese home front as a place of relative peace, which the soldiers are fighting to defend, and the only damage evident here is inflicted by the Imperial regime.[15] The continued omission of the impact of war on civilians feeds neatly into the idea that it is possible to wage war with minimal impact on noncombatants. Furthermore, in both films, civilians are ignorant of the realities of war, which remains the exclusive domain of the suffering soldier. Both films thus preserve the mystique of the battlefield as a space occupied and understood only by soldiers.

By concentrating on the soldier's experiences and memories of combat, *Flags of Our Fathers* and *Letters from Iwo Jima* go beyond *Saving Private Ryan* in absolving the memory not only of the American soldier but of *all* soldiers. The redemption of the citizen soldier on both sides of the fighting is, in one sense, the logical outcome of the separation of the soldier from the ideologies of war that began during the representations of the conflicts in Korea and Vietnam. Eastwood's diptych hints at atrocities committed by soldiers on both sides but preserves the notion that such acts are the result of war's brutalizing impact on men. Any suggestion of moral ambiguity in the architecture of the citizen soldier has been replaced in *Flags of Our Fathers* with the conviction of the nobility of sacrificing your life for the man next to you and in *Letters from Iwo Jima* with the certainty that, as Clint Eastwood puts it in "Red Sun, Black Sand" (Rowen 2007), "rightly or wrongly" the individual sacrifices made by soldiers can be acknowledged regardless of the ideological context of the war itself. *Saving Private Ryan* contracts the wartime generation's experiences of World War II into the soldier's memories of combat, but Eastwood's two films about Iwo Jima take the increasing focus on the citizen soldier's experience of war one step further by privileging the memories of the men who did the fighting above all others of the wartime generation. In both films, civilians appear incapable of challenging official perspectives of the war, and only the soldiers know the truth of the battle. In *Flags of Our Fathers*, the truth of their experiences remains buried in the memories of the three flag raisers, who never succeed in countering the myths created by the military and the press, whereas in *Letters from Iwo Jima*, the truth, in the form of the soldiers' letters home, is literally buried in a cave in the island. Like *Saving Private Ryan*, *Flags of Our Fathers*, and *Letters from Iwo Jima* speak for the veterans and, through them, claim to speak for the entire wartime generation.

As a flashframe, Joe Rosenthal's photograph of the flag raising acts as a kind of lightning conductor in the premediation and remediation of memories of the war, and it illuminates moments in which the three central aspects of the transmedia mnemonic structure are reinterpreted and reconfigured. During the war itself, the photograph functioned as a microcosm of the vision of World War II as constructed in American media. The photograph of anonymous citizen soldiers united in their efforts to achieve victory slotted easily into the national war narrative of a people fighting for the uniquely American ideals of freedom and democracy, as symbolized in the American flag. After the war, the photograph formed the frame for a new iteration of the citizen soldier and individual heroism in the form of John Wayne, a different kind of American icon. *Flags of Our Fathers* and *Letters from Iwo Jima* are part of the ongoing remediation of the photograph, and although they attempt to deconstruct aspects of the photograph's remediation in the transmedia construct of the war, the two films are nevertheless reliant on the construct itself as a measure of authenticity. Eastwood's diptych challenges the wartime definition of both heroism and villainy, but it also reaffirms the configuration of the citizen soldier as a member of a "band of brothers" and the spectacular-authentic nature of the visual construction of the war in the current generation's mediascape.

CONCLUSION

In *Saving Private Ryan*, the citizen soldier solidifies into a contemporary configuration in which traces of the uncommon common man remain. The heroism of the soldier is connected no longer to abstract ideologies such as freedom or democracy but rather to the willingness to sacrifice everything for a comrade in arms. *Saving Private Ryan* recalibrates the visual construction of the war in a hypermediated esthetic that combines imagery from wartime visual media with contemporary technologies of filmmaking. Despite vividly demonstrating the impact of war on the bodies of American soldiers, *Saving Private Ryan* preserves the idea of World War II as a "good war" through the conceptualization of sacrifice as the one "decent" element of war. The war that *Saving Private Ryan* asks the world to remember, therefore, is a conflict made righteous through the sacrifices that soldiers made for each other and for future generations of Americans.

Made in the aftermath of the events of September 11, 2001, and while the US was engaged in the Iraq war, *Flags of Our Fathers* and *Letters from Iwo Jima* confirm the resilience and stability of the structure of the contemporary citizen soldier despite Hollywood's concerns that such events had fundamentally altered the relationship between the American public, soldiers, and mediations of war.[16] When viewed together, *Flags of Our Fathers* and *Letters from Iwo Jima* question the idea of the "good war" and disturb the visual construction of the war; however, the two films also preserve the polarities that characterize the war's visual representation and its spectacular-authentic esthetic. More significantly, in both *Flags of Our Fathers* and *Letters from Iwo Jima*, the citizen soldier is the primary victim of war and of the institutions that sent him out to fight. In all three films discussed in this chapter, the citizen soldier is manipulated by the military and misunderstood by civilians, but he is also a member of a "band of brothers" and a hero simply by virtue of being a soldier. As Marilyn Young (2006, 321) points out, fighting for your brother in arms legitimizes the status of the "nation-at-war" because when the cause is "us," there can be no doubt that the cause is just—an ideological perspective with particular significance in the wars that followed September 11, 2001.

Saving Private Ryan, Flags of Our Fathers and *Letters from Iwo Jima* generate meaning precisely because of their intertextual relationships to an integrated system of mediated memories of World War II. As a master mediation, *Saving Private Ryan* provides a template that premediates aspects of the citizen soldier, the notion of the "good war," and the visual construction of the war for future representations. *Flags of Our Fathers* and *Letters from Iwo Jima* confirm the configuration of the citizen soldier as a hero because of his martial identity and his membership in an exclusive group of brothers in arms, as well as the visual construction of the war as a hypermediated spectacle that combines wartime strategies with contemporary techniques of filmmaking, but the two films also demonstrate that the concept of the "good war" does not fit easily with the extremes of the Pacific theater. Instead, current mediations of World War II are increasingly turning to the Pacific war as the arena in which to explore the ambiguities of conflict and to reflect concerns connected to contemporary wars. While this chapter focused primarily on intertextual relationships in the transmedia mnemonic structure of World War II, the next explores how the industrial contexts and connections operating within the system shape the representation of the conflict on television in two miniseries: *Band of Brothers* and *The Pacific*.

NOTES

1. But not, as we shall see in the next chapter, from television screens.
2. A prime example is the *Enola Gay* controversy mentioned in the Introduction, in which American veteran organizations vehemently opposed the inclusion of

material demonstrating the impact on the Japanese of the atomic bombings of Hiroshima and Nagasaki in a proposed exhibit at the Smithsonian National Air and Space Museum. The excision of the contentious material from the display can be seen as a continuation of the ellipses of the "good war" construct.

3. An extremely rough survey of films set in World War II and released in the 1950s reveals that those set in the Pacific are in the clear majority (at around forty). In the 60s, the balance shifts, with around thirty-five films set in Europe, as opposed to twenty-five in the Pacific. Figures are based on releases per year listed on IMDb (www.imdb.com).

4. The 1984 "Boys of Pointe du Hoc" speech (penned by Peggy Noonan) was delivered by Reagan beneath the cliffs scaled by US Army Rangers during the D-Day landings and was broadcast live across America on the major television networks. Both Douglas Brinkley (2005) and David Greenberg (2004) suggest that this speech triggered the burgeoning interest in the wartime generation and positioned June 6 as a central moment in the American memory of World War II in contemporary US culture. Stephen Ambrose and Tom Brokaw were both present at this event.

5. The choice of shutter speed imparts a staccato quality to movement and the sharpness of its focus gives explosions a particularly frenetic and "crisp" appearance.

6. The sound design for Saving Private Ryan has since attained an iconic status of its own and is now available as a download to be added on to various games, including Call of Duty, replacing the existing gaming composite track.

7. Flashbacks are a phenomenon of memory particularly associated with posttraumatic stress disorder. Previous interpretations based on Freudian analysis understood traumatic memories as "repressed." More recent theories, however, suggest that traumatic memories are those that the individual is unable to process in the normal way and relegate to the past and that paradoxically remain "present." The flashback is therefore characterized as "more detailed and affectladen [sic] than ordinary memories" (Baddeley, Kopelman, and Wilson 2002, 457).

8. I am indebted in my analysis to Janet Walker's (2003) argument that the landing sequence is best understood through a "traumatic aesthetic" rather than through notions of realism.

9. www.imdb.com/title/tt0120815/board/?ref_=tt_ql_5

10. Reviews are organized by user ratings. IMDb considers those who gave the film a rating higher than the general average of 8.6 as "loving" the film and those who scored it lower than the average as "hating" it. For examples of negative reviews, see those posted September 22, 2004 and May 9, 2005. www.imdb.com/title/tt0120815/reviews?ref_=tt_ql_8

11. The comparison between the soldier's role in war and a "job" is a recurring theme in wartime films. It is evident in documentaries such as John Ford's *Battle of Midway*, which portrays the role played by the American GIs during the battle as part of a day's "work," as well as in films such as *The Story of G.I. Joe* (William Wellman, 1945). Such comparisons not only helped create continuity between home front production and the war but also softened the potentially disturbing image of American soldiers as killers.

12. According to Box Office figures (Box Office Mojo), the film performed better in Japan than in the US.

13. The subject of reconciling the memory of the World War II Japanese soldier with the militaristic ideology that produced him is an ongoing political issue not only in Japan but also throughout Asia. These difficulties crystallize around the Yasukuni Shrine, which lists the names of over two hundred thousand men and women who, according to its website (www.yasukini.or.jp,

accessed September 24, 2014), "made [the] ultimate sacrifice for their nation since 1853 during national crises," including those convicted of war crimes after World War II. Controversy surrounds the attendance or nonattendance of various political figures in Japan, most notably the prime minister at the shrine during annual ceremonies of commemoration. This subject has become highly politically charged and is often taken as an indication of how a Japanese prime minister will react to foreign pressure in general.

14. I am drawing here on Robert Burgoyne's interpretation of the two films as moving beyond "codes of realism and authenticity" to invoke "not just the tangible world but its uncanny double" (2010, 166).

15. While the battle for Iwo Jima was taking place, Tokyo was undergoing saturation bombing. Only one day after Rosenthal's photograph was published, the *Los Angeles Times* (1945b) reported that the largest formation of Superfortresses that had ever been launched was "ripping [the] heart of [the] Jap Capital."

16. For an examination of the initial impact of September 11 on the war film, see Lyman (2001).

REFERENCES

Artwohl, Alexis, and Loren W. Christensen. 1997. *Deadly Force Encounters: What Cops Need to Know to Mentally and Physically Prepare for and Survive a Gunfight.* Boulder, CO: Paladin.

American Film Institute. 2011. "Steven Spielberg on *Saving Private Ryan.*" AFI. Posted May 26, 2011. Accessed August 8, 2011. www.youtube.com/watch?v=IuZ7H4ZGI8Y

Baddeley, Alan D., Michael D. Kopelman, and Barbara A. Wilson, eds. 2002. *The Handbook of Memory Disorders.* New York: Wiley.

Basinger, Jeanine. [1986] 2003. *The World War II Combat Film: Anatomy of a Genre.* Middletown, CT: Wesleyan University Press.

Beidler, Philip D. 1998. *The Good War's Greatest Hits: World War II and American Remembering.* Athens and London: University of Georgia Press.

Biguenet, John. 2014. "The Profound Contradiction of *Saving Private Ryan.*" *The Atlantic*, June 5. Accessed September 23, 2014. www.theatlantic.com/entertainment/archive/2014/06/the-false-patriotism-of-saving-private-ryan/371539/?single_page=true#disqus_thread

Bolter, Jay David, and Richard Grusin. 2000. *Remediation: Understanding New Media.* Cambridge, MA: MIT Press.

Bourke, Joanna. 1999. *An Intimate History of Killing: Face-to-Face Killing in Twentieth Century Warfare.* New York: Basic Books.

Bradley, James, and Ron Powers. 2000. *Flags of Our Fathers.* New York: Bantam Books.

Brinkley, Douglas. 2005. *The Boys of Pointe du Hoc: Ronald Reagan, D-Day and the U.S. Army 2nd Ranger Battalion.* New York: Harper Collins.

Burgoyne, Robert. 2010. *Film Nation: Hollywood Looks at U.S. History.* Rev. ed. Minneapolis: University of Minnesota Press.

Burgoyne, Robert. 2012. "Generational Memory and Affect in *Letters from Iwo Jima.*" In *A Companion to the Historical Film.* Robert Rosenstone and Constantin Parvulescu, eds.: 349–364. Malden, MA: Wiley-Blackwell.

Chicago Times. 2006. "Soul of a Nation," August 22. Accessed September 23, 2014. http://articles.chicagotribune.com/2006–08–22/news/0608220252_1_iwo-jima-japanese-defenders-joe-rosenthal

Confessore, Nicholas. 2001. "Selling *Private Ryan*." *The American Prospect* 12, no. 17 (September 24). Accessed February 25, 2010. www.questia.com/magazine/1G1-79026801/selling-private-ryan

Daly, Steve. 2006. "Brothers in Arms." *Entertainment Weekly*, October 19. Accessed June 5, 2009. www.ew.com/ew/article/0,,1548166,00.html

Dick, Bernard F. 1985. *The Star Spangled Screen: The American World War II Film*. Lexington: University Press of Kentucky.

DiGiacomo, Frank. 1998. "Stephen Ambrose Saves Spielberg's Butt." *New York Observer*, July 13. Accessed September 23, 2014. http://observer.com/1998/07/stephen-ambrose-saves-spielbergs-butt/

Dower, John. 1986. *War Without Mercy: Race & Power in the Pacific War*. New York: Pantheon.

Elsaesser, Thomas. 1996. "Subject Positions, Speaking Positions: From *Holocaust, Our Hitler*, and *Heimat* to *Shoah* and *Schindler's List*." In *The Persistence of History*. Vivian Sobchack, ed.: 154–186. New York and London: Routledge.

Fussell, Paul. 1989. "The Guts, Not the Glory, of Fighting the 'Good War.'" *Washington Post*, July 26. Accessed October 11, 2011. http://mises.org/daily/10

Graser, Marc. 1999. "*Ryan*'s Next Attack: Sell-Through Market." *Variety*, July 28. Accessed August 21, 2011. www.variety.com/article/VR1117744320?refCatId=13

Gray, J. Glenn. [1959] 1998. *The Warriors: Reflections of Men in Combat*. Lincoln: University of Nebraska Press.

Gray, Jonathan. 2010. *Show Sold Separately: Promos, Spoilers and Other Media Paratexts*. New York and London: New York University Press.

Greenberg, David. 2004. "D-Day OD: Why World War II Nostalgia Has Gone Too Far." *Slate Magazine*, June. Accessed September 22, 2014. www.slate.com/id/2101752/

Haggith, Toby. 2002. "D-Day Filming: For Real. A Comparison of 'Truth' and 'Reality' in *Saving Private Ryan* and Combat Film by the British Army's Film and Photographic Unit." Special issue: "War and Militarism." *Film History* 14, nos. 3–4: 332–335. www.jstor.org/stable/3815436

Hammond, Michael. 2004. "*Saving Private Ryan's* Special Affect." In *Action and Adventure Cinema*. Yvonne Tasker, ed.: 153–166. Abingdon: Routledge.

Harrison, Simon. 2012. *Dark Trophies: Hunting and the Enemy Body in Modern War*. Oxford and New York: Berghahn Books.

Hayes, Christopher. 2006. "The Good War on Terror: How the Greatest Generation Helped Pave the Road to Baghdad." *In These Times*, September 8. Accessed April 11, 2009. www.inthesetimes.com/article/2788/the_good_war_on_terror/

Hedetoft, Ulf. 2000. "Contemporary Cinema: Between Cultural Globalization and National Interpretation." In *Cinema and Nation*. Metta Hjort and Scott Mackenzie, eds.: 278–297. London: Routledge, 2000.

Hein, Laura. 1995. "Introduction: The Bomb as Public History and Transnational Memory." Special issue, "Remembering the Bomb: The Fiftieth Anniversary in the United States and Japan." Laura Hein, ed. *Bulletin of Concerned Asian Scholars* 27, no. 2 (April–June): 3–15. Accessed September 22, 2014. http://criticalasianstudies.org/bcas/back-issues.html?page=27

Hoskins, Andrew. 2004. *Televising War: From Vietnam to Iraq*, London and New York: Continuum International Publishing Group.

Hughes, Chris. 1998. "Our Private Grief; Spielberg's War Epic Brings Back the Horror of D-Day for Four Veterans." *The Mirror*, September 8. Accessed September 23, 2014. www.thefreelibrary.com/OUR+PRIVATE+GRIEF%3B+Spielberg's+war+epic+brings+back+the+horror+of...-a060608621

King, Geoff. 2006. "Seriously Spectacular: 'Authenticity' and 'Art' in the War Epic." In *Hollywood and War. The Film Reader*. David J. Slocum, ed.: 287–302. New York: Routledge.

Kornbluth, Jesse, and Linda Sunshine, eds. 1999. *Now You Know: Reactions After Seeing* Saving Private Ryan. Compiled by America Online and DreamWorks. New York: Newmarket Press.

Kreidler, Maryhelen C., Melissa K. Zupancic, Cynthia Bell, and Mary Beth Longo. 2000. "Trauma and Dissociation: Treatment Perspectives." *Perspectives in Psychiatric Care* 36, no. 3: 77–85. Accessed September 23, 2014. www.questia.com/read/1G1–66107329

Life. 1945a. "The Famous Iwo Flag Raising." *Life*, March 26. Accessed September 18, 2014. http://books.google.co.uk/books/about/LIFE.html?id=R1cEAAAAMBAJ

Life. 1945b. "A Jap Burns." August 13. Accessed September 18, 2014. http://books.google.co.uk/books/about/LIFE.html?id=R1cEAAAAMBAJ

Los Angeles Times. 1945a. "Marines Capture Half of Last Iwo Airfield." February 25. Proquest Historical Newspapers: *Los Angeles Times* (1881–1987)

Los Angeles Times. 1945b. "Carrier Planes Join 200 'Forts' in Ripping Heart of Jap Capital." February 26. Proquest Historical Newspapers: *Los Angeles Times* (1881–1987)

Lyman, Rick. 2001. "Fewer Soldiers March Onscreen; After Attacks, Filmmakers Weigh Wisdom of Military Stories." *New York Times*, October 16. Accessed January 22, 2009. www.nytimes.com/2001/10/16/movies/fewer-soldiers-march-onscreen-after-attacks-filmmakers-weigh-wisdom-military.html?src=pm

Magid, Ron. 1998. "Blood on the Beach." *American Cinematographer*, December. Accessed February 17, 2009. www.ascmag.com/magazine/dec98/Blood/index.htm

Marling, Karal Ann, and John Wetenhal. 2002. "Patriotic Fervor and the Truth About Iwo Jima." George Mason University's History News Network, March 4. Accessed August 21, 2011. http://historynewsnetwork.org/article/599

Morris, Nigel. 2007. *Empire of Light*. London: Wallflower Press.

Nichols, Bill. 2000. "The 10 Stations of Spielberg's Passion: *Saving Private Ryan, Amistad, Schindler's List*." *Jump Cut* 43: 9–11.

Ohnuki-Tierney, Emiko. 2007. "Letters to the Past: Iwo Jima and Japanese Memory." *openDemocracy*, February 23. Accessed June 18, 2009. www.opendemocracy.net/arts-Film/iwo_jima_4381.jsp

Sturken, Marita. 1997. *Tangled Memories: The Vietnam War, the AIDS Epidemic and the Politics of Remembering*. Berkeley: University of California Press.

Tanaka, Yuki. 1996. *Hidden Horrors: Japanese War Crimes in World War II*. Boulder, CO: Westview Press.

Terkel, Studs. 1985. *"The Good War."* London: Hamish Hamilton.

Torgovnick, Marianna. 2005. *The War Complex: World War II in Our Time*. Chicago: University of Chicago Press.

Walker, Janet. 2003. "The Vicissitudes of Traumatic Memory and the Postmodern History Film." In *Trauma and Cinema: Cross-Cultural Explorations*. E. Ann Kaplan and Ban Wang, eds.: 123–144. Hong Kong: Hong Kong University Press.

Wallace, Amy. 1998. *"Ryan* Ends Vets' Years of Silence." *Los Angeles Times*, August 6. Accessed September 23, 2014. http://articles.latimes.com/1998/aug/06/news/mn-10608/2

Wheeler, Richard. 1980. *Iwo*. Edison, NJ: Castle Books.

Williams, David E. 2006. "Symbolic Victory." *American Cinematographer*, November. Accessed September 24, 2009. www.theasc.com/ac_magazine/November2006/FlagsofOurFathers/page1.php

Young, Marilyn. 2006. "In the Combat Zone." In *Hollywood and War. The Film Reader*. David J. Slocum, ed.: 315–324. New York: Routledge.

Zinn, Howard. 2001. "The Greatest Generation?" *The Progressive*, October 2001. Accessed September 23, 2014. www.progressive.org/0901/zinn1001.html

KEY FILMS

Bataan. Tay Garnett, Loew's, 1943.

The Battle of Midway. John Ford, United States Navy, 1943.

Beach Red. Cornell Wilde, Theodora Productions, 1967.

The Big Red One. Sam Fuller, Lorimer Productions, 1980.

A Bridge Too Far. Richard Attenborough, Joseph E. Levine Productions, 1977.

Black Hawk Down. Ridley Scott, Jerry Bruckheimer and Scott Free Productions. 2001,

Flags of Our Fathers. Clint Eastwood, DreamWorks SKG, Warner Bros, Amblin Entertainment, 2006.

Flags of Our Fathers/Letters from Iwo Jima Extra Features, Collector's Edition DVD 2007, Warner Home Video, produced by Mark Rowen:

"An Introduction by Clint Eastwood."

C:\Users\mwaldren\Desktop\Ramsay Accepted Files\6244-0528-Ref Mismatch Report.docx - LStERROR_94"Red Sun, Black Sand: The Making of *Letters from Iwo Jima.*"

C:\Users\mwaldren\Desktop\Ramsay Accepted Files\6244-0528-Ref Mismatch Report.docx - LStERROR_95"Visual Effects."

Guadalcanal Diary. Lewis Sieler, Twentieth Century Fox, 1943.

Letters from Iwo Jima. Clint Eastwood, DreamWorks SKG, Warner Bros, Amblin Entertainment, 2006.

The Longest Day. Ken Annakin, Andrew Marton, and Bernhard Wicki, Twentieth Century Fox, 1960.

Midway. Jack Smight, Mirisch Corporation, 1976.

None but the Brave. Frank Sinatra, Warner Bros., 1965

San Pietro. John Huston, U.S. Army Pictorial Services, 1945.

The Sands of Iwo Jima. Alan Dwan, Republic Pictures, 1949.

Saving Private Ryan. Steven Spielberg, DreamWorks SKG, Paramount Pictures and Amblin' Entertainment. 1998.

Saving Private Ryan. Extra Feature, Special Limited Edition DVD 1999, Dream-Works Home Entertainment: "Special Message from Steven Spielberg."

Saving Private Ryan. Extra Features, 60th Anniversary Commemorative Edition DVD 2004, Paramount Home Entertainment, writer/producer Laurent Bouzereau:

"Making of *Saving Private Ryan.*"

"Miller and His Platoon"

"Music and Sound."

Spielberg on Spielberg. Richard Schickel, Turner Classic Movies, 2007.

The Thin Red Line. Terence Malick, Fox 2000 Pictures, 1998.

To the Shores of Iwo Jima. Milton Sperling, US Government Office of War Information, 1945.

Wake Island. John Farrow, Paramount Pictures, 1942

Windtalkers. John Woo, MGM, 2002.

With the Marines at Tarawa. U.S. Marine Corps Photographic Unit, 1944.

4   It's Not War, It's HBO's World War II

INTRODUCTION

As a master mediation of World War II, *Saving Private Ryan* reconstructed the citizen soldier, recalibrated the visual construction of the war, and confirmed that, from the perspective of Baby Boomers, World War II was a "good war." Yet in order to tell stories that communicate the scale and breadth of the war in both Europe and the Pacific, Hanks and Spielberg turned to the small screen because, as Hanks puts it, television offers a "luxury of scope and of time" not possible in film (interview in Thompson 2001). Expanding the spectacular-authentic vision of World War II established by *Saving Private Ryan* demands an extraordinary budget for television, yet when Hanks and Spielberg approached cablecaster HBO in 1998 with a proposed adaptation of Stephen Ambrose's book, *Band of Brothers*, HBO agreed to back the project to the tune of $125 million, making it the most expensive television series of its time.[1] Just under a decade later, HBO agreed once again, in Spielberg's words, to make "room on their schedule" and in their budget for *The Pacific*, this time at a cost of $250 million (interview in Wayland 2010). Unlike *Saving Private Ryan*, which follows a fictitious squad on one mission, both *Band of Brothers* (Dreamworks SKG, Playtone, HBO, 2001) and *The Pacific* (Dreamworks SKG, Playtone, HBO, 2010) reconstruct the experiences of real soldiers in the war in campaigns in Europe and the Pacific, respectively. As supposedly "true" stories (as the trailer for *Band of Brothers* describes the series) created with the stated intention of honoring the veterans of World War II, the two miniseries were marketed as event status programs and highlighted as special even in HBO's usual discourses of distinction. This chapter examines *Band of Brothers* and *The Pacific* to investigate how industrial contexts and connections contribute to the evolution of the citizen soldier, the "good war," and the esthetic construct of World War II in television.

Tom Hanks first encountered Ambrose's book, *Band of Brothers*, while researching his role as Captain Miller in *Saving Private Ryan*. He recognized that its story presented an opportunity to explore the entire European campaign, from the US entry into the war until its end. *Band of Brothers* charts the history of an entire company, the 101st Airborne's Easy Company, from training through to the end of the war and the resumption of their lives as civilians. As one commentator notes, *Band of Brothers* is the "bigger story" behind *Saving Private Ryan* because the fictional Ryan, like the men of Easy, is a member of the 506th Regiment (Thompson 2001). *Band of Brothers* is therefore the actual story of what happened to paratroopers like Ryan when they parachuted into Europe, and the television series both draws on and expands the template of war memory established in *Saving Private Ryan*. In a similar way to *Saving Private Ryan, Band of Brothers* was promoted as more than a television program, as part of broader cultural events that recognized the US involvement in the war as "just and honorable" (Paget and Lipkin 2009, 98).

According to Spielberg, because of the response to *Band of Brothers* and repeated requests from veterans, including the director's father, to tell the story of the war in the Pacific theater, it was "inevitable" that he would partner with Hanks and HBO once again to produce *The Pacific* (interview in Wayland 2010). Due to the nature of the fighting in this arena, which involved different units in various island campaigns, *The Pacific* adopts a different approach to *Band of Brothers* and concentrates on the experiences of three individual Marines—Eugene Sledge, Robert Leckie, and John Basilone—rather than an entire company. *The Pacific* is drawn primarily from the memoirs of Sledge (1981) and Leckie (1957), as well as from a series of interviews with veterans conducted by Stephen Ambrose for a book also entitled *The Pacific*, completed after his death by his son Hugh Ambrose and published alongside the series in 2010. Hanks describes the war in the Pacific as "[a] large industrial version of what all future wars were going to be like" (interview in Armstrong 2010a, 4). The series is an example of how the transmedia structure of World War II is used as a framework for understanding or reflecting on current wars. This chapter continues to investigate how the war in Europe accommodates the "good war" concept in the current configuration of the transmedia structure of World War II, while the Pacific arena reflects more ambiguous attitudes toward conflict.

To illustrate how the interconnections between media forms and industries resulted in the production of two series that can in many ways be considered as brand extensions of *Saving Private Ryan*, the chapter begins with an examination of the relationship between Spielberg, Hanks, and HBO. From there, to clarify why the cablecaster agreed to finance projects that verge on prohibitively expensive, I move on to explaining the position HBO occupies in the industry and the kind of television it produces. Having established the industrial context for both series, the chapter situates them in the ongoing televisual discourse relating to World War II. I explain how HBO's preliminary marketing strategies carve out a distinct place for the two series in the transmedia structure of the war by identifying them as event status programs distinguished by connections to cultural processes of memorialization and by marketing them as mementos of those processes. Given the twin luxuries of scope and time that television offers, do the experiences of the citizen soldier remain the defining ones for World War II in these two series? How does the spectacular-authentic esthetic that characterizes the recent cinematic representations of the war translate to television? The analysis of the series themselves explores the answers to these questions and also considers how the "good war" concept evolves in both series. This chapter also examines how DVD and Blu-ray technologies extend the life of both series beyond the moment of broadcast and touches on the impact of these formats on the transmedia structure of the war.

DREAMWORKS SKG, PLAYTONE, AND HBO

The background to the partnership and the industrial positioning of HBO at the time that *Band of Brothers* was produced provides an explanation of why Hanks and Spielberg regarded HBO, of all the networks available to them, as the perfect partner in expanding their vision of World War II from film to television. The industrial context of the two series also sheds light on Hanks and Spielberg's specific approach to the configuration of World War II memory. This section therefore examines the context for the partnership and the position occupied by HBO in the current mediascape.

At the end of the 1990s, DreamWorks SKG, the company Spielberg cofounded in 1994 with David Geffen and Jeffrey Katzenberg, was closing the gap on its competitors in terms of market share. *Saving Private Ryan* was one of only seven films released by DreamWorks SKG in 1998, but in that same year the studio attained 7 percent of the US cinema market share (Krämer 2002, 322). In 1999, a mission statement from Spielberg on the DreamWorks Studios website (DeamworksStudio.com) promised that the studio would "strive to tell great stories and pursue the most talented filmmakers to bring these unique stories to the big and small screen" (this statement has since been removed). However, despite the studio's burgeoning success in the film industry, DreamWorks' forays into television had met with comparatively limited success by the end of the 1990s.[2] For HBO, therefore, the appeal of the partnership on the *Band of Brothers* project lay not so much with DreamWorks' or Spielberg's previous excursions into television but far more firmly with their status in the film industry. Thomas Schatz (2008, 27) argues that the collaboration with DreamWorks and Hanks is part of HBO's "obvious strategy to push more aggressively into the cinematic realm." But at the same time, collaboration with HBO on *Band of Brothers* presented both DreamWorks SKG and Spielberg with a chance to extend their own interests into HBO's particular brand of so-called quality television, a point I will return to later in this section.

Derek Paget and Steven Lipkin (2009, 103) suggest that *Band of Brothers* "might not have acquired financial critical mass were it not for the name Spielberg"—an echo of the same set of circumstances behind the making of

Saving Private Ryan at a time when World War II was regarded as a risky financial subject for the film industry. However, it should not be forgotten that Hanks' star persona also contributes to the status of the project and that the other production company involved in the partnership is Hanks' own. Together with producer Gary Goetzman, Hanks founded Playtone in 1998. By that time, Hanks' career had taken a similar trajectory to that of Spielberg's in terms of work regarded as more serious or culturally significant.[3] Both Hanks and Goetzman are reluctant to hold press conferences or make public announcements regarding Playtone's strategy. The most that Goetzman will admit is that they "just want to tell good stories," although this in itself can be viewed as a strategy, inasmuch as Goetzman goes on to acknowledge in the same interview that Playtone wants to tell good stories in order to make good profits (Manly 2006). Although Hanks previously worked with HBO on *From the Earth to the Moon* (HBO, 1998) as both host of the series and director of one episode, *Band of Brothers* presented an opportunity to further his career not only as a producer but also as a director of HBO's brand of quality television. In addition, the series offered the fledgling production company the opportunity to break into television at a very early stage in its development in order to tell good stories.

What is it about HBO, however, that facilitates the particular kind of authenticity demanded by Hanks and Spielberg for *Band of Brothers*, and why is the channel so eager to align its own interests with the film industry? The answer to these questions lies in the channel's history. Formed early in the 1970s, the channel was, from its beginnings, based on an entirely different economic model to that of the major networks at the time, namely, CBS, NBC, and ABC (Edgerton 2008, 1). As a subscription service, the channel's marketing strategy is aimed predominantly at attracting and retaining a paying audience. As a result, HBO has never been dependent on advertisers for revenue. Initially, its focus and means of differentiating itself from advertiser-based networks was founded on a strong (and continuing) affiliation with the film industry. This affiliation is apparent in its title—Home Box Office—and the channel originally concentrated much of its programming on providing its audience with Hollywood films, as well as on broadcasting popular sporting events and cutting-edge comedy shows. By the time *Band of Brothers* was produced in 2001, however, the channel had revised its strategy to include a focus on its own original programming and had adopted the slogan, "It's not TV. It's HBO."

Much has been written about this particular marketing strategy and how the channel positioned itself as what Gary Edgerton refers to as "the TV equivalent of a designer label" (2008, 9). A full analysis of the creation of HBO's brand of quality television falls outside my remit in this book, but some points from the overall discussion are relevant to *Band of Brothers* and *The Pacific*.[4] Christopher Anderson (2008, 30) identifies a shift in HBO's marketing strategies from the "brand as a corporate trademark to the brand as an integral experience in the lives of consumers." HBO's shift in brand identity was in response to a number of changes in the industry, including an increasingly competitive market, and technological developments that led to a proliferation of media platforms through which programs could be disseminated. The mid-1990s ushered in an era in broadcasting history referred to in media scholarship as the Digital Age, or TVIII.[5] In the US, the development of multimedia conglomerates and a rapid expansion of television networks due to deregulation of the industry are the factors that differentiate the TVIII era from previous years in television history. Up until this point, HBO's management had been content with the channel's status as an " 'occasional use' subscription service," but in 1995, new CEO Jeff Bewkes adopted a strategy in reaction to these changes designed to intensify the relationship between the channel and its existing subscribers, as well as to expand HBO's subscriber base (Teather 2003).

Bewkes's strategy, as described by Christopher Anderson, was based on establishing "a unique cultural value" for the channel's output and positioning it to appeal to "an educated upper-middle class" market (2008, 30). HBO is able to differentiate its original programming from that of other networks for two major reasons. First, as a subscription service, it is not subject to the regulations of the Federal Communications Commission (the US broadcasting regulatory body) and therefore has much more freedom in terms of content (language, violence, and explicit sexual content). Second, the channel is owned by parent company TimeWarner and consequently has the financial weight to enable it to finance ambitious and innovative projects. Even though each HBO series "strives to create a distinctive and highly unique visual style," the one thing the channel highlights consistently is the high production values of its original programming (McCabe and Akass 2008, 88). Both factors facilitate the channel's ability to brand itself and its products as distinct from mainstream television—as the slogan states, "It's not TV. It's HBO."—and to identify its target audience as an educated and refined elite.

The shift in strategy has been a resounding success for the channel, so much so that it is now regarded as being "synonymous with quality," and much of its original programming is hailed as groundbreaking television (McCabe and Akass 2008, 84). The idea of quality television for HBO is predicated on the principle that its original programming is an innovative and unique form of "cultural capital" (Santo 2008, 33). The channel takes pains to suggest that this is made possible through the creative autonomy it supposedly affords its artists, but as Janet McCabe and Kim Akass argue, the potential risks inherent in HBO's strategy are mitigated by the fact that it is frequently "those with established reputations" in the industry who are enlisted by the cablecaster (2008, 87–88). HBO flagship series *The Sopranos* (1999–2007) provides a prime example. HBO's marketing of the show attributes the success of *The Sopranos* to the much publicized creative license afforded to showrunner David Chase. Despite the fact that Chase is a veteran writer/producer in network television, HBO's website for *The Sopranos* (www.hbo.com/sopranos/cast/crew) described his success with the series as due to his "annoyance with network television's rules" (Chase's biography has since been removed). *The Sopranos*, together with other HBO series such as *Sex and the City* (1998–2004) and *Deadwood* (2004–2006), are marketed as controversial and provocative, ultimately presenting a challenge to so-called mainstream television. A number of analysts point out that HBO's marketing strategy conceals a paradox in that, despite attempting to embrace a notion of exclusivity for itself (and, by extension, for its audience), the channel still needs to attract as many subscribers as possible.[6] Like Playtone and DreamWorks SKG, HBO's strategy of telling good stories is part of making good profits.

Although attracting and cultivating a large subscriber base still forms the cornerstone of HBO's economic model, the channel also branched out into other sources of revenue in reaction to the pressures of the TVIII era. Selling shows into syndication is an increasingly important source of income in the industry in general, and the practice raises another paradox for HBO's brand identity. Despite positioning itself as outside mainstream television through its marketing campaigns, the channel sells its products to other television networks. As a result, as McCabe and Akass point out, HBO has to take into consideration "the very working practices and business strategies that it sets itself against" (2008, 86). What this means is that in its pursuit of a unique brand identity in a highly competitive broadcast milieu, HBO walks a fine and difficult line between exclusivity and marketability. HBO's shows may have a designer label, but they have to be accessible enough to sell in various forms to a wide market.

As extensions of *Saving Private Ryan, Band of Brothers* and *The Pacific* fit perfectly in HBO's brand values. The involvement of Hanks and Spielberg presents HBO with the opportunity not only to continue its practice of collaboration with well-known industry professionals but also to maintain the channel's association with the film industry. Drawing on similar tropes to those employed in the publicity for *Saving Private Ryan*, Steven Spielberg maintains that "honoring" the veterans is the primary goal of *Band of Brothers*, which according to Spielberg means that the approach to the series is therefore not "commercial" or "mainstream" (interview in Gritten 2001, 46). Spielberg (interview in TV NZ 2011) describes *The Pacific* in similar terms, as "an honor roll of valor and sacrifice," while Hanks refers to their approach to this series as involving a "quest" for "a certain authenticity" (interview in Armstrong 2010a). Because HBO positions itself as "not TV" and defines quality television through the notion of creative risk taking, the cablecaster facilitates Spielberg and Hanks' insistence on a noncommercial, "authentic" approach, regardless of cost. However, any potential risk for HBO in committing to such costly projects is alleviated not only by the status of Hanks and Spielberg but also through the connections of both series to *Saving Private Ryan*. Avi Santo points out that HBO's definition of quality is heavily linked to esthetics in the emphasis on "high production values and cinematic influences" (2008, 34). *Band of Brothers* and *The Pacific* offer HBO the opportunity to appropriate the spectacular-authentic cinematic techniques employed in *Saving Private Ryan* and to transpose these to television.

HBO is able to provide the budget necessary for the complex, hypermediated, and distinctly cinematic effects that are the touchstone for authentic reproductions of the battleground since *Saving Private Ryan*. In turn, the high production values demanded by the combat sequences in both *Band of Brothers* and *The Pacific* are compatible with HBO's discourse of distinction. As Mary Ann Doane notes, the "activation of special effects and spectacle in the documentary format" is a way for television to counter "its own tendency toward the leveling of signification" (2001, 272). Another way of distinguishing the two series from mainstream television is through the violence of the combat sequences. While the authenticity that Hanks and Spielberg demand necessitates a certain amount of violence in both series, *The Pacific*, according to Hanks, encompasses a "different kind of horror" (interview in Armstrong 2010a). *The Pacific* includes, as Hanks puts it, "some of the most vicious stuff I've ever seen on film" (interview in Das 2010) and is rated TV-MA—unsuitable for children under 17. Because HBO is a subscription channel, it is outside of the FCC's regulations and can therefore facilitate a level of violence that might be considered too extreme for a commercial network. As I demonstrate more comprehensively in the analysis of both series, the deployment of the spectacular-authentic esthetic evident in the cinematic depictions of battle and violence in *Band of Brothers* and *The Pacific* are factors that identify both series as exceptional even in HBO's distinctive programming and that have additionally proved to be selling points for the two series in the home theater market.

Spectacle and violence in representations of war contribute to their traditional association with a male demographic. It could be argued that the audience for *Band of Brothers* and *The Pacific* is therefore limited, but Avi Santo (2008) offers a more subtle reading of HBO's strategies. He notes a preoccupation with "white, middle-class male anxieties" in many of the channel's long running series and suggests that instead of specifically targeting a male demographic, the channel "utilizes masculinity as a site for distinguishing its quality brand and promoting the exclusivity it offers its clientele" (34). The version of World War II memory created and maintained in *Saving Private Ryan* and, as we shall see, continued in *Band of Brothers* and *The Pacific*, depicts the war as an almost exclusively masculine experience. Both series therefore fit in the strategy of using masculinity as a marker of distinction. *Band of Brothers* and *The Pacific* attracted a mixed demographic when broadcast and demonstrate Santo's point that HBO's aim is not necessarily to target a male demographic but to utilize masculinity as a distinguishing characteristic of its "exclusive" audience.[7]

In addition to the appeal of the involvement of Hanks and Spielberg, as well as the distinctly cinematic esthetic and thematic concerns drawn from

Saving Private Ryan, the two series also meet HBO's criteria for products that have potential for development in ancillary markets. *Band of Brothers*, for example, generated what Tom Hanks calls an "an awful lot of attention" for HBO and created a "brand of perennial that people can go back to again and again" (interview in Itzkoff 2010). The connections between both series and the memorialization of World War II are central to the ability of *Band of Brothers* and *The Pacific* to sustain the kind of attention and ongoing interest that Hanks describes. As discussed in the previous chapter, *Saving Private Ryan* was linked to a number of commemorative events. HBO in turn connected both *Band of Brothers* and *The Pacific* to official acts of memorialization. Connections to annual commemorations practically guarantees the series slots for yearly repeats on television, as part of the special programming most networks arrange to acknowledge various anniversaries of World War II, which in turn increases the viability of selling the series into syndication. John Caldwell (1995, 162) points out the importance of emphasizing the "distinctive and original nature" of programming that will be sold into syndication. The status of the two series and, by extension, of the channel producing them is significantly enhanced by their association with historic anniversaries. Additionally (and for similar reasons), the series lend themselves particularly well to being marketed as DVD and Blu-ray box sets. Later in this chapter, I will provide concrete examples of the links between the series and commemorations, but for now suffice it to say that *Band of Brothers* and *The Pacific* both fit HBO's bill of designer products that are paradoxically designed for mass appeal.

The two series exemplify HBO's position on its programming being "not TV." Like *The Sopranos*, which features a number of links to the cream of gangster films, *Band of Brothers* and *The Pacific* are linked to not just any war film but to *Saving Private Ryan*, a film that claims to be an authoritative, definitive account of the American soldier's experience of D-Day.[8] Furthermore, the involvement of Hanks and Spielberg on the two projects cements HBO's alignment with film, a medium widely perceived as having "a higher cultural currency than that of television" (Paget and Lipkin 2009, 95). In return, HBO offered DreamWorks SKG and Playtone access to the quality television market and gave Hanks and Spielberg the opportunity to realize their particular vision of World War II. Having established the industrial context for the two series, the next part of this chapter examines how *Band of Brothers* and *The Pacific* fit into the transmedia structure of World War II and considers the implications of their marketing as event status series.

"BIG, IMPORTANT, POWERFUL" TELEVISION

Describing the marketing campaign for the premier of *Band of Brothers* on HBO (scheduled for September 9, 2001), marketing chief Eric Kessler observed, "We want people to say, 'That looks big, important, powerful, and I need to see that'" (interview in Romano 2001). Yet despite HBO's claims that the series it produces are somehow so big and powerful that they are "not TV," of course both *Band of Brothers* and *The Pacific* are products of the medium. As such, although the two series are integrally linked to cinematic representations of World War II and to *Saving Private Ryan* in particular, they are also part of an ongoing televisual discourse that has a long history of its own in the transmedia mnemonic structure of World War II. In Chapter 2, I examined the contributions made by *Combat!* (ABC, 1962–1967) and *Victory at Sea* (NBC, 1952–1953) to the transmedia structure of the conflict, but to fully understand the position occupied by *Band of Brothers* and *The Pacific* as "big, important, powerful" televisual narratives about the war, it is necessary to examine the relationship between television and World War II in a little more detail.

The past is a lucrative topic for a medium Marita Sturken describes as "relentlessly in the present, immediate, simultaneous, and continuous" (1997, 125)—so lucrative, in fact, that channels solely devoted to programming about history have emerged on television in the last two decades. The first of these, the History Channel, was launched in 1995 and is now part of many standard cable packages in both the US and the UK (Taves 2001, 261). As David Cannadine observes, war in general, and the two world wars in particular, occupy a large portion of historical programming (2004, 4). At least part of the explanation for the predominance of programming related to war lies in the existence of extensive visual and audio archives for industrial warfare, particularly for World War II. The transmedia construct of World War II is a source of endlessly recycled archive footage that is not only readily accessible but also either free or cheap to access and often unrestricted by copyright. Both David Cannadine (2004, 4) and Roger Smither (2004, 61), however, suggest that audience demand also plays a large part in ensuring that such programs continue to be made.[9] Some measure of the popularity of programs about war can be extrapolated from the fact that it is enough to sustain the existence of a dedicated channel in the form of the Discovery Group's Military History Channel, which focuses much of its programming on mechanized warfare.

Jeremy Isaac's production, *The World at War* (Thames Television, 1973), provides the best demonstration of the enduring presence of World War II on television screens. Smither (2004, 54) describes *The World at War* as "probably the most successful television history series ever made," with some justification, inasmuch as it was broadcast in around eighty countries and today runs almost continuously on cable networks in the US. Following in the wake of *Victory at Sea*, *The World at War* demonstrated that "[h]istory on television could be high quality, attract a large popular audience and make a great deal of money" (Downing 2001, 295). More importantly, the format of this twenty-six-part series, with its combination of eyewitness testimony, archive footage, evocative soundtrack, and an authoritative voice-over by Sir Lawrence Olivier, created a template of its own for subsequent documentaries on the subject. The series established what Smither calls "the two foundation stones" of documentary histories about this conflict: the integration of archive footage and eyewitness testimony (2004, 56). Of course, both elements were used in previous documentaries, but in *The World at War* the combination was particularly successful because it treated film footage as another form of historical documentation and used it in conjunction with extensive and exclusive interviews from participants and witnesses. Discussing the series on a Plenary Panel at the Televising History Conference (Lincoln, UK, 2009), Isaacs maintains that his goal was to make the war accessible to the 1970s audience by showing the impact on "ordinary citizens" and by posing an implicit question: "How would I have reacted if this country [i.e., the UK] were occupied?" *The World at War* demonstrated that archival footage of the conflict could be refracted through the eyes and voices of those who directly witnessed or participated in World War II. The series seamlessly conflated individual memory with visual history drawn from the transmedia construct of the war.

The pervasive and persistent presence of televisual representations of World War II in the conflict's transmedia structure extends beyond documentaries like *World at War*, however, as best demonstrated by the long-running series *Combat!* During the 1980s, World War II may have faded from US cinema screens, but the conflict occupied a significant space on television screens in the form of the epic miniseries, *The Winds of War* (ABC, 1983) and its sequel, *War and Remembrance* (ABC, 1989). Although largely fictional, the two series are precursors of *Band of Brothers* and *The Pacific* as epic, event status programming set in World War II. ABC's series illustrate the complex relationships between the subject matter of World War II and commercial concerns in the television industry, as well as the potential use of the conflict to confer a sense of weight and worthiness to programming schedules—points well worth remembering when considering HBO's discourse of distinction for *Band of Brothers* and *The Pacific*.

The adaptation of Herman Wouk's novel, *The Winds of War* was produced by ABC at a time when cable and independent networks were just beginning to make inroads into network prime-time audiences, which reduced the audience share of the three majors (ABC, CBS, and NBC) to 80 percent in 1983 (*Lewiston Daily Sun* 1983). John Caldwell defines event status programs as those marked by "[m]assive investments of budget and production resources; they all are sequestered and marketed in primetime; and they all bring with them significant corporate risks" (1995, 160). *The Winds of War* exemplifies these criteria, with an unprecedented and much publicized budget of $40 million, a production schedule that ran over a year and extended across six countries, with 285 speaking parts and extras numbering in the thousands and requiring around 50,000 costumes (Clarke, Dutka, and Worrell 1983). ABC, together with its affiliates, invested $25 million in an intensive marketing campaign that began almost a year before the series aired and included documentaries and promotional spots aired between regular programming on Pearl Harbor Day in December 1982. Unlike HBO, ABC is an advertiser-based network, but even after selling all the commercial slots available during the series at premium rates, the network only just broke even on its investment (Clarke, Dutka, and Worrell 1983). In a highly unusual agreement with Wouk, ABC gave the author the power to restrict both the kinds of products advertised during the series and the frequency of advertising breaks, suggesting not so much that the subject matter was beyond commercial exploitation but rather that only products of a certain kind were permitted to occupy the same airspace as the series itself (Wouk objected to items such as toilet paper and fast food, for example). The cost of the series was eventually justified by its substantial audience figures, which allowed ABC to gain more than a full point in that season's ratings war with CBS (*Spartanburg Herald-Journal* 1983). According to ABC's president, Brandon Stoddard, who also produced the series, *The Winds of War* proved that network television could still attract a massive audience if it presented something "important and special" (interview in Prial 1983). The success of *The Winds of War* proved that World War II could provide the television industry with "important and special" material.

The Winds of War was part of a shift in network programming toward extravagant, large-scale series. Between them, ABC, CBS, and NBC had over two dozen such projects in development in 1983 (Bedell 1983). Six years later, therefore, when ABC produced the sequel to *The Winds of War*, the marketing was at pains to stress that *War and Remembrance* was even more "important and special" than its predecessor and could stand out even in a crowded field of similar programming. Foreshadowing similar rhetoric around the release of *The Pacific*, ABC promised producer Dan Curtis "a budget far above the ordinary" and stated that it was "more than willing to suspend its usual restrictions" in terms of censorship to allow him to include graphic depictions of the horror of the Holocaust (Haithman 1988). Caldwell points out that ABC (foreshadowing HBO's approach) defined *War and Remembrance* as more than "just" television in marketing campaigns, which described the series as "the motion picture event of a lifetime" and an "ABC novel for television" (1995, 167). The financial risk of investing in the most expensive series of its time did not pay off for ABC in the case of *War and Remembrance*, however; the series did not attract the desired audience figures and pushed the network to the brink of bankruptcy. In the years separating the two series, the mediascape had altered, and a proliferation of cable channels contributed to widespread declines in viewership and revenues for network television. Ian Wurzel, senior vice president for research at ABC, observed at the time that it was "extremely unlikely anything like this will ever be made again" (quoted in Carter 1989)—a prediction regarding the end of event status programming that proved premature.

Despite the fact that, in the era of TVIII, audiences are far more splintered than they were in the 1980s, event status programming retains its importance and enables channels to distinguish their product in a highly competitive media milieu. Caldwell suggests that cable companies in particular "have come to ritualize the very secret of event status televisual programming" (1995, 167). This is certainly true of HBO, whose entire marketing strategy revolves around programming that is presented as special or distinct. Yet even in HBO's overall discourse of distinction, *Band of Brothers* and *The Pacific* were marketed in very particular ways to differentiate them from the cablecaster's usual programming. From one perspective, the limited nature of the ten-episode miniseries format does not appear to fit well with HBO's primary goal of attracting and, more importantly, retaining subscribers through long-running series such as *The Sopranos* and *Sex and the City*. Thomas Schatz, however, argues that *Band of Brothers* offered HBO the opportunity to "both counter and complement its growing reliance on original long-form series" (2008, 27). Although that might have been the case at the time *Band of Brothers* was made, when *The Pacific* went into production, prestige projects were even more critical for HBO. In 2007, HBO was facing what *Newsweek* refers to as "the biggest crisis of its 35-year history" (Devin and Roberts 2007). Chris Albrecht, HBO's chief executive and the architect behind the cablecaster's programming structure and creative ethos, resigned at almost the same time HBO's long-running flagship series *The Sopranos* came to an end. In addition, HBO's strategy of innovative original programming was facing strong competition from series such as AMC's *Mad Men* (2007–present), a project that HBO had turned down, and Fox's *24* (2001–2010). A series that could be marketed as high-profile and socially significant could go some way to restore confidence in HBO's reputation as a purveyor of quality television.

As with *The Winds of War* and *War and Remembrance*, both *Band of Brothers* and *The Pacific* were heavily publicized as the most expensive television productions of their time. Caldwell points out that event status series perform much the same function as retail loss leaders because the value of the series is not only in its ability to attract viewers but also in its capacity to generate "regular transfusions of attention-getting marketing fodder" and to function as "high-profile banner carriers" of the channel's brand identity (Caldwell 1995, 162). Chris Albrecht, who originally agreed to the production of *Band of Brothers*, acknowledged the potential of the miniseries to enhance and promote HBO as a brand. *Band of Brothers*, according to Albrecht, was an opportunity to "have the audience see the kinds of projects that HBO stands for" (interview in Kronke and Kuklenski 2001). Because of their subject matter, *Band of Brothers* and *The Pacific* identify HBO as a producer of "big, important, powerful" television that people "need" to see and enable the cablecaster to reach far beyond its subscriber pool to build its brand identity.

The trailer for *Band of Brothers* refers to the series as the "true story" of Easy Company. As true stories of World War II, *Band of Brothers* and *The Pacific* occupy a different position to that of fictional series such as Wouk's or documentaries such as *The World at War*. Because the series are intended to honor the veterans who fought in World War II, they are easily incorporated into moments of memorialization, and HBO mounted intensive campaigns to create widely publicized links between *Band of Brothers* and *The Pacific* and commemorative events. In the case of *Band of Brothers*, HBO spent over a year arranging for the premiere of the series to be held as part of the celebrations for the fifty-seventh anniversary of D-Day in Normandy at Utah Beach in 2001. In partnership with American Airlines, HBO arranged for forty-seven of the surviving veterans of Easy Company and their families to fly out for a special screening of the episode in the series that deals with D-Day. In addition to the veterans, invitations were extended to various heads of state, as well as to the progeny of Winston Churchill, Franklin D. Roosevelt, and Dwight D. Eisenhower. The veterans agreed "to a man" that "the insistence on authenticity that became the hallmark of *Saving Private Ryan* had been, if anything, refined with *Band of Brothers*" (Thompson 2001). Similarly, for the premiere of *The Pacific*, HBO flew 250 veterans to Washington, D.C., for a special wreath-laying ceremony held at the World War II veteran's memorial, an event covered live by news channel CNN and therefore expanding HBO's promotion of the series to a national audience far greater than its subscriber base. The memorial itself has connections to *Band of Brothers*. Announcements advocating support for the creation of the memorial were tacked on to the initial advertising for *Band of Brothers* in the US. Hanks was the national spokesperson for the campaign, and HBO is listed on the memorial's website (www.wwiimemorial.com) as one of the donors. The wreath-laying was followed by a special screening of an episode from *The Pacific* hosted by President Obama at the White House and attended not only by Hanks and Spielberg but also by HBO president Richard Plepler, as well as National Security Adviser General Jim Jones and members of the Joint Chiefs of Staff and Congress. In addition to establishing the importance of the two series, the premieres of *Band of Brothers* and *The Pacific* allow HBO to align itself with notions of public service and to expand its brand identity significantly on both the national and international stages.

The notion of honoring the veterans does not preclude commercial tie-ins. *Band of Brothers* marked HBO's first commercial sponsorship in the form of a partnership with Jeep (a company that owes its success directly to World War II) at a time when, according to Peter Arnell, chairman and chief executive of the agency that brought the two companies together, "people are looking for ideas and not ads" (interview in Elliott 2001). The central idea around which the partnership between HBO and Jeep revolves is commemoration. HBO's $10 million-plus advertising campaign for the series displayed the Jeep logo with this sentence: "The Jeep brand is honored to celebrate the men of Easy Company and all those who served in WWII," while Jeep reciprocated by running six commercials on network television emphasizing not only the vehicle's history in World War II but also explicitly mentioning HBO and *Band of Brothers*, thereby extending HBO's marketing reach to nonsubscribers. Although Jeff Bell, vice president for marketing communications at Chrysler Group, argues that "this is more a touchstone to our brand values and heritage than it is to try to sell Jeeps," it cannot be denied that both Jeep and HBO are utilizing commemoration to bolster their respective brand identities (interview in Elliot 2001). The partnership and marketing campaign illustrate Caldwell's point that the advertising around event status programs such as *Band of Brothers* is "self-consciously designed as a device that both markets a retail product and that is marketed *by* products in point-of-sale promotional campaigns" (Caldwell 1995, 163). Honoring the veterans thus becomes a commercial exercise linking brands to the social and national values inherent in the processes of commemoration.

If the carefully orchestrated links to commemorative events established the two series as important television, the remainder of the marketing for *Band of Brothers* and *The Pacific* was designed to complete the remaining requirements on Kessler's list of how viewers should regard both series—as big and powerful. The promotion of *Band of Brothers* in particular is a prime example of the synergistic benefits of media conglomeration in the TVIII era, following the merger of TimeWarner (HBO's parent company) with AOL. In addition to billboards and print adverts, *Band of Brothers* was featured on AOL's welcome screen, reaching around thirty million subscribers every time they logged in (Beatty 2001). AOL additionally constructed a separate website (no longer running) for *Band of Brothers*, through which viewers could "experience the war" (Beatty 2001). In addition, other cablecasters in TimeWarner's network were utilized in promoting *Band of Brothers*. TBS (Turner Broadcasting System) scheduled a war film every Monday, and Turner Classics held a thirty-six-hour marathon of war films in the days before *Band of Brothers* was due to air in September 2001, interspersed with behind-the-scenes inserts on the making of *Band of Brothers*. *Band of Brothers* was therefore thoroughly integrated into the transmedia structure of World War II, in the form of history on AOL's website, and the legacy of "classical" World War II films on the TimeWarner network. Originally scheduled to air in June 2001, HBO pushed the debut of the series back to September, reasoning that audiences in the summer were more inclined to want lighter fare. In addition, by delaying the airdate to autumn, the start of *Band of Brothers* coincided with the start of schools, not only opening up an additional market but also implying that the series has an educational value. *Band of Brothers* aired in a prime time slot on Sunday evenings previously reserved for prestige, long-form series such as *The Sopranos* and *Sex in the City*, leaving no doubt as to its significance in HBO's schedule.

While *Band of Brothers* was marketed as the expanded story of *Saving Private Ryan*, *The Pacific*, in turn, was promoted as television on a different scale to *Band of Brothers*. If *Band of Brothers* was an "epic miniseries event," as its trailer proclaims, *The Pacific* had to exceed it in scale to be "beyond epic" (Armstrong 2010a, 4). Furthermore, the subject matter of

The Pacific is used to distinguish it from its predecessor. Although Hanks and Spielberg suggest that the war in the two theaters should not be contrasted in terms of brutality, both make exactly those kinds of comparisons. Hanks (interview in Armstrong 2010a, 4) describes the war in Europe as "recognizable version of the terror of war" but points out that in the Pacific, the fighting was based on racial hatred, with the result that "horrible things were done on both sides to human beings both dead and alive." Spielberg, in turn, notes that in contrast to his determination in *Saving Private Ryan* not to shy away from depicting the horrors of war, the war in the Pacific was so extreme that "we pulled ourselves back from what we could have shown . . . we had a line we wouldn't cross" (interview in TV NZ 2011). *The Pacific*, in other words, goes further than either *Band of Brothers* or *Saving Private Ryan* in its spectacular-authentic depiction of the horror of warfare, a point driven home by references to the scale of the production as the costliest television series to date, with a budget "usually reserved for Jerry Bruckheimer blockbusters" (Block 2010). With $10 million of that budget allocated to promotion, HBO's event-level multimedia campaign for *The Pacific* included sponsorship of national war-related events like the wreath-laying ceremony in Washington, together with high-profile prelaunch advertising in prime placements on radio and television, such as a key slot during the 2010 Super Bowl. HBO's own website for *The Pacific* (www.hbo.com/the-pacific) featured a link to episodes from the series inviting subscribers to "witness the conflict." Like AOL's website for *Band of Brothers, The Pacific*'s website implies that the series offers direct, unmediated access to World War II. In addition to the wealth of historical detail on the website, such as extensive interactive "battle maps" and expanded historical backgrounds of the characters and the battles in the series, the online marketing drive incorporated social media sites such as Facebook (www.facebook.com/thepacific) and Twitter (#ThePacific), which invited viewers to share their own stories, photographs, and memories of the war, as well as their reactions to the series. *The Pacific*'s preliminary marketing thus embeds the series in a complex web in which national and individual histories and memories are comprehensively intertwined in the broader transmedia structure of the war. *Band of Brothers* was rebroadcast by HBO early in 2010 both as a reminder of the brand identity of the series and as an extended preview for *The Pacific*. In the case of *Band of Brothers* and *The Pacific*, event status television thus promotes and premediates event status television.

The status of *Band of Brothers* and *The Pacific* as true stories about World War II facilitates powerful emotional connections to memorialization and imbricates both series in historical discourses both inside and outside of television. Both series negotiate the space between the documentary format of programs such as *The World at War* and fictional dramatizations such as *The Winds of War*. Moreover, despite their vaunted cinematic connections, *Band of Brothers* and *The Pacific* are distinguished, as Tom Hanks notes, through the televisual affordances of time and scope, and it is around these two factors that I structure my analysis of the series themselves. According to Charles McGrath, time is the "great advantage" of the television series (2000, 205). With ten hours at its disposal, *Band of Brothers* has the capacity to reduce the Omaha Beach landing in *Saving Private Ryan* to "the chapter in the long war that it is" (Thompson 2001), whereas the campaign for Iwo Jima is just one of many in *The Pacific*. Although ten hours may be an unthinkable running time for a film, compared to *War and Remembrance* (with thirty episodes) and to long-running HBO series such as *The Sopranos*, *Band of Brothers* and *The Pacific* are nevertheless relatively limited in the context of televisual narratives. As a result, they offer highly concentrated versions of what Caldwell refers to as "excessive narrative" (1995, 164). In other words, the two series offer in compressed form "so much incident and so many people that the effect is a kind of hyper-reality, an adrenaline rush" (McGrath 2000, 246).[10] But what happens to the configuration of the citizen soldier, the visual construction of the war, and the notion of the "good war" in the "hyper-reality" of *Band of Brothers* and *The Pacific*? The next section of this chapter moves on to an analysis of the series themselves and demonstrates that, although undoubtedly influential, the master mediation of World War II created by *Saving Private Ryan* is not a fixed, immutable template. Instead, it functions as a reference point in the transmedia structure of the conflict around which other lodes of memory may develop.

BAND OF BROTHERS

Jeanine Basinger points out that *Saving Private Ryan* replicates many aspects of the classic World War II combat film; the narrative follows a squad of soldiers, containing a familiar ethnic mix, on a specific mission through a wartime landscape, during which they moan about their situation, reminisce about their home lives, and face an uncertain future between bouts of intense combat ([1986] 2003, 259–261). The expanded time frame available to *Band of Brothers* explodes these classic conventions and enables the series to develop the scope of its narrative far beyond that of film. Instead of following one small representative group of recognizable individuals, the series follows an entire company through the course of not one mission but many, from their training through to the end of the war. Because of its episodic structure, the series is able to generate a sense of the inch-by-inch, moment-by-moment nature of winning a war not possible in film. The incremental nature of televisual narrative in turn facilitates a close examination of the impact of these moments on the characters who inhabit them.

Of course, multiple characters and storylines are typical of most televisual narratives, but they are configured differently in *Band of Brothers*. According to Spielberg, *Band of Brothers* follows the "rules" not of conventional drama but of a narrative imposed by "the veterans of the 506th" (interview in Gritten 2001, 46). One of the first points of departure is that, unlike *Saving Private Ryan*, which used the authority of Tom Hanks' star persona to generate a certain level of identification with his character, in *Band of Brothers* almost none of the large ensemble is recognizable. With the exception of David Schwimmer who plays Herbert Sobel, Easy's first commanding officer (but who features significantly only in the first episode) and one or two others including Damien Lewis, who plays Richard Winters, the bulk of the cast is relatively unknown. Each episode foregrounds different characters, and others fade to the background in an approach that attempts to present a range of different perspectives on various moments of the conflict. As they would in reality, some characters appear only to be eliminated immediately; their deaths made all the more powerful by this abruptness. Easy Company sustained a massive 150 percent casualty rate, and the fluidity with which characters come and go throughout the duration of the series reflects the churn of replacements in a way that would not be possible for film.

In the first viewing of *Band of Brothers*, therefore, individual characters do not register with the same significance as they do in film or in other television series. Richard Winters (Damien Lewis) is certainly one of the central figures, but in almost half the episodes he is in the background. The shifting perspective of the conflict evident in *Saving Private Ryan* is taken to extremes in *Band of Brothers*. Moments in which the action is viewed from the point of view of individual soldiers in *Saving Private Ryan* are splintered into seconds and minutes, but in *Band of Brothers* such moments are expanded to hour-long episodes. "Carentan" (Episode 3:10) and "Bastogne" (6:10) provide the best examples, where events are viewed from the perspectives of Corporal Blithe (Marc Warren) and Medic Eugene Roe (Shane Taylor), respectively, neither of whom features prominently in other episodes of the series. The extended temporal canvas of television thus has the capacity to explore how various events affect individuals with different degrees of intensity. John Creeber (2004, 43) regards the idea that the past is experienced and interpreted differently by numerous different individuals as "one of the most important insights" into memory and history that the epic miniseries can offer. However, as with *Saving Private Ryan*, the multiple perspectives of World War II in *Band of Brothers* raise the question: Whose memories are represented here?

Like *Saving Private Ryan*, *Band of Brothers* is framed by moments in the present. Surviving members of Easy Company feature at the beginning of every episode and at the close of the final one, talking about their experiences and memories of the war, which connect to the specific events covered in the narratives of each episode. They are unidentified until the very last episode, so for first-time viewers of *Band of Brothers*, the veterans are anonymous, and it is difficult, if not impossible, to link all of them to·the actors playing the younger versions of themselves. With nothing to identify them as individuals, the veterans become defined through their generation. These are old men, talking about the past, in contrast to the young men in the series itself, living it. The choice to keep their identities obscured until the final episode blurs their individuality in the present, and they are absorbed into a group identity as members of the Greatest Generation, with their individual testimonies merging into one agreed, negotiated version of the past.

The presence of the veterans or "the Private Ryans grown old," as Derek Paget and Steven Lipkin (2009, 103) refer to them, therefore frames the narrative of *Band of Brothers* in a different way to the bookend scenes of *Saving Private Ryan*. The importance of the veteran as a survivor was mentioned in the previous chapter, but to recap, survivors are "awarded moral authority, and their experience carries the weight of cultural value" (Sturken 1997, 255). The use of the individual testimony of the veterans in *Band of Brothers* underscores the series' claim to being the "real" story of Easy Company and also adds cultural weight to its narrative. The very presence of the veterans allows viewers to feel that they have access to what Marita Sturken (1997, 120) calls the "site of truth" that the survivor represents and imbues the footage that follows their testimony with a sense of authority. As Paget and Lipkin suggest, the interviews with the veterans create a "sober, documentary *frame*" (2009, 103, emphasis in original) that is missing in *Saving Private Ryan*. From the opening of the first episode to the close of the final one, *Band of Brothers* signals that it is both memory and history, and as such, it is "bracketed-off from everyday experience" (Caldwell 1995, 188).

The bracketing off of *Band of Brothers* from everyday experience and everyday television is further emphasized by its title sequence. From the moment the title sequence of *Band of Brothers* begins, the series employs what Caldwell refers to as "exhibitionist history" in that televisual techniques are used to "strip, manipulate and refabricate historical images from archival fragments" in ways that are designed to create a narrative world *"more ontologically real* than the world surrounding the more strictly fictional characters in other genres" (Caldwell 1995, 188, emphasis in original). As the titles roll, scenes from the series are rendered either as faded and folded photographs or as scratched, monochromatic film strips. Like the trailer for *Saving Private Ryan*, the title sequence draws on and is informed by the memory of mediated images of World War II. The titles are hypermediated in that they remediate scenes from the series and render them as other media forms. But in addition to locating the events in the past, the title sequence locates the series in the legacy of the visual structure of the war and encodes *Band of Brothers* as history.

The remediation of aspects of the transmedia construct of the war continues in the series itself, with *Saving Private Ryan* exerting a clear influence in the series' esthetic approach. Echoing Spielberg's comments on the camera crew operating as combat photographers for *Saving Private Ryan*, Ken Dailey, digital effects supervisor, observes, in the "Making of *Band of Brothers*" feature (Finn) for the 2002 release of the DVD box set, that shooting *Band of Brothers* was "as though you were actually back in the 1940s with a

1940s camera actually shooting stuff for real." While *Saving Private Ryan*'s key battles take place at two locales, each episode of *Band of Brothers* deals with a different aspect of the conflict and takes place in different settings, ranging from Easy's training camp in Georgia, to the D-Day parachute jump in Normandy, and the winter whiteout of the woods of Bastogne. Each episode has a distinctive esthetic, but all draw on the desaturated color palette used in *Saving Private Ryan* and therefore reference the visual structure of the war in the work of photographers and filmmakers such as John Ford, Frank Capra, and John Huston. Deborah Jaramillo suggests that such references are integral to the creation of a niche audience in HBO's already "exclusive" audience—that of the film aficionado. To paraphrase Jaramillo (2002, 69), *Saving Private Ryan* and the films of Ford, Huston, and others represent what *Band of Brothers* aspires to be in terms of esthetics, as well as what HBO hopes the series will become: the televisual equivalent of a film classic of World War II.[11]

The battle sequences in *Band of Brothers* remediate the dense, hypermediated esthetic deployed in *Saving Private Ryan*. However, as the "Making of *Band of Brothers*" feature (Finn, 2002) stresses, the series *surpasses* the film in its depiction of the spectacle of battle in terms of scope. According to information provided in the "Making of *Band of Brothers*," the production crew had gone through more pyrotechnics than the entire shoot of *Saving Private Ryan* by the time the third episode, "Carentan" (3:10) was completed. Like *Saving Private Ryan*, *Band of Brothers* includes graphic depictions of the violent impact of weapons of war. "The Breaking Point" (7:10), for example, vividly illustrates both the seductiveness of the destructive spectacle of a German bombardment in the Ardennes and its terror, as one soldier (Carwood Lipton, played by Donnie Wahlberg) huddles in a foxhole in the woods laughing in horrified delight at what he calls the "most awesome and terrifying display of firepower," while elsewhere in the forest, another member of the unit is blown almost in half in the same attack. Thomas Schatz sees the "quest for cinematic spectacle" as incompatible with television, and he therefore suggests that *Band of Brothers*' attempts to outdo *Saving Private Ryan* undermine the series (2008, 133). However, given technological developments in terms of image and sound quality in television sets, together with the increase of home theater systems that closely approximate the cinematic experience, the old maxim that spectacle is lost on the small screen can no longer be said to hold true. On the contrary, the televisual use of hypermediated spectacle is a marker of significance that delineates the series from the flow of mainstream television. Furthermore, as I will discuss in more detail in the analysis of *The Pacific*, the spectacular aspect of the visual construction of World War II is a selling point for products of television in the home theater market, where it is used to showcase new media technologies such as high-definition (HD) television.

Band of Brothers not only remediates the spectacular-authentic esthetic that characterizes the visual construction of World War II since *Saving*

Private Ryan; the series also replicates the familiar elisions and divisions between home and war, chaos and order, soldier and civilian. Although *Band of Brothers* includes scenes with civilians, most notably in "Replacements" (4:10), which features encounters between members of Easy Company and Dutch citizens in Eindhoven during Operation Market Garden, the brunt of the damage inflicted by the war in the series is borne by the US soldiers. The series' depiction of geographical space sustains the sense that the GIs carry the sole cost of the war. England and Paris are shown as refuges from the fighting; England in particular is painted as a rural idyll, a retreat for the soldiers from combat. There is no hint of the ravages of the sustained bombing suffered by this country or of the losses it sustained. By refracting the many experiences of the conflict, including that of the Holocaust, through the eyes of the American citizen soldier, *Band of Brothers* becomes less *a* depiction of the American experience of World War II and more a depiction of World War II *as* an American experience.

Band of Brothers expands the vision of warfare established in *Saving Private Ryan* over a broader canvas, but it also embellishes the film's themes of brotherhood and sacrifice in relationship to the citizen soldier. The previous chapter demonstrated how the "delight in comradeship," as Glenn Gray ([1959] 1998, 29) refers to it, has become a recurring feature of American representations not only of World War II but also of contemporary conflicts. As is evident from its title, the main theme of *Band of Brothers* consists of the masculine bonds formed during combat. In the absence of a central character with whom to identify, attention shifts to the brotherhood and to the collective identity of Easy Company in both the present and the past. Despite being members of an elite regiment, the men of Easy Company are, like the soldiers in Shakespeare's *Henry V* from which the series draws its title, portrayed as "working-day" warriors (Act IV, Scene III, line 109). The description of the men of Easy as "ordinary men" asked by "the world" to do "extraordinary things," as one of the taglines used on the theatrical promotional posters puts it, invokes the wartime identity of the citizen soldier as the extraordinary ordinary man. A large part of what makes the soldiers in *Band of Brothers* extraordinary is the bond between them. However, whereas *Saving Private Ryan* and *Flags of Our Fathers* suggest that the primary motivation for soldiers to fight was for their brothers in arms, *Band of Brothers* recalls an older layer of meaning associated with the citizen soldier in the transmedia construct of the war.

Band of Brothers makes clear reference to Frank Capra's series of wartime documentaries, *Why We Fight*, in an episode of the same name in which members of Easy Company discover and liberate a concentration camp (9:10). As mentioned in Chapter 2, Capra's series of seven films was made in an attempt to explain the reasons behind America's involvement in the war and was initially intended for the military but later released for public consumption. There is no mention of Nazi atrocities against the Jews and other groups in Europe at all throughout Capra's films, but the film series identifies ideals such as freedom and democracy as a defining and unifying force. One of the films, *War Comes to America* (1945), describes the American nation as a "brotherhood." Derek Paget and Steven Lipkin echo the idea of the citizen soldier as representative of the "brotherhood" of the American nation by suggesting that "[t]he experience of Easy Company testifies to the value of a democracy when it is truly participatory" (2009, 102). Before the patrol stumbles across the camp in the *Band of Brothers* episode, "Why We Fight" (9:10), one of the band (David Webster, played by Eion Bailey) questions why the Americans are in the war at all. The episode offers itself as an answer by rearticulating the cultural memory of the US citizen soldier as represented in Capra's films as liberator of the oppressed and defender of democracy. *Band of Brothers* therefore rescues the memory of the US soldier from the troubling memories of the Vietnam War through the very medium that (arguably) contributed to the introduction of moral ambiguities in the citizen soldier in the first place.

Band of Brothers consequently preserves the notion of World War II as the "good war," in which US soldiers fight to save the world for democracy. Although the series includes references to friendly fire incidents and reveals the widespread practice of looting by GIs, the elisions critical to the maintenance of the "good war" structure persist, most notably in the absence of any significant indication of the damage inflicted by the war on Europe's civilian population. *Band of Brothers* reflects the influence of its source material in its exaggeration of the role played by the US in the war and in the minimization of the role of both Britain and the Soviet Union. Furthermore, because the individual identities of the soldiers are folded into that of the Greatest Generation, the story of this generation becomes one in which white male voices are dominant and the cost of the war appears to rest almost entirely on their shoulders. In *Band of Brothers*, that cost is made all the more poignant because the affordances of televisual narrative enable it to be rendered incrementally, "the way such things happen in life, and not the way they typically happen in movies, for example, or even in books" (McGrath 2000, 249).[12] For example, the series charts the changes in men who are horrified by mere stories of German prisoners being summarily executed at the beginning of the war (in "Day of Days," 2:10) to men who are unmoved when they actually witness this happening in front of them ("Why We Fight"). That the impact of these events still resonates in the present is illustrated by the sometimes emotional testimony of the veterans. The emotional affect of this confluence between past and present is intensely persuasive and encourages its own kind of forgetfulness for the members of the Greatest Generation excluded from the brotherhood: the African Americans and Native Americans who also fought in this war, and the women who did the same.

The complex array of characters, hypermediated effects, and stylistic flourishes combine to provide an authoritative framework for the representation of the citizen soldier, the visual construction of the war, and the "good war" in *Band of Brothers*, but the structural composition of the series also encourages a particular kind of spectatorial engagement. It is only through repeat viewings that individuals gradually become more recognizable in the brotherhood, and character trajectories, such as Neal McDonough's subtle portrayal of Buck Compton's gradual descent into combat fatigue, become apparent. To assemble the disparate narratives in the series into a collective whole to create a complete picture of the band of brothers, it is necessary to view the series more than once. Spielberg suggests that the series requires "concentration" because it "is not like *The Sopranos*, with the same faces every week" (interview in Gritten 2001, 46). Spielberg's observation implies that the spectator of event status television is more than a mere consumer, and it also fits with HBO's brand identity of delivering quality television to a discerning viewership. By encouraging repeat viewings, the composition of *Band of Brothers* facilitates an extension of the life of the series into syndication and into the DVD and Blu-ray market.

Despite the fact that in the era of TVIII it has become evident that the moment of broadcast is no longer the "primary site of importance" for television (Bennett and Brown 2008, 6), studies on television and memory tend to focus on the individual program as broadcast. Thomas Schatz, for example, suggests that the events of September 11, 2001, which occurred just two days after *Band of Brothers* premiered on HBO, overshadowed the broadcast of the series as a whole and made it seem "oddly anachronistic" (2008, 127). In contrast, Paget and Lipkin suggest that the series was particularly apposite at the time of broadcast, in the light of "a post–September 11 US audience's need for effective leadership and rescue in an atmosphere of victimization" (2009, 98). Either way, although the pilot for *Band of Brothers* drew a respectable audience of around ten million, viewing figures tapered off in subsequent weeks (Schatz 2008, 127). The DVD of *Band of Brothers* went on to become not only HBO's best-selling DVD but one of the highest grossing TV-to-DVD releases to date (Keveney 2010).

The introduction of home video significantly impacted viewing practices by facilitating the possibility of time shifting viewing, but digital technology extends the life of the television series far beyond the moment of broadcast, not least because, unlike video, the digital does not degrade with time. In the case of *Band of Brothers*, must-see TV transformed easily into must-have TV. HBO positioned the DVD and Blu-ray box sets of the series not only as collectibles but as mementos of larger processes of commemoration. First released early in November 2002 in both the US and the UK, the series was packaged as a Commemorative Gift Set to coincide with Remembrance Day (UK) or Veterans Day (US) on November 11. Successive rereleases of the DVD as a limited edition packaged in a metallic box in 2007 and on Blu-ray in 2008 have also been timed for release just before or on November 11. As mentioned previously in this chapter, HBO's preliminary marketing inscribed the series into commemorative processes, and the DVD and Blu-ray sets of the series are subsequently identified as mementos of those processes. Hanks attributes the success of the series in the DVD and Blu-ray market precisely to the links between *Band of Brothers* and commemorative anniversaries. According to Hanks, unlike other series, *Band of Brothers* "keeps churning right along because people keep buying it every Veterans Day, every Christmas, every D-Day" (interview in Itzkoff 2010).

A discussion thread on IMDb's message boards for *Band of Brothers* addressing the subject of repeat viewings, entitled "Sign here if you watch BOB at least once a year" (started August 8, 2008), demonstrates exactly how the box sets have allowed the series to become incorporated into highly individual rituals of commemoration.[13] One user posts that "we watch it once a year, sometimes on D-Day, or sometimes Veteran's day" (posted November 16, 2008), while another starts his/her viewing of the series "ten days before Memorial Day, it makes the day even more meaningful" (posted May 14, 2009). Furthermore, a brief survey of reviews of the *Band of Brothers* box sets on websites, such as amazon.co.uk, indicates that the hyper-reality of the series also encourages repeat viewing. For example, one reviewer writes that since first viewing the series at the age of eleven when it was broadcast in 2001, he/she has watched *Band of Brothers* "at least 15 or so times" (posted April 8, 2009), noticing something different with each viewing. Repeat viewings of the series therefore not only recall the individual's first experience of viewing the series but also become part of personal processes of commemoration.

DVD and Blu-ray technologies have not only impacted viewing practices but have also facilitated the proliferation of so-called ancillary material around the series itself. Extra features are a standard, if not mandatory, element of DVD and Blu-ray sets. According to Caldwell (2008, 161), extra features extend the marketing of a product to *after* its broadcast date and include the consumer in a discourse about "artistry, quality and cultural significance." The extra features available on the DVD and Blu-ray sets of *Band of Brothers* can be understood as extensions of HBO's preliminary marketing of the series and illustrate how these formats support the further distribution of such material. For example, both formats include a segment devoted to the premiere in Normandy in 2001. "Premier in Normandy" (Entertainment News 2001) focuses on the "special HBO screening" of what the voice-over describes as the cablecaster's "most important project to date." In addition to interviews with the veterans and actors, the segment features Susan Eisenhower, who refers to *Band of Brothers* as "powerful" television, together with Winston S. Churchill and Anna Eleanor Roosevelt who all endorse the series and, by extension, the channel itself. "Premier at Normandy" bolsters the sense of the series as culturally valuable and significant television and also ensures that nonsubscribers are made aware of HBO's role in a prestigious international commemorative event.

The extra features on the *Band of Brothers* sets all undoubtedly perform a promotional function to a lesser or greater degree; however, they also constitute a complex paratextual network through which consumers are encouraged to interpret the series and assess its status in the televisual land-scape. Memory and memorialization feature prominently throughout the bonus features of both DVD and Blu-ray sets but are particularly empha-sized in the documentary "We Stand Alone Together: The Men of Easy Company" (Mark Cowen, 2001) and the "Making of *Band of Brothers*" (HBO, 2001), available in both formats. "We Stand Alone Together" inte-grates interviews with the veterans of Easy Company, some of whom are featured holding faded, tattered photographs of their younger selves, with archive footage of the war, in an approach that is reminiscent of *The World at War*. The voices and images of the veterans literally overlap as one inter-view fades into the next, and, as in *Band of Brothers*, it is difficult to dis-tinguish individuals. Like *Band of Brothers*, "We Stand Alone Together" transforms personal memories into a totalized and unified narrative. "We Stand Alone Together" integrates *Band of Brothers* with archival footage of the war and transforms the series from a semidocumentary into history. The Blu-ray discs additionally offer a "field-guide" option, which includes a timeline running at the bottom of the screen with icons supplying vari-ous historical details such as maps and general information about weapons and a pop-out window in which veterans reminisce about their personal experiences of the events onscreen. The field guide seamlessly integrates individual memory and history, knitting both into the very fabric of the series itself.

The "Making of . . ." feature, in turn, emphasizes the status of *Band of Brothers* as "special TV," as actor Neal McDonough puts it, designed with memorialization in mind. For those members of the audience who may have missed the marketing at the moment of broadcast, the "Making of . . ." reasserts the status of *Band of Brothers* as event status television. From the outset, the series is described in the voice-over as "epic," and interviews with the various directors underscore the size and scope of the series. Hanks describes the series as "five times bigger than what we had on *Saving Private Ryan*," drawing attention not only to the scale of the project but also to its connections to the film. Director David Frankel refers to the concentration camp set in "Why We Fight" as "a monument to people who died in camps rather than a movie set," and actor Richard Speight (who plays Sgt, Warren "Skip" Muck) urges those who watch the series to commit to memory the actions of Easy Company. The extra features position the viewer not only as a consumer of quality products but also as the curator of a valuable cultural artifact.

The success of the series in the syndication market is a further illustra-tion of the value of *Band of Brothers* as a cultural commodity for HBO because of its subject matter. In a press release on November 17, 2003, the History Channel announced a multiyear deal with HBO for the rights to both *Band of Brothers* and the documentary feature "We Stand Alone Together." Described as a "Basic Cable Network Premiere Event," the debut of the series on the History Channel in November 2004 (timed to coincide with Memorial Day) marked the first time *Band of Brothers* aired in the US on any other network besides HBO (History Channel Press Release 2003). The $6.5 million fee was more than the History Channel had ever paid for any series up to that point. The agreement provides an example of how an event status series may be used by subsequent networks to attract viewers, to market network brand identities, and to promote original programming. Dan Davids, executive vice president and general manager of the History Channel at the time, describes the series in the release (ibid.) as the "perfect match for The History Channel brand." Scott Carlin, president of domestic programming for HBO, both justified the sale and underscored the status of *Band of Brothers* by stating in the same release that the History Channel "has the same values of historical accuracy" that are present in the series. *Band of Brothers'* construction of the citizen soldier as a member of a special brotherhood united by the exclusive bonds of combat, its hypermediated representation of European battlefields as the spaces in which those bonds were forged and its continuation of the "good war" narrative are all endorsed by the extra features on the DVD and Blu-ray sets and the sale of the series to the History Channel as "the true story of Easy Company."

Toward the end of "The Last Patrol" (8:10), one of Easy Company's brotherhood wonders how anyone will ever know "the price paid by soldiers in terror, agony and bloodshed if they'd never been to places like Normandy, Bastogne or Haguenau?" *Band of Brothers* offers itself as the answer to this question. The series utilizes the luxuries of scope and time to expand the version of World War II memory established in *Saving Private Ryan* and creates a narrative replete with multiple characters, intertwining storylines, and hypermediated displays of historicity that combine to produce a compelling impression of World War II as an American experience. The paratextual network developed through the preliminary marketing of the series, together with the extra features on DVD and Blu-ray, as well as the publicity surrounding the sale of the series into syndication, generates a network of texts that positions the series not only as big, important, and powerful television but also as a significant part of the transmedia mnemonic structure of the war. According to its paratextual network, *Band of Brothers* is the "true" story of the experience of an entire generation. Yet it is precisely the smoothing over of individual experience into the story of a generation that Tom Hanks cites as one of the main reasons for making *The Pacific*. Speaking almost a decade after the broadcast of *Band of Brothers*, Hanks suggests that the reasons why US soldiers went to war in the first place have been lost in the plethora of books and museums dedicated to the Greatest Generation (Noble 2010). Consequently, *The Pacific* follows three Marines of the 1st Marine Division—Eugene Sledge, Robert Leckie, and John Basilone, played by Joe Mazzello, James Badge Dale, and Jon Seda, respectively—into a war Hanks describes as "a different beast from the conflict in Europe" (interview in Lawrence 2010).

THE PACIFIC

According to much of the publicity surrounding *The Pacific*, the soldiers who fought in Europe really can be considered, like Henry V's band of brothers, as the "happy few" (Act IV, Scene III, line 60). In contrast to *Band of Brothers, The Pacific*, according to Tom Hanks, is "not about a gang of elite paratroopers who discovered themselves on the greatest camping trip of their lives" but presents an under-the-helmet perspective of a war considered far more brutal than the war in Europe (interview in Armstrong 2010a, 4). Due to the increasing focus on D-Day in Normandy and the war in Europe in memorialization, in popular history, and in films such as *Saving Private Ryan* and series like *Band of Brothers*, the war in the Pacific has become characterized in US media as an unfamiliar and forgotten war. As one reviewer observes, by the time the Baby Boomers came of age, the war against the Japanese had "essentially been reduced to two events and one iconic image: the attack on Pearl Harbor, the dropping of atomic bombs on Hiroshima and Nagasaki, and the photograph of Marines raising the American flag atop Mt. Suribachi on Iwo Jima" (Franklin 2010). Whereas Pearl Harbor and Rosenthal's photograph feature prominently in films such as *Pearl Harbor* (Michael Bay, 2001), *Flags of Our Fathers*, and *Letters from Iwo Jima* (Eastwood, 2006), the time and scope afforded by television allows *The Pacific* to expand its narrative to include battles that have recently not featured as regularly as D-Day in Normandy on US screens, both small and large.

Like *Band of Brothers, The Pacific* takes advantage not only of the expanded temporal and spatial canvas offered by television but also of the relative creative freedoms offered by HBO in order to tell its story. Most films dealing with ground combat in the Pacific tend to focus on the intense nature of fighting in a single locale, as demonstrated by the Eastwood films in the previous chapter but also evident in older films such as *Beach Red* (Cornel Wilde, 1967) and *None but the Brave* (Frank Sinatra, 1965). The narrative affordances of television, combined with HBO's substantial financial backing, allow *The Pacific* to explore the exponential effect of the multiple D-Days and invasions that characterized the fighting across the islands in this arena of World War II on its three central characters. Echoing Spielberg's comments on the unconventional narrative structure of *Band of Brothers*, Hanks suggests that *The Pacific* "break[s] every narrative rule" because the series devotes attention to battles that eventually proved unimportant in the larger framework of the war (interview in Armstrong 2010b, 26). Close to two and half episodes (5–7:10) are devoted to the battle for Peleliu Island, for example, a campaign that proved to be of little strategic importance in the overall war but that obviously had great significance for the soldiers involved, including Leckie and Sledge. In devoting considerable attention to the individual soldier's perspective of a battle with no wider historical impact, *The Pacific* not only continues but also intensifies the crystallization of World War II around the experience of the American soldier that is evident in the current configuration of the transmedia structure of the war.

Although *The Pacific* concentrates on three central characters, the stories of Sledge, Leckie, and Basilone connect in the loosest of intersecting narratives as the three Marines fight in different campaigns across the Pacific theater. *The Pacific* consequently fractures the notion of the brotherhood of combat and challenges the idea that soldiers fight and die for the man next to them. Instead, the narrative arc of *The Pacific* echoes the wartime construction of the citizen soldier by first establishing the civilian identities of Sledge, Leckie, and Basilone in scenes that emphasize their family relationships and that demonstrate their innocence. Leckie, for example, is introduced in a scene at a church, where he shyly engages in conversation with a girl who lives next door to him ("Guadalcanal/Leckie," 1:10). Whereas Easy Company's training is the subject of the entire first episode of *Band of Brothers* ("Currahee," 1:10), *The Pacific* devotes very little time to sequences involving the three central characters in training. Consequently, the transition from civilian life to war is jarring, mirroring the shock that the Marines themselves felt at their first experience of combat against the Japanese. The character trajectories of Sledge, Leckie, and Basilone consequently read as a fall from innocence. As Steven Spielberg puts it, *The Pacific* is about the "corruption of the human spirit" in the "hell" of war (interview in TV NZ 2011).

The omission of any indication of serious crimes committed by American citizen soldiers remains one of the most persistent elisions in the transmedia structure of the war, and it has significantly contributed to the development of the idea of World War II as a "good war." *The Pacific* introduces a level of ambiguity into the structure of the "good war" by acknowledging that US Marines in World War II were capable of committing atrocities, but it frames any such actions in a larger narrative of the war's brutalizing impact. The series reflects Spielberg's assertion that the Marines were "trained by the enemy" not only in how to fight but also in how to fight like the enemy (interview in Wayland 2010). Consequently, *The Pacific* echoes representations of soldiers in the Korean and Vietnam wars by portraying its citizen soldiers as victims of war who are driven to commit atrocities. Crucially, the most disturbing atrocities in *The Pacific* are not committed by the central characters but by those around them. In what Jon Zobenica (2010) describes as a mechanism "akin to employing the passive voice," *The Pacific* shies away from depicting the full impact of the war on Sledge, Leckie, and Basilone, instead displacing the worst of the moral corruption onto their fellow Marines. For instance, in "Okinawa" (9:10), when Eugene Sledge reaches his lowest point and attempts to remove a gold tooth from a corpse, Snafu, a member of his squad (played by Rami Malek), prevents him from doing so, even though Snafu himself regularly engages in such activity. Sledge and Leckie ultimately emerge from the war damaged but not beyond redemption, and the series demonstrates that both go on to become productive members of society. As Joanna Bourke points out, "The 'before and after' drama, with innocence shattered by a great trauma offers a certain narrative satisfaction and coherence" (1999, 356). Confrontation with the more difficult aspects of war in *The Pacific*, including racial hatred and the complex reasons why Marines found it acceptable to collect Japanese body parts as trophies, are therefore either avoided or smoothed over in a before-and-after drama of their loss of innocence.[14] Despite disrupting the "good war," *The Pacific* preserves the reputation of the Greatest Generation because the citizen soldiers of the series emerge as the victims of war who sacrifice their innocence in the hell of war but retain their humanity. Just as *The Pacific* reconstructs aspects of the citizen soldier familiar from wartime media, the series also remediates the visual construct of the war.

In acknowledgment of the theater's sharp visual contrast to the European war, with its bright blue skies and vivid shades, *The Pacific*'s spaces of battle are drawn with a different color palette to that of *Saving Private Ryan* and *Band of Brothers*. Douglas Brinkley (2010) calls this a "faded Hawaiian postcard look," but it is more accurate to say that *The Pacific*'s construction of World War II remediates the faded imagery of films such as *The Battle of Midway* (John Ford, 1943) and *With the Marines at Tarawa* (USM.C.,1944) as they look today. In its visual construction of landing sequences and battles, *The Pacific* draws on and expands the esthetic construction of combat sequences in *Saving Private Ryan* and *Band of Brothers*, deploying similar techniques to mimic combat photography. In the tradition of epic status television, however, *The Pacific* attempts to create even more spectacular battlefields than either its companion series or film. Filming D-Day on Peleliu, for example, involved detonating 150 pyrotechnics every two minutes and was so overwhelming that actor Joe Mazzello, who plays Eugene Sledge, reportedly fled the beach (Armstrong 2010a). The under-the-helmet perspective that the series cultivates ensures that the spaces of combat are seen only from the Marines' perspective.

The Pacific's visual construction of war therefore not only preserves the polarization that characterizes World War II in the transmedia structure of the conflict but deepens the divisions between its binaries. The distinctions between the spaces of war and those of peace were, by nature, particularly extreme in the Pacific theater. To a certain extent, the war in Europe was conducted in a topography and against an enemy that appeared familiar to many Americans, but the diverse terrain of the Pacific islands, which could vary from tropical jungles to the black and barren beaches of Iwo Jima, created a series of landscapes that were alien to most of the wartime generation. Whereas the scarcity of civilians in *Saving Private Ryan* and *Band of Brothers* represents an active absence in the visual construction of the war, many of the islands featured in *The Pacific*, with the exception of Okinawa, were in actual fact devoid of civilians. With most of the fighting taking place on island settings with unfamiliar flora and fauna and few civilians, the battles that *The Pacific* covers really did occur in exclusive spaces known primarily to soldiers. According to the main tagline for the series, which appears on all the posters and DVDs, "Hell was an ocean away."[15]

However, it is not so much through its depiction of the hell of war in the Pacific that the series intensifies the binaries inherent in the visual construction of World War II as through its nostalgic depiction of 1940s America as a peaceful and untroubled idyll. In "Home" (10:10), the series hints at some of the difficulties faced by citizen soldiers in assuming their civilian identities once again, as well as at the disruption caused by the strikes that plagued the US in the wake of the war, but the spaces of the home front for the most part represent recovery, particularly for Eugene Sledge, whose healing process is very much connected to the tranquil pastoral environment of his home in Alabama. The extreme contrast created by the idealization of home front America and the nightmarish Hieronymus Bosch–type landscapes of warfare in *The Pacific*, as Spielberg describes them (interview in TV NZ 2011), reinforces the perceptual polarities of the visual construction of World War II between concepts of civilization and savagery, us and them, good and evil. If hell was an ocean away, *The Pacific* suggests that for those who survived, escaping hell was simply a matter of traversing that same ocean and returning to the USA, which, according to its depiction in *The Pacific*, was not that far from heaven.

The Pacific's representation of war as a series of battles waged for territory in spaces inhabited only by soldiers is similar to the construction of conflict evident in first-person shooters, as I discuss in more detail in the next chapter. As in *Saving Private Ryan*, Eastwood's two films, and *Band of Brothers*, the cost of the war in *The Pacific* is born by the soldiers. Even though the series includes a scene in which a civilian woman on Okinawa is used by the Japanese as a suicide bomber ("Okinawa," 9:10), because of *The Pacific*'s resolute under-the-helmet perspective, civilian deaths have meaning only in terms of their impact on the American soldiers who witness them.[16] The series extends the same perspective to the dropping of the two atomic bombs, which are important only in terms of what they mean to the US Marines. The intense focus on the perspective of the soldiers is a deliberate narrative choice intended to reflect solely what American soldiers knew or felt at the time, but it preserves critical elisions in the transmedia structure that enable the continuation of the narrative of the role of the US in World War II as a peaceful nation goaded into war through the treacherous and violent actions of others. As in wartime representations, the citizen soldier's loss of innocence in the hell of war in *The Pacific* mirrors the greater national narrative of the perceived loss of innocence of the US itself after the attack on Pearl Harbor.

The tension between acknowledging the savage behaviors that characterized the war in the Pacific theater yet at the same time continuing to honor the Greatest Generation results in an uneasy mix of nostalgia and graphic brutality, which the series does not succeed in reconciling. Consequently, although the notion of the "good war" is not replicated in *The Pacific*, neither is it significantly challenged. Central to the architecture of the "good war" construct is the idea that the US cause in World War II was unquestionably just. *Saving Private Ryan* and *Flags of Our Fathers* rearticulate the justness of the USA's cause in the war through the notion that citizen soldiers fought for their fellow Americans. *Band of Brothers* expands on the theme of brotherhood but also reinvokes the fight for freedom and democracy as the central cause of the war. The reasons behind the US involvement in World War II in *The Pacific* are never as clearly articulated. In the first episode, "Guadalcanal/Leckie" (1:10), a Marine asks, "Remind me what we're doing here?" Leckie responds, rather vaguely, with a quote from the Iliad: "Without a sign his sword the brave man draws, and asks no omen, but his country's cause." Similarly, after the particularly brutal battle for the airfield on Peleliu, Sledge's captain (played by Scott Gibson) reassures him by telling him that "history is full of wars fought for a hundred reasons, but this war, our war . . . [is] all worthwhile because our cause is just" ("Peleliu Airfield," 6:10). A part of the captain's speech to Sledge is also used in voice-over in the trailer for *The Pacific*, combined with an evocative score to buttress the elegiac beauty of the sacrifices made by the Greatest Generation in the service of a just cause in "their" war. Yet the cause itself is never clearly defined.[17] Despite Hanks' assertion that *The Pacific* investigates what motivated Marines to join up, the series never explains in any detail why Leckie, Sledge, and Basilone were so eager to fight. In the final episode, Leckie implies that his personal reason for fighting was because of his love for Vera, the girl next door ("Home," 10:10). Ultimately, the reasons for the US presence in the Pacific are neither articulated nor questioned. The "good war" may not be clearly discernable in *The Pacific*, but its ghostly outline is still evident in the implication that the USA's reasons for fighting, whatever they may be, are unquestionably "just" and that the sacrifices made by the Greatest Generation, including the innocence of its citizen soldiers in the service of such a cause, are "all worthwhile."

The resurrection of the loss of innocence trope in *The Pacific* is particularly significant in the wake of the attacks on the World Trade Center and the Pentagon on September 11, 2001, events repeatedly associated with the bombing of Pearl Harbor by the Bush administration.[18] In a similar fashion but for very different reasons, Tom Hanks makes frequent claims that *The Pacific* is "about *today*" and represents the War on Terror (interview in Vary 2010, emphasis in original).[19] Hanks suggests that the war in *The Pacific* should be "familiar" because it is a "war of racism and terror," during which US forces are "terrorize[d] with suicide attacks" and "reduced to subhuman levels in order to survive" (ibid.). Whether Hanks' analogy is appropriate or not is open to debate. In contrast to *The Pacific*'s depiction of battles for territory in contained island settings with almost no civilians, the War on Terror is an ideological war waged without a front, in which territory does not have the same significance as it did in any theater of World War II. Furthermore, unlike the war in the Pacific, the War on Terror is waged against different nations and ethnicities, frequently in areas densely inhabited by civilians. Analogies between World War II and current conflicts, whatever their political purpose or suitability, illustrate the way in which the visual construction of World War II, together with its crucial absences and polarities has become, as George Roeder suggests, a way of seeing war not only for the generation that fought it but also for subsequent generations (1993, 81).

Regardless of whether *The Pacific* is a successful analogy for current wars, the importance of the series for HBO relates to attracting subscribers and developing ancillary revenue streams. The DVD and Blu-ray sets of *The Pacific*, according to TimeWarner, HBO's parent company, contributed to an increase in content revenue sales for 2011, while subscription revenue climbed 9 percent for the company (Elis 2011), suggesting that *The Pacific* had the intended effect of contributing to maintaining HBO's reputation as a supplier of quality television after the crises it faced toward the end of 2007 in the wake of Albrecht's departure and the end of *The Sopranos*. The paratextual network generated by the features on the Blu-ray and DVD box sets of *The Pacific* echoes that of *Band of Brothers* in a comparable mixture of production history, history of the war, and affirmations of the series' status as epic and important television. *The Pacific*, however, provides a good example of how the spectacular-authentic depiction of combat in World War II functions as a selling point in the contemporary mediascape. Barbara Klinger observes that the rhetoric surrounding the marketing of home entertainment systems often emphasizes spectacle, suggesting that the effects-laden cinematic blockbuster is therefore ideal for showcasing media center technologies (2006, 49–49). *The Pacific*'s extended, hypermediated battle sequences illustrate that HBO's brand of quality television can perform much the same function. According to one review of the series on Blu-ray (Swanson and Henderson 2010), *The Pacific* is neither as compelling as *Band of Brothers* nor as innovative as *Saving Private Ryan* but nevertheless delivers a "stunning home video experience" that "inserts viewers . . . fully into the sensation of battle" through "flawless" video transfers and "fiercely directional" sound mixes. Another predicts that *The Pacific* on Blu-ray will "end up being your demo disc when you want to show off what your sound system can do" (Hickman, Brown and Peck 2011). Such reviews indicate how the element of spectacle in the visual construction of World War II can be abstracted from its context and appropriated in unexpected ways completely divergent from the empathic emotional responses intended by the makers of the series. The commercial success of *Band of Brothers* and *The Pacific* in the Blu-ray and DVD markets, according to Tom Hanks, illustrates that "great television can be something that lives on people's library shelves, much like classic literature" (interview in Lawrence 2010). Both series therefore exemplify what Christopher Anderson identifies as a "crucial step" in HBO's creation of a brand identity: the creation of a "television culture in which it is possible to think of a television series as work of art" (2008, 35).

CONCLUSION

In a perfect example of Marita Sturken's (1997) notion of entanglement between individual memory, history, and cultural representations, *Band of Brothers* was incorporated into the memory processes of Easy Company's surviving veterans.

The image of the band of brothers that ends the title sequence in the series (Figure 4.1) and that is also on the cover of the DVD box set was featured on the welcome page to Easy Company's official website (www.menofeasy company), which was set up after the series and continued to operate at least until the end of 2010. In addition to information about Easy Company's veterans, the site included interviews with some of the actors who played them in a blending not only of past and present but also of historical and televisual narratives. The welcome page featured a letter from the veterans, which quoted World War I veteran and Congressional Medal of Honor winner, Alvin York, stating that although the veterans are honored by the attention given to them by both Ambrose's book and the HBO series, the memory of the fallen is not "for buying and selling." Regardless of Hanks and Spielberg's obvious reverence for the Greatest Generation, buying and selling remain an important feature of how World War II memory is produced and disseminated by HBO, Playtone, and DreamWorks SKG.

Band of Brothers and *The Pacific*, despite all claims to the contrary, are most certainly products of television. As event status series that lay claim to both history and memory, they allow HBO to legitimate its status as a purveyor of meaningful, distinctive, and valuable cultural commodities. Overt ties to the film industry and the paratextual network created by the DVD and Blu-ray box sets position the series as a blend of history, memory, and

Figure 4.1   Final shot of the title sequence for *Band of Brothers.*

art. The links between the series and processes of commemoration, both official and private, enhance the idea that HBO, DreamWorks, and Playtone have created not just television series but memorials. *Band of Brothers* and *The Pacific* consequently produce a version of World War II memory that resists critique and disguises the commercial and industrial goals of each of the producers.

According to David Noon, the drive toward memorializing the events of World War II in the US includes a tendency to define the conflict "in predominantly military terms and in ways that emphasize the ideological unity of the nation in the face of 'evil' " (2004, 348). Echoes of the original war narrative developed by the Roosevelt administration (as discussed in Chapter 2) can be heard in what Noon refers to as the "impulse" to commemorate World War II (ibid.). Both *Band of Brothers* and *The Pacific* are products of the commemorative impulse, and, as such, they blend aspects of the wartime mediated construction of World War II with those that have emerged more recently. *Band of Brothers* recalls the wartime rationale for America's involvement in the conflict as a fight for freedom and democracy and simultaneously constructs the citizen soldier as a member of a brotherhood forged in combat. In the absence of that brotherhood, *The Pacific* casts the citizen soldier as a victim of war's brutalizing influence and reproduces the wartime narrative of the US's "loss of innocence" through the nation's encounter with the Japanese. Drawing on *Saving Private Ryan*'s spectacular-authentic battlefield esthetic, both series amplify the divisions inherent in the visual construction of the war in their composition of the spaces of conflict. Marginalizing civilians and other nationalities involved in the fighting, they preserve the critical elisions that allow the "good war" construct to continue to exist and be visible even in the Pacific theater. The presence of veterans, historians, and historical material in the paratextual network that surrounds the two series confirms their version of the citizen solider, the "good war," and the esthetic composition of the war as history. As both must-see and must-have television, both series lay claim to being memorable in their own right. *Band of Brothers* and *The Pacific* possess what Peter Rollins calls a "dangerous beauty" identifiable in the "drama of commemoration" that diverts attention from the causes of war and the complexities of soldiers' relationship to combat (2001, 117).

In stark contrast, the emotional trappings of commemoration are not quite as much in evidence in the digital gaming industry—the focus of the next chapter. Despite suggestions in the marketing of *The Pacific* that the Pacific theater is a forgotten and unfamiliar facet of World War II, the war against Japan features prominently in the first-person shooter *Call of Duty: World at War* (Activision, 2008). *World at War* is the fifth installment in a franchise of computer and video games described by Bobby Kotick, the CEO of Activision, as "one of the most viewed of all entertainment experiences in modern history" (interview in Ivan 2009). The next chapter examines what digital games, a component of the mediascape so significant to the current generation that they are sometimes referred to as the Gamer Generation, adds to the transmedia construct of World War II.

NOTES

1. To put the cost of the series into perspective, at an average of around $12 million per episode, *Band of Brothers* cost almost ten times more than an hour of standard network television drama at the time and three or four more times the cost of prestige series such as *The Sopranos* (Carter 2001).
2. Collaboration with ABC produced *Spin City* (1996–2002), while Spielberg's own production company, Amblin' Entertainment, joined forces with Warner on *E.R.* (1994–2009), a long-running series that also did well in syndication.
3. For a detailed examination of Spielberg's films and the balance between those taken "seriously," as well as those dismissed by critics as trivial or escapist, see Morris (2007). Morris argues that Schindler's List (1993) marked the point at which Spielberg successfully crossed over into "mature" cinema (2). For Hanks, the shift happened with Philadelphia (Jonathan Demme, 1993).
4. For a detailed analysis of HBO's slogan and marketing strategies, see Leverette, Ott, and Buckley (2008).
5. The first is known as the Broadcast Age (1950–1975), the second as the Cable Age (1975–1995), and the Digital Age started as of 1995 (Todreas 1999, 6).
6. See Leverett, Ott, and Buckley (2008) for a good selection of articles that support this perspective.
7. Evidence of female interest in *Band of Brothers* can be found in *The Chick's Guide to Band of Brothers*, a movie group on Yahoo. Accessed September 24, 2009. https://groups.yahoo.com/neo/groups/ChicksGuideToBandOfBrothers/info
8. Deborah Jaramillo (2002) cites a number of intertextual references in *The Sopranos* to seminal films in the gangster genre.
9. Tony Soprano frequently watches the History Channel's documentaries on World War II in HBO's *Sopranos*, illustrating not only the ubiquitous nature of this conflict on television but also subtly commenting on the History Channel's demographic.
10. The author is referring to *E.R.*, but the same applies to *Band of Brothers* and *The Pacific*.
11. Original reads: "They are what *The Sopranos* aspires to be and what HBO is betting *The Sopranos* will become" (Jaramillo 2002, 69).
12. Again, the author refers specifically to *E.R.*, but the description is equally fitting for *Band of Brothers*.
13. Thread has since been archived.
14. For an examination of some of the reasons behind the collection of body parts by Marines in the Pacific, see "Skull Trophies of the Pacific War" (Harrison 2012, 129–140).
15. In an example of compact marketing synergies, the tagline is also part of the title of Hugh Ambrose's book (2010).
16. Considering the fact that ninety-five thousand civilians died on Okinawa (Dower 1986, 45), *The Pacific*'s acknowledgment of the civilian presence on the island is marginal, to say the least.
17. The lack of a clear definition of what the Marines are fighting for allowed for the series to be advertised on Channel 7, the network that coproduced and broadcast *The Pacific* in Australia, as a war that "changed Australia's destiny," as the voice-over for the trailer in this region suggests, and in which

American Marines "risked everything to save us." The trailer implies that the "cause" was to save the world in general and Australia in particular.
18. For an investigation of the uses of Pearl Harbor in particular and the memory of World War II in general by the Bush administration, see Noon (2004).
19. See also Armstrong (2010a) for further references by Hanks to the War on Terror.

REFERENCES

Ambrose, Hugh. 2010. *The Pacific*. Edinburgh: Canongate Books.
Anderson, Christopher. 2008. "Overview: Producing an Aristocracy of Culture in American Television." In *The Essential HBO Reader*. Gary R. Edgerton, and Jeffrey P. Jones, eds.: 23–41. Lexington: The University Press of Kentucky.
Armstrong, Stephen. 2010a. "The Mother of All Wars." *The Sunday Times: Culture*, March 14, 4–5.
Armstrong, Stephen. 2010b. *The Pacific. Radio Times*, April 3–9, 24–26.
Basinger, Jeanine. [1986] 2003. *The World War II Combat Film: Anatomy of a Genre*. Middletown, CT: Wesleyan University Press.
Beatty, Sally. 2001. "HBO Marches into Battle." *Wall Street Journal*, July 18. Accessed September 24, 2014. www.sddt.com/News/article.cfm?SourceCode=20010718fn#.VARBEfldXax
Bedell, Sally. 1983. "For the TV Networks, the Key to Success is a Long Story." *New York Times*, April 24. Proquest Historical Newspaper: *New York Times* (1851–2008).
Bennett, James, and Tom Brown. 2008. "Introduction: Past the Boundaries of 'New' and 'Old' Media: Film and Television *After* DVD." In *Film and Television After DVD*. James Bennett and Tom Brown, eds.: 1–18. New York: Routledge.
Block, Alex Ben. 2010. "How HBO Spent $200 Million on *The Pacific*." *The Hollywood Reporter*, October 14. Accessed October 22, 2011. www.hollywoodreporter.com/news/how-hbo-spent-200-million-27133
Bourke, Joanna. 1999. *An Intimate History of Killing: Face-to-Face Killing in Twentieth Century Warfare*. New York: Basic Books.
Brinkley, Douglas. 2010. "How Tom Hanks Became America's Historian in Chief." *Time Magazine*, March 6. Accessed September 25, 2014. http://content.time.com/time/magazine/article/0,9171,1969719,00.html
Caldwell, John Thornton. 1995. *Televisuality: Style, Crisis and Authority in American Television*. New Brunswick, NJ: Rutgers University Press.
Caldwell, John Thornton. 2008. "Prefiguring DVD Bonus Tracks: Making-ofs and Behind-the-Scenes as Historic Television Programming Strategies Prototypes." In *Film and Television After DVD*. James Bennett and Tom Brown, eds.: 149–171. New York: Routledge.
Cannadine, David. 2004. "Introduction." In *History and the Media*. David Cannadine, ed.: 1–7. Hampshire: Palgrave Macmillan.
Carter, Bill. 1989. "A Mini-Series Teaches ABC Hard Lessons." *New York Times*, May 8. Accessed September 24, 2014. www.nytimes.com/1989/05/08/business/the-media-business-a-mini-series-teaches-abc-hard-lessons.html
Carter, Bill. 2001. "On Television." *New York Times*, September 3, 2001. Accessed September 24, 2014. www.nytimes.com/2001/09/03/business/on-television-hbo-bets-pentagon-style-budget-on-a-world-war-ii-saga.html
Clarke, Gerald, Elaine Dutka, and Denise Worrell. 1983. "The £40 Million Gamble: ABC Goes All Out on Its Epic *The Winds of War*." *Time*, February 7. Accessed October 18, 2011. www.time.com/time/magazine/article/0,9171,923330,00.html

Creeber, Glen. 2004. *Serial Television: Big Drama on the Small Screen*. London: BFI (British Film Institute) Publishing,

Das, Lina. 2010. "Spielberg Marches On: It Cost $150 million and *The Pacific* Promises to Be the Most Realistic War Drama Ever Made." *Daily Mail*, April 2. Accessed January 1, 2012. www.dailymail.co.uk/tvshowbiz/article-1262972/ Steven-Speilbergs-The-   Pacific-cost-151million-promises-realistic-war-drama-made.html

Devin, Gordon, and Johnnie L. Roberts. 2007. "A Whacking Leaves HBO in Crisis." *Newsweek*, May 21. Proquest Historical Newspapers: *Newsweek*.

Doane, Mary Ann. 2001. "Information, Crisis, Catastrophe." In *The Historical Film: History and Memory in the Media*. Marcia Landy, ed.: 269–285. London: Athlone Press.

Dower, John. 1986. *War Without Mercy: Race & Power in the Pacific War*. New York: Pantheon Books.

Downing, Taylor. 2001. "History on Television: The Making of *Cold War*, 1998." In *The Historical Film: History and Memory in the Media*. Marcia Landy ed.: 294–302. London: Athlone Press.

Edgerton, Gary R. 2008. "Introduction: a Brief History of HBO." In *The Essential HBO Reader*. Gary R. Edgerton and Jeffrey P. Jones, eds.: 1–22. Lexington: University Press of Kentucky.

Elis, Blake. 2011. "Time Warner Tops Wall Street Forecasts." *CNN Money*, February 2. Accessed October 20, 2011. http://money.cnn.com/2011/02/02/news/ companies/time_warner_earnings/

Elliott, Stuart. 2001. "Jeep's Manufacturer Seeks to Capitalize on the Vehicle's Featured Role in *Band of Brothers*." *New York Times*, September 10. Accessed September 10, 2010. www.nytimes.com/2001/09/10/business/media-business-advertising-jeep-s- manufacturer-seeks-capitalize-vehicle-s.html

Franklin, Nancy. 2010. "Hell on Earth: HBO's *The Pacific*." *The New Yorker: On Television*, March 15. Accessed October 20, 2011. www.newyorker.com/arts/ critics/television/2010/03/15/100315crte_television_franklin?currentPage=all

Gray, J. Glenn. [1959] 1998. *The Warriors: Reflections of Men in Combat*. Lincoln: University of Nebraska Press.

Gritten, David. 2001. "In Good Company." *Radio Times* 2 (September 29–October 5): 42–46.

Haithman, Diane. 1988. "The Long March of *War and Remembrance*." *Los Angeles Times*, November 10. Accessed January 18, 2011. http://articles.latimes. com/1988-11-10/entertainment/ca-21_1_war-and-remembrance

Harrison, Simon. 2012. *Dark Trophies: Hunting and the Enemy Body in Modern War*. Oxford and New York: Berghahn Books.

Hickman, Luke A, Kenneth Brown, and Aaron Peck. 2011. "*Band of Brothers/The Pacific*: Special Edition Gift Set (Blu-ray) Review." *High-Def Digest*, October 25. Accessed January 2, 2012. http://bluray.highdefdigest.com/5742/ brothers_pacific_se.html

History Channel. 2003. "*Band of Brothers* Marches over to the History Channel(R) In a Basic Cable Network Premiere Event; The History Channel Acquires Award-Winning Landmark Miniseries from HBO." Press Release. *The Free Library*, November 17. Accessed February 7, 2010. www.thefreelibrary. com/BAND OF BROTHERS Marches Over to the History Channel(R) In a Basic. . .-a0110231477

Ivan, Tom. 2009. "*Call of Duty* Tops 55 Million Sales." *Edge*, November 27. Accessed September 25, 2014. www.edge-online.com/news/call-duty-series-tops-55-million-sales/

Itzkoff, Dave. 2010. "Tom Hanks Returns to *The Pacific*." *New York Times: Arts Beat*, June 3. Accessed October 8, 2011. http://artsbeat.blogs.nytimes. com/2010/06/03/tom-hanks-returns-to-the-pacific/

Jaramillo, Deborah L. 2002. "The Family Racket: AOL Time Warner, HBO, *The Sopranos*, and the Construction of a Quality Brand." *Journal of Communication Inquiry* 26, no. 1 (January): 59–75. DOI: 10.1177/019685990202600100

Keveney, Bill. 2010. "Hanks and Spielberg Return to WWII Together for *The Pacific*." *USA Today*, December 3. Accessed January 22, 2011. www.usatoday.com/life/television/news/2010-03-12-Pacific12_CV_N.htm

Klinger, Barbara. 2006. *Beyond the Multiplex: Cinema, New Technologies, and the Home*. Berkeley: University of California Press.

Krämer, Peter. 2002. "Steven Spielberg." In *Fifty Contemporary Filmmakers*. Yvonne Tasker, ed.: 319–328. London: Routledge.

Kronke, David, and Valerie Kuklenski. 2001. "Television Notebook Fox Exec Tout Fiction, Succumb to Reality." *Daily News (LA California)*, July 18. Accessed October 12, 2009. www.thefreelibrary.com/TELEVISION+NOTEBOOK+FOX+EXECS+TOUT+FICTION%2c+SUCCUMB+TO+REALITY.(L.A. . . .-a079094844

Lawrence, Will. 2010. "Tom Hanks Interview on *The Pacific*." *The Telegraph*, April 1. Accessed October 8, 2011. www.telegraph.co.uk/culture/tvandradio/7527926/Tom-Hanks-interview-on-The-Pacific.html

Leckie, Robert. 1957. *Helmet for My Pillow*. New York: Bantam Books.

Leverette, Marc, Brian L. Ott, and Cara Louise Buckley, eds. 2008. *It's Not TV: Watching HBO in the Post-Television Era*. New York: Routledge.

Lewiston Daily Sun. 1983. "*Winds of War* Tops ABC Forecast," February 10. Accessed October 18, 2011. http://news.google.com/newspapers?id=rTEpAAAAIBAJ&sjid=hGQFAAAAIBAJ&pg=1223,1740584&dq=winds+of+war&hl=en

Manly, Lorne. 2006. "For Tom Hanks, Just Another Day at the Office." *New York Times*, July 30. Accessed October 23, 2009. www.nytimes.com/2006/07/30/movies/30manl.html?pagewanted=all

McCabe, Janet, and Kim Akass. 2008. "It's Not TV, It's HBO's Original Programming." In *It's Not TV: Watching HBO in the Post-Television Era*. Marc Leverette, Brian L. Ott, and Cara Louise Buckley, eds.: 83–93. New York: Routledge.

McGrath, Charles. 2000. "The Triumph of the Prime-Time Novel." In *Television: The Critical View*. Newcomb, Horace, ed.: 242–253. New York: Oxford University Press.

Morris, Nigel. 2007. *Empire of Light*. London: Wallflower Press.

Noble, Elliott. 2010. "World Exclusive Interview: Tom Hanks on *The Pacific*." Skymovies.com, February 22. Accessed December 31, 2011. http://skymovies.sky.com/world-exclusive-interview-tom-hanks-on-the-pacific

Noon, David Hoogland. 2004. "Operation Enduring Analogy: World War II, the War on Terror, and the Uses of Historical Memory." *Rhetoric & Public Affairs* 7, no. 3 (Fall): 339–364. DOI: 10.1353/rap.2005.0015

Paget, Derek, and Steven N. Lipkin. 2009. "'Movie-of-the-Week' Docudrama, 'Historical-Event' Television, and the Steven Spielberg Series *Band of Brothers*." *New Review of Film and Television Studies* 7, no. 1 (March): 93–107. DOI: 10.1080/17400300802603047

Prial, Frank. 1983. "*Winds of War* May Start Blowing Winds of Change on Network TV." *Miami News*, February 15. Accessed October 18, 2011. http://news.google.com/newspapers?id=LrslAAAAIBAJ&sjid=EfMFAAAAIBAJ&pg=6341,4320849&hl=en

Roeder, George. 1993. *The Censored War: American Visual Experience During World War II*. New Haven, CT, and London: Yale University Press.

Rollins, Peter. 2001. "*Victory at Sea*." In *Television Histories: Shaping Collective Memory in the Media Age*. Gary R. Edgerton and Peter Rollins, eds.: 103–122. Lexington: University Press of Kentucky.

Romano, Allison. 2001. "On HBO, War Is Hype." *Broadcasting and Cable* 131, no. 34 (August 13): 18. Accessed September 24, 2014. www.broadcastingcable.com/news/news-articles/hbo-war-hype/69371

Santo, Avi. 2008. "Para-Television and Discourses of Distinction: The Culture of Production at HBO." In *It's Not TV: Watching HBO in the Post-Television Era.* Marc Leverette, Brian L. Ott, and Cara Louise Buckley, eds.: 19–45. New York: Routledge.

Schatz, Thomas. 2008. "*Band of Brothers.*" In *The Essential HBO Reader.* Gary R. Edgerton and Jeffrey P. Jones, eds.: 125–134. Lexington: University Press of Kentucky.

Sledge, Eugene. 1981. *With the Old Breed at Peleliu and Okinawa.* New York: Presidio Press.

Smither, Roger. 2004. "Why Is So Much Television History About War?" In *History and the Media.* David Cannadine, ed.: 51–66. Hampshire: Palgrave Macmillan.

Spartanburg Herald-Journal. 1983. "'Winds of War' Sweeps Ratings to Win for ABC," February 18. Accessed September 24, 2014. http://news.google.com/new spapers?nid=1876&dat=19830219&id=6VEsAAAAIBAJ&sjid=Vc4EAAAAIBA J&pg=6832,3573943

Sturken, Marita. 1997. *Tangled Memories: The Vietnam War, the AIDS Epidemic and the Politics of Remembering.* Berkeley: University of California Press.

Swanson, Peter, and Eric Henderson. 2010. "*The Pacific.*" *Slant Magazine,* November 3. Accessed October 8, 2010. www.slantmagazine.com/dvd/review/the-pacific/1853

Taves, Brian. 2001. "The History Channel and the Challenge of Historical Programming." In *Television Histories: Shaping Collective Memory in the Media Age.* Gary R. Edgerton and Peter Rollins, eds.: 261–281. Lexington: University Press of Kentucky.

Teather, David. 2003. "US TV Special: HBO's Boss of Bosses." *Broadcast,* July 8. Accessed November 6, 2009. www.broadcastnow.co.uk/news/multi-platform//usnews-tv-special-hbos-boss-of-bosses/1122238.article

Thompson, Chuck. 2001. "Army Buddies." *American Way,* September 1. Accessed March 29, 2009. www.americanwaymag.com/tom-hanks-saving-private-ryan-jay-leno-america

Todreas, Timothy M. 1999. *Value Creation and Branding in Television's Digital Age.* Westport, CT: Quorum Books.

TV NZ. 2011. "Interview with Steven Spielberg." Accessed October 8, 2011. http://tvnz.co.nz/the-pacific/interview-steven-spielberg-3403539

Vary, Adam B. 2010. "Steven Spielberg and Tom Hanks Talk About *The Pacific.*" *Entertainment Weekly,* March 21. Accessed October 22, 2011. http://popwatch.ew.com/2010/03/21/spielberg-and-hanks-the-pacific/

Wayland, Sara. 2010. "Steven Spielberg Interview HBO's *The Pacific.*" *Collider.* February 4. Accessed October 13, 2011. http://collider.com/steven-spielberg-interview-hbo-the-pacific/15813/

Zobenica, Jon. 2010. "Getting Their Guns Off." *The Atlantic Monthly,* April 13. Accessed September 25, 2014. www.theatlantic.com/magazine/archive/2010/05/getting-their-guns-off/308030/

KEY TELEVISION SERIES

Band of Brothers. HBO, DreamWorks SKG, DreamWorks Television, Playtone, 2001.

Band of Brothers Extra Features, Commemorative Edition DVD Box Set. HBO, Warner Home Video, 2002.

"The Making of *Band of Brothers.*" Writer/producer, Joan Finn, 2001.

"Premiere at Normandy." *Entertainment News.*

"We Stand Alone Together: The Men of Easy Company." Director Mark Cowen. 2001

Combat! ABC, 1962–1967.
The Pacific. HBO, DreamWorks SKG, DreamWorks Television, Playtone, 2010.
Victory at Sea. NBC, 1952.
War and Remembrance. ABC, 1989.
The Winds of War. ABC, 1983.
The World at War. Thames Television, 1973.

5 Brutal Games

INTRODUCTION: THE MEDIUM OF THE MOMENT

Saving Private Ryan's influence on the transmedia construct of World War II extends beyond film and television into what Sheldon Brown terms "the medium of our moment"—the videogames industry (quoted in The Entertainment Software Association's 2005 report). Even before the end of production on *Saving Private Ryan*, Spielberg expressed an interest in attempting to create a game that would bring gamers "to the same place we're trying to put Capt. Miller and his Rangers" (quoted on Dale Dye's webpage, www.warriorsinc). In the spring of 1997, Spielberg took the idea for such a game to DreamWorks Interactive, a division of the company devoted to the creation of games for PCs and consoles, formed through a partnership between Microsoft and DreamWorks. The resulting game, *Medal of Honor*, was published by Electronic Arts (EA Games) in 1999. *Medal of Honor* was the first World War II game of its kind specifically designed for the console, in this case the Sony PlayStation, rather than the PC. At the time, first-person shooters (FPSs) were a rarity on consoles, and the PlayStation itself was still a relatively new system, having been launched in September 1995. *Medal of Honor* draws on similar ideas of authenticity and verisimilitude as *Saving Private Ryan*. The film and the game share the same military consultant in the form of Dale Dye, who put the developers through a scaled-down version of boot camp, a technique familiar to film and television but unprecedented in gaming. Dye also provided advice on gaming scenarios, weapons, and how soldiers would actually react in the field. The result was a game that emphasized its connections to history and created an evocative atmosphere through a combination of grainy visuals, distinctive sound effects, evocative soundtrack, and actual World War II footage.

Released into a market where FPSs were generally restricted to science fiction, as in *Doom* (ID Software, 1993) or the fantastic, as in *GoldenEye 007* (Rare, 1997), *Medal of Honor*'s combination of history and gameplay had no comparison. One review described it as "the most genuine reproduction of World War II in any videogame on consoles today" (Perry 1999). The game's technical innovations, particularly in sound, and the relative sophistication of its artificial intelligence (AI), which was more developed than any other FPS of the time, are part of why it became the foundation of a multimillion dollar franchise for EA Games. Glenn Entis, head of DreamWorks Interactive in 1999, consequently credits Spielberg with bringing World War II to interactive entertainment (quoted in Kennedy 1999). Although *Medal of Honor* introduced World War II to console gaming and arguably established a template of its own for subsequent FPSs, the conflict has a history in gaming that predates Spielberg's intervention in the industry.

From the earliest years of the games industry, World War II was the conflict of choice for games set in real-world conflicts. In a cursory sampling of all types of war games released across various platforms from 1980 to 2009, games writer Scott Sharkey (2009) demonstrates that out of 223 sampled games, 183 are set in World War II, with a noticeable spike in releases in the late 1990s, which Sharkey attributes to the success of *Saving Private Ryan*. No other war features nearly as often, with the next highest being 18 games set in World War I, and 16 set in the Vietnam War. Sharkey (ibid.) speculates that the dominance of World War II in gaming could be due to the fact that World War II was the last war in which the US was clearly victorious and also ascribes it to the perception of the conflict as a "good war," with Nazis ranking "just above robots and zombies on the list of evil things we can guiltlessly cap in the head." A more recent and detailed study conducted by Johannes Breuer, Ruth Festl, and Thorsten Quandt (2011) concentrates only on the FPS. Breuer, Festl, and Quandt found that, of games released between 1992 to early 2011, the majority (62 percent) of those set in a clearly identifiable conflict are set in World War II. At 16 percent, games set in the Vietnam War account for the next highest percentage. Similar to Sharkey, Breuer and colleagues suggest that a perceived lack of ambiguity and controversy associated with World War II make it more attractive for game developers. However, online responses to Sharkey's articles from gamers point to additional reasons for the dominance of World War II in the FPS.

The responses to Sharkey's article indicate an awareness of the characterization of World War II as a "good war." They discuss why the perceived clear definition of good and evil associated with World War II, as opposed to the ideological minefields of the conflicts in Vietnam and Iraq, lends itself particularly well to gameplay. While they demonstrate an awareness of the influence of other media operating in the transmedia construct of the war—*Saving Private Ryan*'s success is cited as a contributing factor to the endurance of this conflict in gaming a number of times—they also provide a sense of what gamers look for in a war games. In the case of the FPS in particular, the criteria are organized around depictions of space and weaponry.

The scope of World War II means that the games can be set in a number of environments, ranging from jungles to beaches and urban cityscapes, with a number of familiar "set pieces," described by one commentator (posted August 13, 2009) as "well-known, explicitly resolved conflicts," such as the

Normandy beach landings. In general, the comments on Sharkey's article suggest that the nature of the trench warfare in World War I and the jungle settings of Vietnam limit the games that use these conflicts as contexts. Varied terrain facilitates different styles of gameplay in the FPS. Playing as a sniper in the ruins of Stalingrad, for example, offers a different gaming experience in comparison to the close-quarters combat of the Pacific islands. In terms of weaponry, one respondent (posted August 14, 2009) notes that the versatility of the weaponry available during World War II makes the conflict ideal for the FPS because "[i]t's harder for a game designer to translate the subtle differences of modern weapons." Of course, a number of games, which have ardent supporters, are set in more current conflicts. The *Medal of Honor* franchise itself departed from a World War II setting for the first time in 2010, in favor of the war in Afghanistan. However, the responses to Sharkey's article illustrate some of the reasons why World War II is such a dominant presence in the FPS format. The significance of space and weaponry will be explored in more detail later in this chapter, but from the outset it is important to note that gamers themselves consider these elements crucial to what makes World War II a particularly ideal scenario for the FPS. Which raises the following question: if World War II is particularly suited to the first-person shooter, what is the first-person shooter doing for the memory of World War II?

Despite interest in the academic field in the pedagogic potential of games, shooters like the *Medal of Honor* (DreamWorks Int., EA Games, 1999–present) and *Call of Duty* (Infinity Ward, Activision, 2003–present) franchises are generally dismissed as having little to offer in the way of memory or historical significance, particularly when contrasted with World War II strategy games. "There is nothing to be learned from this kind of history," writes Jerome de Groot, who reluctantly goes on to acknowledge that there is nevertheless a kind of "ontological kick" to be gained from playing them (2009, 38). Niall Ferguson (2006) is even more vehement in his dismissal of the FPS. "I hate them," he says, referring specifically to *Medal of Honor* and *Call of Duty*, although he acknowledges that "they have taught my sons an amazing amount about World War II hardware" (ibid.). There is an ambiguity at the heart of comments such as these; both object to the FPS, but there is a grudging acknowledgment of a certain kind of historical engagement in these games that other forms of media perhaps do not offer. However, neither de Groot nor Ferguson fully define nor explore what form of engagement the FPS offers.

To explore the question of what the FPS brings to the transmedia structure of World War II, this chapter begins by briefly examining the history of World War II in gaming and the role played by games in developing the cultural narrative of World War II. The previous chapters illustrated that as the transmedia structure of World War II evolved over the last two decades, the experiences and memories of the US citizen soldier have become increasingly dominant within the cultural narrative of the conflict. During the war itself, combat was emphasized as the defining experience of World War II in US media. In current representations, combat forms the basis of a unique and exclusive bond of brotherhood among soldiers, forged in the spaces of the battlefield. With the notable exception of *Letters from Iwo Jima* (Clint Eastwood, 2006), the war memories of civilians and the experiences of soldiers and resistance fighters outside the US do not feature prominently in the transmedia structure of the war. The films and television series discussed so far are all positioned as reverential tributes to the Greatest Generation and are linked to public commemorative events and memorials. My approach throughout has been to illustrate the connections and interrelations among particular media as they formulate various iterations of World War II memories and to argue that it is unfeasible to consider any medium in isolation. The gaming industry is no different from other media industries in that it not only remediates other media, such as television and film, but also emphasizes these connections as a measure of authenticity. The outline of the organizational framework of World War II memory in the form of the citizen solder, the visual construction of the war, and the structure of the "good war" is therefore identifiable in games. However, it is important to bear in mind that digital games introduce a different element into the transmedia structure of the war in the form of play. With reference to the *Medal of Honor* games but moving on to focus particularly on *Call of Duty: World at War* (Activision, 2008), I draw on Paul Connerton's (1989) notion of "habit memory" to examine the particular kind of engagement with World War II that the FPS engenders. As simulations, FPSs reduce war to the basic components of space and weaponry, but in doing so, they facilitate connections to aspects of war memory obscured by other mediated representations of World War II. Not least among these is the acknowledgment that, as Vietnam veteran William Broyles (1984) suggests, while it is "no mystery why men hate war," there may also be "strange and troubling" reasons for loving the experience of war, particularly when it is rendered as a game without risk.

THE CULTURAL STORY OF WORLD WAR II FOR THE NEXT GENERATION

Even a brief survey of some of the facts and figures of the industry vindicates the idea of games as the medium of our moment. The games industry is the fastest growing sector of entertainment media with the retail side of the business showing a massive 250 percent growth from 1999 to 2009, despite a dip in 2008 (NPD Group Press Release 2009). By May 2009, 10 percent more adults in America played games than went to the cinema (NPD Press Release 2010). Watching television is also the activity most likely to be displaced by gaming, particularly for youths (Jones 2002, 179). In terms of gender, women make up 48 percent of gamers, and women aged eighteen or older form a significantly larger portion (36 percent) of the gaming population than males aged seventeen or younger (Entertainment Software Association Report, 2014, 3). The phenomenally rapid growth of this sector of the media is a vital distinguishing factor between the current mediascape and that of previous generations. Games are so significant in the current mediated milieu that John Beck and Mitchell Wade (2004) refer to today's generation as the Gamer Generation. Digital games are played by all generations, but, as Beck and Wade argue, "a boomer who can feel natural playing a video game—or a member of the game generation who *can't*—is a real anomaly" (19).

For the Gamer Generation, therefore, the *Medal of Honor* and *Call of Duty* franchises are potentially as significant, if not more so, than any other mediation in the transmedia construct of World War II. Bobby Kotick, CEO of Activision, highlights the importance of games in today's mediascape by claiming that *Call of Duty* is not only "one of the greatest entertainment franchises of all time" but also "one of the most viewed of all entertainment experiences in modern history" (quoted in Ivan 2009). Yet despite the pervasive presence of World War II games in the war game sector of the game industry, as well as the sheer size of the markets they attract, significantly less academic attention has been devoted to digital games than has been given to representations of the conflict in media such as film and television. It is not my intention to redress this imbalance here, but it is important to examine in brief some of the games that precede both *Medal of Honor* and *Call of Duty* in order to explore the gaming industry's version of the cultural story of World War II and also to establish the significance of these two franchises for the transmedia structure of the war as a whole.

Sebastian Deterding notes that early war games developed for the PC were "little more than digitized board games" and points to an "industrial continuity" between the settings and publishers of both board games and digital games (2010, 31). Such connections go some way toward explaining why most early computer war games, including those set in World War II, were strategy based. Similar to the strategy board games they are drawn from, early computer games present a linear history of the conflict, where cause follows effect. The gamer either occupies a god-like perspective of the entire conflict or is a commander in the field of a specific battle. In 1981, for example, of the five war games set in World War II released in that year, only one, *Castle Wolfenstein*, developed by Muse Software, can be considered a shooter (according to Mobygames.com). By 1984, as the market began to expand, and the number of games in general increased, the number of World War II games doubled. Although most of these are still either strategy games or flight simulators, some include elements of the shooter (ibid.). Examples include *Battle for Midway* (published and developed by Personal Software Services), in which gamers assume command of two task forces of the Pacific fleet and at one point have to man the guns and shoot down attacking Japanese aircraft, and *Night Gunner* (published and developed by Digital Integration Ltd.), a flight simulator in which gameplay primarily consists of shooting at other aircraft or undertaking bombing runs. Like *Castle Wolfenstein* in 1981, *Beyond Castle Wolfenstein* was the only World War II game in 1984 that can truly be considered an FPS. Both *Castle Wolfenstein* and *Beyond Castle Wolfenstein* established the groundwork for *Wolfenstein 3D*, developed by ID Software in 1992.

Wolfenstein 3D was key to popularizing the FPS and to establishing its significance within the gaming industry. *Wolfenstein 3D* pioneered many of the features now taken for granted in the form, such as the ability to select weapons, to pick up both health and ammunition while moving through levels, as well as the ability to save progress anywhere during the course of the game. The game features a US soldier in the form of BJ Blaskowicz, who navigates the maze-like structure of Castle Wolfenstein in what can only be described as a typical B-movie plot, collecting treasure and shooting guards. Despite an unprecedented level of gore in the game, the limits of graphics capabilities of the time reduce both BJ and his Nazi opponents to cartoon-like proportions. As Ed Halter observes, "there is something both creepy and funny about seeing the perpetrators of the Holocaust reduced to icons of near-cuteness" (2006, 156). *Wolfenstein 3D* was nevertheless taken seriously enough in Germany, where it was banned it due to the game's display of the swastika and use of the Nazi Party's anthem. Of all the game's innovations, the ability to navigate a three-dimensional environment, rather than being restricted to a single screen, is perhaps the most significant. In that respect, *Wolfenstein 3D* provided a template for the navigation of space still utilized by the contemporary FPS.

Wolfenstein 3D's developer, ID Software, continued its innovations of the FPS with *Doom* (1993). ID made the unusual decision to release *Doom* as unlimited shareware on the Internet, allowing gamers to modify the game at will. Although this is not a World War II game, it is worth mentioning briefly that its capacity for modification led to *Marine Doom* (1996), which Ed Halter describes as "a boots-on-the-ground combat simulator" for the "PC Generation" (2006, 168). *Marine Doom* is a much cited early example of the US military's interest in the FPS and its adaptation of the form for its own purposes, including training and recruitment.[1] However, the modification of *Doom* was not intended to teach marines to shoot but to train them in teamwork and cooperation (Halter 2006, 168). Despite the fact that *Marine Doom* was ultimately not officially incorporated into widespread training within the Marine Corps, it is an indication that even at this early stage of the FPS's development, the military had identified the potential of the form to do more than simply generate knowledge about weaponry. Whereas most strategy games provide a perspective of the bigger picture of the war from the point of view of Navy commanders or Army generals, the FPS, as the creators of *Marine Doom* identified, provides the under–the-helmet viewpoint of combat of the ordinary soldier.

As established in previous chapters, Spielberg similarly cultivates the under–the-helmet perspective of war in *Saving Private Ryan, Band of Brothers*, and *The Pacific*. It is perhaps unsurprising, therefore, that when the director developed the idea for a World War II game, the FPS rather than the online strategy game was a natural fit for a perspective of war that favors the ordinary soldier's point of view. Glenn Entis, CEO of DreamWorks Interactive at the time *Medal of Honor* was developed, points out that the core ideas for the game, from the title, to the setting and the mission structures were entirely Spielberg's (interview in Elliot 2008). According to Entis, EA regarded Spielberg not only as having particular insight into the US soldier's experience of World War II because of his work on *Saving Private Ryan* but also as someone who understood the constraints and the possibilities of gaming because of his own interest in the technology (ibid.). As the company proclaimed in an ad appearing in *Creative Computing* magazine (June 1983) in the early years of its inception, the PC was more than "a medium for blasting aliens" and posed the question "can a computer make you cry?" EA in turn seemed particularly compatible with Spielberg's concept of creating a game that would echo the emotional resonance of *Saving Private Ryan*. Although DreamWorks Interactive was sold to EA before the first *Medal of Honor* game was completed, the influence of *Saving Private Ryan* throughout the franchise is undeniable.[2]

As with *Saving Private Ryan* and *Band of Brothers*, the idea of honoring veterans is at the heart of the *Medal of Honor* franchise. Twelve of the franchise's fourteen releases are set in World War II, and all of these remediate the trademark desaturated visuals of both *Saving Private Ryan* and *Band of Brothers*, as well as the evocative film and television music scores that form the background to the games. The same veneration for the citizen soldier is evident throughout all the games in the franchise, including those set in more recent wars. According to EA executive producer Greg Goodrich, "What defines *Medal of Honor* is the reverence for service and sacrifice, and those stories of brotherhood and honor and respect . . . the same as *Band of Brothers*" (in Garratt 2012). Despite initial opposition from Paul W. Bucha, the president of the Congressional Medal of Honor Society (CMOHS) to the development of the first game, the CMOHS now fully endorses the franchise and even features the games on one of the pages of its website (www. medalofhonornews.com). Bucha himself identifies the franchise as "a new avenue to send our message to upcoming generations that the medal itself represents ordinary people doing extraordinary things for their country" (interview in *IGN* 1999). Rather than the detached perspective offered by strategy games or the quirky esthetic of *Wolfenstein 3D*, *Medal of Honor* offers an engagement with the conflict designed to be emotionally affecting. As the copy on the packaging for the PlayStation game *Medal of Honor: Frontline* (2002) proclaimed: "You don't play, you volunteer."

Despite *Medal of Honor*'s promise of an emotionally laden experience of war, however, "play" remains central to the way in which games configure their version of the cultural story of World War II, and the franchise therefore departs from the way in which World War II is represented in other media in a few significant ways. In contrast to film or even to the expanded time and scope offered by televisual narratives, *Medal of Honor* games cover many more battlefields, ranging from Europe through to Africa (an arena neglected in contemporary film and television) and shifting in later games to the Pacific. In addition to an expanded geographical canvas, the games offer a variety of campaigns. Gamers can play as an officer for the OSS (Office of Strategic Services, in *Medal of Honor*, 1999), a female resistance fighter (in *Medal of Honor: Underground*, 2000), or as a paratrooper (in *Airborne*, 2007), for example. With the franchise's emphasis on narrative, some of these characters reappear in other installments of the games, challenging Espen Aarseth's (2004, 48) assertions that intertextuality is not significant to games. *Heroes* (2006), for example, connects various characters and narrative threads, including Lieutenant Patterson from *Frontline* (2002), who proposes to Manon Batiste, the French resistance fighter in *Underground*. *Medal of Honor* thus offers a range of perspectives and physical locations throughout a selection of campaigns from World War II, in contrast to the highly concentrated representations of the American soldier's experiences of specific moments in the conflict evident in the other media discussed in this book. The overall emphasis throughout the franchise, however, remains on the heroic actions of individuals.

Medal of Honor may have set the bar for World War II FPSs, but it is generally acknowledged to have suffered a decline in both popular and critical acclaim—possibly a consequence of the pressures of releasing a game roughly every six months.[3] Following the release of the franchise's third installment, *Allied Assault* (2002), most of the team responsible for the development of *Medal of Honor*, including all the project leads, broke from EA and developer 2015 Studios after disputes over game design to form their own studio, Infinity Ward. With backing from publisher Activision, they released the first *Call of Duty* in October 2003. In stark contrast to *Medal of Honor*'s overriding theme, *Call of Duty* was released with the tagline "In war, no one fights alone," and Activision's page for the game on its website (https://store.activision.com) promises a perspective on the war "through the eyes of citizen soldiers and unsung heroes from an alliance of countries," including American, British, and Russian soldiers.

Given the prevalence of World War II in the FPS format, by 2003 there was a sense among gamers that the conflict was, as games magazine *Computer and Video Games* (CVG) put it, "tired, unoriginal and generally done to death" (2008a, 87). The first *Call of Duty* was one of about twenty-three games set in World War II released that year, most of which were strategy games (according to Mobygames.com).[4] The only other significant World War II FPS released in 2003 was *Medal of Honor: Rising Sun*, which was widely criticized for its weak gameplay.[5] The first *Call of Duty* was credited with reinvigorating the World War II FPS, largely because of its innovations to the FPS format. In a sense, *Call of Duty*'s technological success mirrors *Saving Private Ryan*'s achievements in remodeling the perspective of the World War II battlefield through technical innovation. Winning more than eighty game-of-the-year awards, including the industry's first from the British Academy of Film and Television—significant at the time as a belated acknowledgment of gaming in the general mediascape—the first *Call of Duty* "redefined realism and the concept of war gaming to balance it better with fun . . . the reason we all play games" (*CVG* 2008a, 123). Examples of *Call of Duty*'s improvements to game mechanics include a visual reference indicating which direction damage is coming from, as well as regular, auto-saved checkpoints conveniently spaced to forestall the necessity for constant quicksaves, thus preventing tedious replays through swaths of gameplay to reach the same point.[6] Such innovations enhance the gamer's involvement in the game by reducing the necessity of focusing on the actual mechanics of gameplay. Making the game easier to play also broadened its appeal to include casual gamers as well as those more proficient (*CVG* 2008a, 123).

But in addition to technical innovations and the focus on the mechanics of gameplay, the first *Call of Duty* also introduced changes into the cultural narrative of World War II. One of the key ways in which *Call of Duty* recalibrated the cultural narrative of the conflict was by offering shifting perspectives of the war in the same game. As the game changes geographic locations or fronts, it forces gamers to adopt a new "character" in the form of American, Russian, or British soldiers, along with a different outlook on the war. Forcing gamers to switch among soldiers of various nationalities broadens the perspective of the war in general and, more importantly, dilutes the possibility of individual heroism. In most FPSs, including *Medal of Honor*, playing as a single character throughout one game allows gamers to collect weapons and accumulate skills until their avatar is practically invincible by the end of the game. Because Infinity Ward made the unusual decision to compel gamers to switch characters in the same game, *Call of Duty* counters the archaic notion that the actions of individuals matter on the industrial battlefield and instead emphasizes the insignificance of the soldier as one small part of a massive operation.

Although the first *Call of Duty* reintroduces soldiers of other nations to the transmedia structure of the war, the game also reconstitutes one of the key attributes of the citizen soldier in its current configuration: the idea of the soldier as a member of a "brotherhood." *Call of Duty* was the first FPS to feature sustained, plausible behavior in nonplayer characters (NPCs). For much of the game, gamers fight as part of a squad in support and defense of one another. Unlike other games that also feature squads (one example would be Ubisoft's *Brothers in Arms*, released in 2005), the squad in *Call of Duty* does not require controlling or ordering. Squad members act independently to provide covering fire, shout warnings, and even put themselves at risk to save the gamer. Each individual has a distinct personality that emerges during the course of the game, facilitated by a feature dubbed by the developers as "battlechat," which allows NPCs to talk to one another and to the enemy. Through the squad, *Call of Duty* creates the sense that the gamer is not an isolated individual but rather a member of a group of soldiers, all of whom are caught up in massive events beyond their control.

The *Call of Duty* franchise's dilution of heroic individuality has an additional consequence. In the absence of one central soldier as a focal point of identification, *Call of Duty* shifts attention to the spectacle and magnitude of industrialized warfare. As CVG puts it, *Call of Duty* made "war" itself the hero, rather than the citizen soldier (2008a, 120). The first game of the franchise marshaled cinematic standards of realism in war to generate a sense of the scale and chaos of World War II. For example, the first *Call of Duty* introduced an effect called "shellshock" by drawing on similar techniques used in *Saving Private Ryan*'s landing sequence. A grenade or explosion near the gamer produces momentary auditory and visual distortion; a feature that complicates gameplay by reducing reaction time but that also forges a deeper connection between the gamer's senses and the world of the game. The world created by the developers of the first game was also unusual in that it extends beyond the immediate vicinity of gameplay into a vast background filled with visual and sound effects, such as distant explosions or gunfire. The spectacle of industrialized warfare, a key component in the visual structure of World War II, is used throughout the *Call of Duty* World War II games to situate the gamer as a "tiny man trapped in miles of exploding chaos" and to generate an unusual sense of extreme vulnerability, as opposed to the feelings of invincibility more common to the FPS in general (*CVG* 2008a, 119).

In addition to its remediation of cinematic effects, the *Call of Duty* franchise as a whole has multiple connections and references to other mediations of World War II. The first *Call of Duty* includes some of the exploits of the 506th Parachute Regiment, familiar from both *Saving Private Ryan* and *Band of Brothers*, and features Giovanni Ribisi, who plays Medic Irwin Wade in *Saving Private Ryan* as the voice of Private Elder. *Call of Duty 2: The Big Red One* (Activision, 2005) not only references Sam Fuller's film in its title but also uses Mark Hamill, one of the actors from the film, to provide the voice-over narration of the game. *Call of Duty: The Big Red One* additionally features seven of the actors from *Band of Brothers* who provide voices for various characters in the game. There are overt references to scenes from films throughout the franchise. The hand-to-hand combat of *Call of Duty 3* (Activision, 2006), for example, is unmistakably modeled on the scene in *Saving Private Ryan* in which Corporal Mellish grapples with a German soldier, and the opening cutscene (cutscenes are cinematic sequences during which the gamer is forced to relinquish control of the game) of the Stalingrad sequence in *Call of Duty: World at War* practically replicates the opening scene from *Enemy at the Gates* (Jean-Jacques Annaud, 2001).

Such references not only place the *Call of Duty* franchise in the historical framework of World War II but also integrate the games into the network of mediated representations of the conflict. Subtly alluding to the recent trend in the transmedia structure of World War II to represent the war as an exclusively American experience, the *Call of Duty* World War II games trade on the idea that, as the *Call of Duty* webpage (https://store.activision. com) puts it, "no one soldier or nation single-handedly won the war" to distinguish themselves. In contrast to Aarseth's view that intertextual references have no impact on gameplay (2004, 48), Henry Jenkins suggests that references such as these create a "dialogue" with other mediated texts and that games ultimately convey "new narrative experiences through [their] creative manipulation of environmental details" (2004, 124). The World War II *Call of Duty* games convey new experiences of the war's history through the gamer's manipulation of and interaction with the gameworld. In *Call of Duty*, the "environmental details" of World War II are broken down into contested spaces and weaponry.

The sales figures and audiences commanded by the *Call of Duty* games appear to support Kotick's hyperbolic statement regarding the games as "one of the most viewed of all entertainment experiences in modern history" (quoted in Ivan, 2009). Releases of new installments of the franchise exceed opening weeks for cinematic blockbusters in terms of promotion, scale, and initial profits (for one example, see Stuart 2011). On average, six and a half million people play a *Call of Duty* game online per day (Boxer 2011), making the franchise as much a social networking phenomenon (an aspect of the game that offers a potentially rich area for future exploration) as it is a gaming one. It should be noted, however, that the *Modern Warfare* installments of *Call of Duty*, which are set in hypothetical conflicts of the near future, are a large source of the franchise's overall revenue. Despite the critical and commercial success of the first *Modern Warfare* (*Call of Duty 4*, released in 2007), *Call of Duty 5: World at War* marked a return to World War II. Similar to the DVD and Blu-ray sets of *Band of Brothers* and *The Pacific*, *World at War* was timed for release on November 11 in 2008 to utilize the general publicity for World War II during times of commemoration, but the return to World War II in the franchise was a move greeted with skepticism by both gamers and critics alike (for examples, see Thorsen 2008 and comments). Yet despite the initial misgivings of some players and commentators, *World at War* outsold *Modern Warfare* by more than two to one in the first week of sales in the UK alone (Martin 2008). The game eventually went on to sell more than eleven million copies worldwide, ending not far behind the first *Modern Warfare* in terms of overall sales (Fahs 2009).

As the last *Call of Duty* to be set in World War II, *World at War* continues the franchise's recalibration of aspects of the transmedia structure of the conflict, but it does so at a moment when the ongoing presence of World War II in the FPS was under scrutiny. As a result, the tension between gameplay (always a focus for the franchise) and historical context is evident in both the game and the discourse surrounding it. The use of historical content in gaming inevitably raises aspects of the debate concerning the nature and purpose of narrative in games. Although *World at War*, like all games in the franchise, references other visual media, it cannot be analyzed purely in terms of the narrative it constructs, or even through its visual or auditory content, but must be considered in terms of gameplay. As Henry Jenkins notes, "the experience of playing games can never be simply reduced to the experience of a story" (2004, 120). My approach is to consider *World at War* as a simulation; however, this does not preclude a discussion of the narrative components of the game. As part of a franchise that consistently emphasizes the thrill of gameplay, *World at War* is an ideal example of what happens to the citizen soldier, the idea of the "good war," and the war as a visual construct when these three elements are translated via a technology that introduces "play" to the memory of the conflict. The next section will investigate how *World at War* represents World War II as a series of responsive environments that are contested and explored by the gamer primarily through the use and deployment of specific weapons.

WORLD AT WAR: "THERE'S A SOLDIER IN ALL OF US."

World at War expands *Call of Duty*'s global perspective of World War II to include not only the Russian campaign, which features in both *Call of Duty 1* and *2*, but also the war in the Pacific. Until the release of *World at War*, the majority of games set in the Pacific arena were flight simulators or strategy games based on naval battles. The most notable exception is *Medal of Honor: Rising Sun*, but like the rest of the *Medal of Honor* franchise, *Rising Sun* involves covert missions, such as the infiltration of a top-secret Axis summit in Singapore in 1943 and air strikes on gold-smelting operations in Burma. Such specialized missions were far from the experiences of ordinary marines, who faced an unrelenting series of amphibious landings and pitched battles in attempts to take and hold islands such as Guadalcanal (August 1942), Peleliu (November 1944), and Iwo Jima (February 1945). Similar to the approach subsequently adopted by Tom Hanks and Steven Spielberg in their publicity for *The Pacific*, Activision and Treyarch, the developers of the game, suggest that the experience of the US marines in the Pacific is a neglected dimension of World War II history in gaming. *World at War*'s military adviser, Lieutenant Colonel Hank Kiersey, observes that "[n]obody knows how brutal and tough and gritty and demanding and environmentally challenging the fight in the Pacific theatre was" (interview in *CVG*, 2008b, 53). Similarly, Keirsey describes the Russian campaign as particularly brutal because, at different stages of the conflict, both the Russians and the Germans were fighting to defend their home countries (ibid.). The choice of the Pacific and the Russian theaters, according to Mark Lamir, head of Treyarch at the time *World at War* was developed, resulted in a game "scarier" than any other in the franchise, with a "grittiness" that made even the developers "uncomfortable" (quoted in *XBOX* 2008). As the copy on the

Xbox 360 box of the game (2008) proclaims, *World at War* is "war like you've never experienced before."

Despite claims that *World at War* offers a unique gaming experience, the game uses a slightly enhanced version of the same proprietary game engine used in *Modern Warfare*, known as the IW.4.0 (Infinity Ward.4.0). What this means, in effect, is that the game mechanics are notably similar in both games.[7] So similar, in fact, that games reviewer John Funk (2008) suggests that *World at War* is *Modern Warfare* with a different "skin." The IW.4.0 enabled the use of a dynamics physics engine for the first time in the franchise, facilitating the creation of detailed and responsive environments. These include intricate lighting and particle effects, as well as physical effects such as variations in bullet impacts on different surfaces—a feature that forces gamers to make careful decisions about where to take cover because they have to allow for destructible materials. For *World at War*, the engine was enhanced to accommodate different weapons, the flamethrower being the most notable in its impact not only on the enemy but also on the environment. Furthermore, the IW.4.0 enabled behavior modifications for enemy AI, creating resourceful and unpredictable opponents in *World at War* and facilitating the startling "banzai" attacks in the Pacific theater. With only slight variations in the game mechanics of *Modern Warfare* and *World at War*, context takes on a particular significance inasmuch as gamers familiar with the former would most certainly have experienced "war like this" before, at least in terms of gameplay.

In line with the rest of the franchise, *World at War* does not permit gamers to play through World War II as a single soldier. In single-player mode, the game opens in the Pacific on Makin Island on the night of August 17, 1942. The gamer starts out as Private Miller, a member of the US Marine Corps. The game begins with Miller in a position of vulnerability as a prisoner of war captured by the Japanese. Bound, weaponless, and helpless, the gamer is forced to watch the brutal execution of a fellow prisoner in one of the game's most violent and disturbing scenes before being rescued by US forces. As Miller, gamers fight their way through the Pacific campaign, accompanied by rescuer and mentor Sergeant Roebuck, voiced by Keifer Sutherland. During the battle for Peleliu Island (which takes place two years after the events on Makin), the game shifts from the Pacific theater to return to 1942 and the campaign in Russia. Here the gamer fights as Private Dmitri Petrenko, who is also introduced in a position of helplessness. The Russian campaign begins with the aforementioned reference to *Enemy at the Gates*. Petrenko gradually regains consciousness in the debris of a fountain, while German soldiers shoot the dead and wounded soldiers lying around him. Hiding among the bodies is Sergeant Reznov, voiced by Gary Oldman, who becomes the gamer's comrade in arms for the duration of the Russian campaign. Roebuck and Reznov act as mentors to the gamer throughout the game, the familiarity of their voices adding an additional dimension of intermediality to gameplay. After all, "who *wouldn't* go to war with Jack Bauer?" asks one reviewer of the game (Robinson 2008, emphasis in original), referring to Kiefer Sutherland's role in the series *24* (Fox Network, 2001–2010). Another notes that Sutherland's and Oldman's voice skills enable the gamer to be drawn "into the intense mindset of these soldiers" (Watters, 2008). A third playable character in the solo campaign is available on all platforms except the Wii. In a short but intense diversion from the other campaigns, the gamer plays as Petty Officer Locke, a gunner on a Catalina "flying boat" in the only mission set on the Pacific Ocean.

Like all games set in real-world conflicts, *World at War* encourages what Patrick Crogan refers to as a particular kind of play with the mediated past: "[p]lay in and with a reconstruction of historical temporality drawn from the narrative modes of more traditional media such as historical discourse, historical archives, war films and documentaries" (2003, 282). The way in which *World at War* "plays" with aspects of the transmedia construct of the war is evident from the start of the game. Throughout *World at War*, each new campaign is introduced with a sequence of historical facts and statistics that flash onscreen over maps and stylized graphics with images, such as the Japanese rising sun or the Nazi swastika, interspersed with archive footage of the war itself.

Some of the archive material used in these scenes is relatively explicit and includes scenes of actual mass executions conducted by the Japanese, as well scenes of combat and evocative images of soldiers. These scenes contextualize *World at War* in much the same way as the mini documentaries at the beginning of *Band of Brothers* and *The Pacific*. The opening of the game, for example, includes images and information regarding Pearl Harbor as well as some details of the impact of the war on the US manufacturing

Figure 5.1   Stylized graphics in opening cutscene of *Call of Duty: World at War*.

industry, hinting that the reasons behind the US involvement in the war were not necessarily altruistic. They add what game reviewer Chris Watters (2008) calls a "sobering realism" to the game.

Both the factual sequences and the filmic scenes introducing Miller and Petrenko are cutscenes. The difference between the narrative that plays out in the cutscenes and the story that unfolds in the gameplay itself, or ludonarrative, contributes to the problematic nature of conceptualizing narrative in games. Games designer Clint Hocking (2007) refers to the incongruity between cutscene and gameplay as "ludonarrative dissonance" and argues that the "leveraging of the game's narrative structure against its ludic structure" has the potential to inhibit the gamer's ability to interact with either. In the case of *World at War*, the nature of the ingame violence is for some at odds with the somber tone of the cutscenes, leading one reviewer to conclude that "any message that Treyarch wished to tell about the brutality of war is lost as it revels in the ridiculous violence" (Robinson, M. 2008). For others, however, the inclusion of the documentary inserts is precisely what imbues the gameplay with emotional resonance. Rather than generating ludonarrative dissonance, a cutscene with archival footage of recruits heading off to war, for example, makes it easier for gamers to imagine themselves in the "skin" of the characters of *World at War*, according to John Funk (2008). Rune Klevjer (2002) offers a more conciliatory perspective of cutscenes than Hocking, arguing that they should be regarded as an "integral part of the configurative experience" of gameplay and that they often perform functions that gameplay does not.

The cinematic cutscenes in *Call of Duty* demonstrate Klevjer's point because they elicit emotional responses that differ from the overall experience of gameplay. The cinematic cutscenes, such as the prisoner of war sequence on Makin island or the scene in the fountain that opens the Russian campaign, are significant not only because they represent another way in which games "play" with different media forms but also because they are moments in the game over which the gamer has no control. In *World at War*, there are also cutscenes *within* gameplay itself in single-player mode when the gamer loses control of the game. These occur at points in the narrative when Miller or Petrenko is helpless—when Petrenko is trapped under a burning beam in a house in Stalingrad, for example, or when Miller is shot and wounded during the escape from Makin Island. Cinematic cutscenes in *World at War* thus coincide with moments in the overarching narrative when the soldier the gamer embodies has lost control over his situation. Unlike some FPSs, *World at War* does not allow gamers to skip through these scenes. The game designers therefore utilize that sense of frustration the gamer may feel at having been forced to relinquish control in the game as a small reflection of the frustration and fear soldiers are subject to when placed in situations that render them powerless. These particular moments in *World at War* create something that James Newman (2002) refers to as "experiential cohesion" by blurring the boundaries between filmic cutscenes and gameplay.

I want to push Newman's notion a little further to suggest that in *World at War*, cutscenes also create experiential cohesion between past and present, as both the documentary style inserts and the cinematic sequences connect aspects of the mnemonic structure of World War II to the immediate experience of gameplay. The cutscenes contextualize gameplay and provide a narrative framework, but they also, as Rune Klevjer suggests, serve a different purpose by allowing gamers to get "under the skin" of soldiers in extreme situations. The emotional impact of the experiential cohesion between past and present created by the cutscenes and their interaction with gameplay is illustrated by game reviewer Chris Watters's (2008) observation that the facts and statistics presented in the documentary inserts are abstractions until the gamer actually plays the game. For example, the odds of survival for marines on Peleliu (which were one in five), start to "hit a little closer to home" when the gamer plays through the campaign and experiences the near overwhelming barrage of Japanese artillery while witnessing allies and squad mates fall to surprise banzai attacks and sniper fire (ibid.). Rather than viewing Iwo Jima from John Bradley's perspective or seeing Peleliu through the eyes of Eugene Sledge, the gamer in *World at War* is indivisible from Miller or Petrenko and has, as the term "FPS" suggests, a first-person perspective.

The citizen soldiers in *World at War* cannot, therefore, be considered in the same way as those represented in other media. Roebuck and Reznov are the most fully realized characters in the game, yet even they serve a purpose that sets them apart from characters such as Miller in *Saving Private Ryan* or Winters in *Band of Brothers*. Roebuck and Reznov are emotional barometers in that their voice-overs in the cutscenes establish the tone of each campaign, but once gameplay in the single-player mode starts, they function as guides, directing the gamer through the game. In this sense, they are enabling features of the gameworld, as functional as the compass in the corner of the screen directing the gamer toward the location of the objective in a particular campaign. The central characters of *World at War*, Miller and Petrenko, are the least realized. They are by necessity abstractions, ciphers through which the gamer experiences the gameworld. There are FPSs that create some sense of character for the avatar through techniques like shifting to a third-person perspective during cutscenes and allowing gamers to see the character onscreen, but apart from one short glimpse of Miller, *World at War* maintains a first-person perspective throughout. The gamer is never represented onscreen as a fully rendered avatar but always as an arm and hand, which is invariably in possession of a weapon. James Newman goes so far as to suggest that, for the controlling player during sequences of gameplay, the very notion of "character" is therefore inappropriate and misleading. Instead, Newman posits that "character" in gameplay is better considered "as *a suite of characteristics or equipment* utilized and embodied by the controlling player" (2002, my emphasis). As Newman goes on to note, in their recollections of gameplay in games such as *World at War*, gamers refer to "being" in the game (ibid.) rather than to playing or directing Miller or Petrenko.

The experience of being Miller or Petrenko is illustrated by the numerous online cheats and walkthroughs of *World at War*. These contain detailed instructions regarding gameplay that address gamers directly, as this sample from games magazine *IGN*'s walkthroughs (uk.guides.ign.com) indicates: "Once the coast is clear, walk into the fenced-in area and head left, and you'll descend into the bunker. Kill the single soldier within, walk up to the charges, and press Use to activate them." As such walkthroughs suggest, the gamer's knowledge and memories of *World at War* are drawn from his/her individual actions and experiences within the game and not through second-hand observations of the actions of characters. *World at War* effectively reconstitutes the citizen soldier in the civilian gamer; as the tagline in the trailer for *Call of Duty: Black Ops* (Activision, 2010) puts it, "There's a soldier in all of us." Rather than identifying with characters such as Sledge or Leckie and seeing events through their eyes, the gamer "encounters the game by relating to everything in the gameworld simultaneously" (Newman 2002). The citizen soldier is thus replaced by the civilian gamer who gains specific firsthand experience of a simulated version of World War II by relating not only to the various characters of the game but also to the construction of the world they inhabit. By simulation, I mean the reproduction through a particular material technology of part of a system or set of systems in order to extract and highlight the relationships and behaviors of its perceived essential components. I am not drawing on Baudrillard's (1981) conceptualization of the term here. My definition has more in common with Gonzalo Frasca's: "To simulate is to model a (source) system through a different system which maintains (for somebody) some of the behavior of the original system" (2003, 223). The reduction of war to space and weaponry in *World at War* should therefore be understood as part of the functionality of simulations. The ways in which gamers relate to these elements of the gameworld are as important, if not more so, as the gamers' relationships to *World at War*'s soldiers.

According to Espen Aarseth, it is the "preoccupation with space" that distinguishes digital games from all other forms of cultural media (1998, 161). Aarseth draws on Henri Lefebvre's distinction between representations of space and representational spaces to construct a hypothesis of the representation of space in games as symbolic and rule based. The notion that space in games is the means by which gameplay is achieved is central to Aarseth's approach because the rules of the game are inseparable from the gameworld. Aarseth is not alone in identifying space as fundamental to all digital games. Henry Jenkins and Mary Fuller (1995) map Michel de Certeau's conceptualization of spatial stories onto what may appear to be two diverse mediations: Nintendo's *Mario Brothers* (1983–present) and a collection of written accounts of the European discovery and colonization of the New World in the sixteenth and seventeenth centuries. Fuller and Jenkins argue that their very different protagonists enact de Certeau's transformations of *place*, characterized as a stable site existing only in a conceptual sense until it has been experienced and colonized, into *space*, the meaningful location of an experiential event. According to Fuller and Jenkins, De Certeau's distinction between the map, described as an abstract representation of space, and the tour, which details a personalized journey through space, is applicable to both the explorer and the gamer, each of whom constructs an individualized account of geographical encounters. Their argument is premised on the notion that the nature of the transformation of place to space and map to tour involves an active, if not aggressive, desire for the possession and consumption of new territories.

Both these approaches offer useful perspectives for the consideration of space in *World at War*. Learning how to navigate space in the gameworld is the most fundamental skill required by digital games of all kinds. It is perhaps even more vital to the FPS, inasmuch as these games demand that gamers move through space at speed and with dexterity, generally while being fired upon by enemy AI. In *World at War*, stillness is actively punished by the game mechanics, particularly in single-player mode. If the gamer takes cover in one place for too long or moves in the wrong direction, the game will spawn opponents in increasing numbers until the gamer is overrun.[8] Through obstacles such as ditches, tangled shrubbery, or doors that will not open, the environment itself also prevents gamers from moving in particular directions. *World at War*, like the other games in the series and many other FPSs, is therefore not an open-world game but one that directs gamers through particular routes or corridors within the gameworld. Space in the game is controlled and manipulated by the game designers in order to facilitate a channeled, linear trajectory through the game's narrative world.

World at War therefore reflects Aarseth's position that games do not so much *represent* space as invoke it as a symbolic fabrication because the difference between the rules of the fabrication and the rules of real space makes gameplay possible. Some view the construction of space in *World at War* as restrictive, with one review suggesting that "the levels rigidly herd you in the right direction" (Whitehead 2008), but games designer Eugene Jarvis's general observation on the purpose of rules in digital games suggests an alternative viewpoint. For Jarvis, "games are about limitations. Not only what you can do but what you can't do. Confining your world and focusing someone in that reality is really important" (interview in Herz 1997, 79). The gamer's focus in *World at War* is directed onto the violent conquest of space. Fuller and Jenkins' conceptualization of the aggressive consumption of space is thus exemplified in the FPS because, whatever the mode of play or campaign, the basic goal of *World at War* is first to traverse successfully the corridors of the game and then to take control of particular spaces before achieving the required objective. The online walkthroughs for *World at War* illustrate the importance of aggressive conquest within the FPS; they are at once highly personalized tours describing journeys through space and instructions on how to master it.

Aarseth and Fuller and Jenkins differ radically in their conclusions on the significance of space in the construction of narratives in games. For Aarseth, gameplay and narrative are "like oil and water" (2004, 51). Fuller and Jenkins (1995), in turn, reason that the privileging space over characterization is not a negation of narrative but part of a long tradition of spatial storytelling. However, although both consider the movement of gamers through the spaces of the gameworld as central to their arguments, neither addresses the actual nature of kinesthetic activity and its consequences. Kinesthetic activity is central to the gamer's experiences of *World at War* and is comprised of a complex series of interactions between the gamer's own body, the interface, and the game. Whether in the form of a console controller or PC mouse and keyboard, gamers have to master the interface until its operation ceases to be a conscious activity and becomes a form of embodied kinesthetic memory. For experienced gamers, the movement of the avatar becomes as unconsciously directed as the movement of the gamer's own body. Rather than become transparent, however, the interface acts as the nexus for what Newman calls a "feedback loop" that links gamers to the space of the gameworld and vice versa (Newman 2002). *World at War* enhances the feedback loop through a number of techniques, particularly when it is played on a console.

These techniques are aimed at engaging gamers' senses, beginning with touch. When the gamer hitches a ride on a tank in the Seelow Heights campaign, for example, the controller vibrates in his/her hands, mimicking the vibration of the tank. Similarly, when calling down airstrikes, the controller vibrates in sympathy with the percussion of the resulting explosion, making it difficult to move or take aim. The development of gaming chairs extended these effects to the entire body. Some are designed not only to deliver surround sound but also to connect with the controller, allowing gamers to "move with the action and feel every bank, turn, dive, and climb," according to the ad for the X-Dream Gyroxus Gaming Chair (on www.boystuff.co.uk), which also proclaims that "you and the game move in tandem!" Moving beyond the haptic, other techniques involve sight and hearing, such as the aforementioned shellshock, which mimics the visual and auditory disorientation caused by a nearby explosion through blurred and vacillating visuals and the temporary loss of sound. Similarly, when using a sniper rifle, the sights will sway and dip to mimic breathing, which can also be heard on the audio track. The gamer can stabilize this movement by "holding" his or her breath via the controller but only for short periods. At these moments in the game, if the gamer even blinks at the wrong time, the shot will be missed, creating a powerful causal link between the gamer's body and the space of the gameworld. In *World at War*, therefore, machinery and spectacle, the basic building blocks of the visual construction of the war, are still present but take on different dimensions in terms of sensory experience for the gamer than they do in other visual media.

James Newman (2004, 124) notes that the importance of positional audio clues in extending the gamer's spatial awareness should not be overlooked, particularly since contemporary consoles support surround sound capabilities. *World at War* generates ambient sound in real time as the game is played. What this means is that the sound matches the gamer's movements and visual perspective—sound increases or decreases in volume depending on where the gamer moves in the game. Sound designers for *World at War* also developed a so-called occlusion system that allows sounds to react to the environment, echoing off some surfaces, for example, but becoming absorbed by others. Both the ambient and the occlusion system create a dynamic soundscape that allows the gamer to trace specific sounds back to their source (*CVG* 2008c, 57–58). The soundscape has a direct impact on gameplay because it allows gamers to identify where enemies are located through the sound of their voices, for example, or to establish the direction from which sniper fire is coming. The visual, haptic, and auditory techniques combine to extend the awareness of space beyond the screen and to create a visceral experience involving the entire body. The gameworld of *World at War* is consequently more than a set of rules with which the gamer engages and also more than a series of places to conquer and occupy. It is a dynamic and fluid "lived space," to borrow a term from Bernadette Flynn (2008, 143), that the gamer is able to influence and that in turn affects the gamer.

As a number of theorists point out (see Aarseth 2004, 52 and Newman 2002, for example), the pleasures of gaming are therefore not only visual but kinesthetic. In the FPS format, the primary way the gamer connects with the space of the gameworld is through weaponry. Martti Lahti (2003, 161) describes the representation of the gamer onscreen as an arm and a weapon as "a sort of imaginary prosthesis" that links the gamer's body to the gameworld. In this sense, in *World at War*, the gamer is a weapon rather than an avatar, and Miller and Petrenko really have significance only in that each offers a different set of weapons and different scenarios in which to deploy them. Gamers can "carry" two weapons at a time. Although these are predetermined at the start of every campaign in single-player mode, gamers may change these for any found on the battlefield during the course of the game. At times, the game dictates the use of a specific weapon against a particular threat, such as the flamethrower to clear out the bunkers on Peleliu or the *panzerschreck* to destroy tanks in the Russian campaign. In the online multiplayer mode, achievements in the game unlock access to different weapons, and gamers are allowed far more choice, facilitating customized gameplay. Such choices are extremely significant because they are components of a reward and recognition system that is part of what makes gameplay compelling: The more skillful you are with your current weapon, the more chance you have of being rewarded with a better one. In either mode, the world of the game is viewed over the barrel or through the sights of a weapon, and the choice of gun influences the way in which gamers engage with the gameworld. For example, selecting one of the many sniper rifles on offer during online multiplayer matches may lead to a particular kind of strategic interaction with the environment involving locating and settling into a good sniping position, rather than rushing the enemy. Selection and skillful use of the most effective weapon at appropriate times in the game can therefore give gamers the edge over their opponents, whether these are in the form of other gamers in multiplayer mode or in the form of enemy AI in single-player mode.

Although critics of the FPS like Niall Ferguson and Jerome de Groot acknowledge that *World at War* consequently has the potential to teach gamers a great deal about World War II hardware, they do not consider the significance of this knowledge. There is an undeniable degree of fetishization in the discussions of weapons evident in the many online communities that have grown up around *World at War*. These discussions may involve listing the weapons available in the game in various ways. Montages of real-world photographs and/or game images of some of *World at War*'s weapons, usually set to music, can be found on sites such as YouTube, while tabulated lists of favorite weapons are common on forums.[9] The latter are significant in that the language used to discuss virtual weapons echoes that used in discussions of real-world weapons. For example, one gamer on a *Call of Duty* thread for PlayStation 3 (www.avforums) observes that "the Type 100 is a nice sub machine gun, it is more accurate than the MP40 and more powerful than the Thompson," while another notes that "after trying all the guns in single-player, I reckon the best ones are the PPSH and the STG44—the[y] seem to have the best combined recoil, accuracy, and fire rate" (both posted November 18, 2008). Such discussions illustrate an acute awareness of the nuances of each weapon, as well as of their strategic uses in the game. Perceived errors or discrepancies in either image montages or in discussions sometimes meet with vehement derision. The lists of weapons are demonstrations of knowledge, but they are also indicative of deeply individual approaches to gaming in which the choice of weapons is an expression of the gamer's personal style of play, as suggested by the occasionally passionate debates on which weapons are the best. In addition to listing or discussing favorite weapons, gamers may also showcase their proficiency with weaponry and attendant idiosyncratic styles of gameplay in *World at War* and other FPSs through videos posted on sites such as YouTube.[10] Videos of ingame footage illustrate the performative dimension of gameplay, in which the skillful choice and use of weapons play an essential role.

The lists of weapons, videos of gameplay, and articles on weaponry may have an element of what Ed Halter refers to as the "artillery nerd-factor" (2006, 258), but they also point to the development of a culture around the fetishization of weaponry that Scott Lukas suggests bears a distinct resemblance to cultures within military organizations that revolve around the accoutrements of warfare (2010, 78). Matthew Payne's (2010) study of the behavior of gamers in a gaming center bears out Lukas's suggestion that knowledge of gaming weaponry can have real-world social consequences. In the community that Payne observed, understanding which weapons are best suited for what scenario or mode of play was perceived as "vital, if not sacred" knowledge, with a particular cultural currency that enhanced individual status within the group (2010, 212). Writing on real-world citizen soldiers in World War II, Glenn Gray noted that the gun could serve as "an extension" of the soldier and help to "cement the wall of comradeship that encloses him and ties him to his own side" ([1959] 1998, 178). In a similar way, the gamer's knowledge, use, and choice of weaponry not only reflect an individual style of gameplay but may also be an extension of personality, informing social interactions with other gamers. Weaponry, as one component of the machinery of warfare so vital to the visual construction of World War II, consequently has a tangible significance, albeit in virtual form, in the lives of gamers in the present.

The gamer's experience of lived space in the FPS is thus inseparable from the operation of the game weapons of the game. The interface is a means not just of moving through space but also of operating the array of weapons in the game. To engage with all the elements of the gameworld simultaneously, the gamer first has to master the control of both movement and weapons via the interface. The mastery of weapons, like the mastery of movement, is something that for experienced gamers becomes a matter of reflex rather than of conscious thought. For veteran gamers, as for touch typists or musicians, the mechanical operation of their chosen object is habitual. According to Paul Connerton, such habitual knowledge is a form of memory "sedimented in the body" (1989, 72). Habit memories are more than dispositions or technical abilities; they are patterns of behavior intimately ingrained within the body itself. Habit memory develops through "knowledge bred of familiarity in our *lived space*" (Connerton 1989, 95, my emphasis). Because the simulated, weaponized spaces of *World at War* extend into the lived space of the gamer, the development of habit memory takes on a specific significance. The habit memories of simulations are not just about operating the interface; they are also about internalizing behaviors such as "tactics, approaches, ways of thinking about a crisis" (Halter 2006, 201).

As a result, simulations made as games for the entertainment industry and those made for military purposes have a vital intersection. According to Michael Macedonia, the technology officer for the US Army's Simulation, Training and Instrumentation (STRI) office, both are concerned with "making memories" (interview in Halter 2006, 198). Macedonia links this to a term in virtual reality research known as "presence"—defined by Ed Halter as "a kind of ineffable sense of reality—not necessarily produced through visual fidelity, but from a gut feeling of *being there*" (2006, 201, emphasis in original). To explain the significance of presence, Macedonia (ibid., 200) refers to a scene in *Patton* (Franklin J. Schaffner, 1970) in which the general, played by George C. Scott, commands his driver to stop at the site of an ancient battleground and, after a cryptic speech describing a battle between Carthaginian and Roman forces, comments, "Two thousand years ago. I was here." For Macedonia, who is partly responsible for the military turning to off-the-shelf games and developers rather than relying on internally developed product for its simulators, Patton's response to a site of battle describes the goal of simulations of warfare for the military: to manufacture "moments of déjà vu" that enable soldiers to perform effectively in any situation (ibid.).

An ideology is at work in creating a sense of presence in *World at War*, enmeshed in the game's symbolic representation of space. Although *World at War*, like others in the *Call of Duty* franchise, includes other than US soldiers as playable characters and therefore dilutes the perception generated through the films and television series discussed in this book of World War II as an American experience, the spaces the gamer explores in *World at War* are scrubbed of noncombatants. The impact of war is therefore evident only on the environment or on the bodies of soldiers. For the most part, *World at War* depicts enemy soldiers in terms that recall their representation in wartime media: The Japanese soldiers are little more than racial stereotypes filled with cruelty and mindless fanaticism, and the Germans are brutal fascists. The lack of detailed characterization in enemy NPCs, and the complete absence of civilians in *World at War* can partly be explained by the technical difficulties and expense involved in integrating different forms of AI.[11] Nevertheless, *World at War* reduces a total war to nothing other than combat between soldiers. The crystallization of World War II around the experience of the soldier is evident throughout the transmedia structure of the war, but *World at War* is an extreme iteration of this feature of World War II mediated memory. The game's relentless progression through contested space leaves very little room for anything other than an intense focus on combat.

Although the promotional material surrounding *World at War* claims that the game reveals the more brutal aspects of World War II, *World at War* limits this exposure to combatants and ignores the civilian face of suffering. The only death to register with any significance in the Okinawan campaign in the game is either that of Miller's mentor, Roebuck, or that of Polonsky, his squad mate. Depending on the gamer's choices and skill levels at this stage of the game, he or she can save only one or the other, and the outcome of either's death is the same—whoever survives urges the gamer and the squad to show no mercy and kill all the remaining Japanese soldiers in the fight that, in the context of the game, marks the climax of the Pacific campaign. *World at War* therefore reiterates the idea that victory must always be total, but it fails to address the cost of total victory to civilians. The absence of civilians in *World at War*'s Russian campaign is perhaps even more critical than in the Pacific, where many islands really were empty of noncombatants.

William Hitchcock describes the scale of Soviet losses as one of the most "incomprehensible facts" of World War II (2009, 131). Of the estimated twenty-three to twenty-six million Soviet deaths, "only" close to nine million of these were soldiers. To put that figure in perspective, the total US service deaths for all theaters in World War II is around 405,400 (132). As Hitchcock points out, all these figures of loss are indicative of great sorrow and suffering, but they also illustrate the differences in the scale of the war on the two fronts (ibid.). Unlike the soldiers of the US and Britain, many Russian soldiers witnessed firsthand the impact of the German invasion on their own country, and as a result, the Russian advance into German territory was a "tidal wave of rape, beatings, wanton violence, looting, destruction, murder" (160). But while Reznov's exhortations to "show no mercy" and to "kill them all" echo much of the anti-German rhetoric evident in Russia in 1945, it is only on German soldiers that the Russians take their vengeance in *World at War*. The buildings and streets of both Stalingrad and Berlin in *World at War* are eerily empty of civilians. In the Russian campaign, it is also a soldier's death that is positioned as the "ultimate" sacrifice in war. Petrenko dies just before the Russian flag can be raised above the Reichstag, and gamers cannot avoid his death. Although Petrenko's death serves as a vivid reminder of industrialized warfare's negation of individual heroism and the random nature of the industrialized battlefield, where even the most experienced soldiers can die at any time, it also emphasizes the soldier's suffering over the civilian's. The absence of civilian suffering in a game designed to be an "adrenaline-filled, epic struggle," as Activision's website (http://store.activision.com/store) describes it, is perhaps unsurprising, even without the technical concerns, but the magnitude of the civilian losses associated with *World at War*'s two central campaigns throws into sharp relief the size of the elision in the broader transmedia structure of the war. Although *World at War* replicates existing absences in the structure, it also intensifies them.

Because there is no way to navigate the landscape of *World at War* except to fight through it and because these battles involve neither civilians nor friendly fire, some have suggested that games like *World at War* justify an aggressive militaristic ideology. Richard King and David Leonard (2010, 91), for instance, argue that the absence of civilians and even of "civilization" in the spaces of FPSs like *World at War* justifies the "intervention, control, and mastery of unused space," a position that echoes the argument made by Fuller and Jenkins that certain representations of space dovetail with an aggressive impulse to conquer and control territory. A similar line of reasoning leads to the assumption that games like *World at War* literally turn civilian gamers into soldiers who enact their own violent transformations of place to space but without a military context to direct and contain them. This point of view is endorsed by David Grossman (2000), a retired US lieutenant colonel, who argues that the FPS mirrors the military's method of "operant conditioning"—a method of training based on a repetitive "stimulus–response" cycle, which ultimately enables soldiers to kill reflexively. The FPS, according to Grossman, created "a generation of barbarians who have learned to associate human death and suffering with pleasure" (ibid.). Grossman's perspective is echoed in the popular press, where generalized anxieties about violence in shoot-'em-up games make no distinction between games like *Unreal Tournament* (Epic Games, 1998-present) and *Halo* (Bungie Studios, 2001), which have science fiction settings, and *Medal of Honor* and *Call of Duty*.[12]

Such assumptions, however, fail to take into account both the complexities of gameplay itself and the importance of context. In terms of the former, violence has a very different function within the FPS than it does within other visual media and may be read in unexpected ways by gamers. "The purpose of the blood," as one notes, "is just so you can see if you've hit your target. You need to be able to tell that to play the game" (interview in Jones 2002, 173). Similarly, in online multiplayer mode, gamers may engage in vicious onscreen combat while simultaneously working as a team and forming social bonds. There is no denying the online space's well deserved reputation for displays of homophobia, racism, and misogyny, but anecdotes such as Chuck Wendig's (2010) description of an online game of *Call of Duty 4: Modern Warfare* demonstrate the potential for the blurring of social and cultural boundaries through war-gaming. Wendig describes a young boy who led a disparate and desperate team of gamers through "our D-Day, our beaches of Normandy moment" as a "critical thinker" and "excellent communicator" (ibid.). In contrast to Grossman's "generation of barbarians," Wendig concludes by suggesting that it is in vast online gaming communities that "some of the leaders of the next generation [are] going to be born . . . and it [is] in this place that these leaders would find their voices" (ibid.). Anecdotes such as Wendig's illustrate that the behaviors and habit memories created by gameplay in the FPS are more complex and subtle than critics of the form suggest. Even though there are studies that attempt to establish a causal link between violence in digital games and a tendency toward violent behavior in the real world (see Anderson and Dill 2000 for one example), other studies demonstrate that the behaviors instilled by FPS games have less to do with learning how to kill and more to do with the ability to process and respond to potentially overwhelming amounts of information while under pressure (for example, see Green, Pouget, and Bavelier 2010). Both positions, however, tend to ignore the significance of context, the second factor that critiques of the FPS often overlook.

In *World at War*, the sense of *being there* is inevitably connected to a sense of *being then*, of experiencing simulated recreations not only of places but also of actual moments from the past. The same reviewer who describes the impact of gameplay on the understanding of the difficulties faced by Marines on Peleliu goes on to point out that the World War II setting of *World at War* contributes to making the game "arguably more emotional" than *Modern Warfare*, which involves fictional countries and is set an in unspecified time in the near future (Watters 2008). A study conducted by Joel Penney (2010) confirms that context can influence emotional engagement. Penney's study compares two groups of gamers: those with a preference for science fiction games, such as *Halo* and *Gears of War* (Epic Games, 2006–present), and those who prefer games set in real-world historical settings, such as *Medal of Honor* or *Call of Duty*. Context was of primary importance for the latter group. Gamers who play FPSs set in World War II regarded them as a source of "authentic historical experiences" and reported a deeper emotional engagement with the games as a result (2010, 198). Penney consequently identifies "empathy with real-life soldiers, past and present" as a key theme in the group that preferred games set in real-world conflicts (ibid.).

Games in general, and FPSs in particular, are frequently criticized for a perceived inability to generate complex emotional responses, particularly that of empathy. For example, in an article questioning the enduring appeal of war games, game writer Leigh Alexander (2010) mourns the "the absence of emotional connection, of conscience and of discussion" among FPS wargamers. The lack of complex characters in the FPS is often cited as a reason for the supposed inability of the form to elicit complex emotional responses. Games designer Will Wright (2007), for example, suggests that films are more successful at generating empathy than games because the actors function as "emotional avatars." Penney's study demonstrates, however, that games such as *World at War* generate empathy through the powerful connections made by gamers between the simulation of warfare in the game and the real-life actions of soldiers in combat. One respondent admits to gaining a "greater appreciation of the dedication, effort and fighting spirit of the previous generation and [I have] come to believe we could learn a lot from them" (quoted in Penney 2010, 201). Rather than identifying with Miller or Petrenko as characters, gamers gain an understanding of the difficulties faced by soldiers in general in World War II through engaging with all aspects of the gameworld in *World at War*, including the particular challenges of the weapons of the time, as well as the procedures and behaviors necessary to achieve military objectives. In other words, empathy is created through presence; from personal memories of having been in a similar but simulated situation.

Previous chapters illustrated that a number of spectators attest to a sense of "knowing" what it must have been like to fight in World War II as a result of their viewing experiences of *Saving Private Ryan, Band of Brothers*, and the other case studies. The sense of knowing they describe meets with Alison Landsberg's definition of "prosthetic memories" in that it is not derived from lived experience but is dependent on an "intellectual and emotional negotiation with the plight of the 'other'" (2004, 128). Recognition of the other is central to the very idea of empathy in Landsberg's model, and empathy in turn is a key element of prosthetic memory. In contrast, the memories generated by *World at War* are based on lived experiences within a virtual environment and are not concerned with the other but with the self. As Penney's study demonstrates, this does not preclude the presence of empathy, but empathy generated through gaming has its source in lived experience rather than in identification with the vicarious experiences of the other.

For gamers such as Tom Bissell, the power of the experience of simulation in gaming is so compelling that it generates "not surrogate experiences, but actual experiences, many of which are as important to me as any real memories" (2010, 182). For others, such as the gamer who first played *World at War* in the basement of his/her synagogue, picking up a controller led to a feeling of empowerment; "as a kid you get tired of being reminded how powerless and weak your people were, so the ability to pick up a controller and kill fascists was always a great feeling" (comment posted August 13, 2009 in response to Sharkey 2009). Similarly, a rabbi who had been haunted throughout his life by an irrational phobia of Nazis (he had no experience of Nazi Germany and had acquired the fear through learning history) finally overcame it by playing *World at War* (Plunkett 2009). The potential of virtual environments to combat phobias is acknowledged by the US military in the development of programs using simulations of Iraq and Afghanistan in order to treat post-traumatic stress disorder. The experience of playing *World at War* is in all likelihood more prosaic for most gamers, but what these kinds of stories indicate is the potential of the game to create an engagement with the past with significant real-world emotional impact.

Although it is important to acknowledge the capacity of *World at War* to generate empathic connections to the past because these are often marginalized in discussions of the FPS format, emotional reactions such as those described by Penney's respondents are only one possible set of responses to games like *World at War*. Film critic Roger Ebert (2010) began an impassioned debate with a public claim that games could never be classified as "art" because they are incapable of generating empathy.[13] Earlier, however, in a review of *Saving Private Ryan*, Ebert (1998) obliquely acknowledged the limits of empathy by pointing out that "weeping is an incomplete response, letting the audience off the hook." The most significant contribution of the World War II FPS to the transmedia mnemonic structure of the conflict is the recognition that war is, for some soldiers and for some of the time, fun. The idea that war in general and that World War II in particular could be fun for soldiers is an aspect of war memory that has been "hiding in plain sight," as Marianna Torgovnick describes those ellipsis that "have never registered in America's image of World War II or in America's image of itself" (2005, 4). Joanna Bourke identifies the "enjoyment of killing" as a persistent theme in the memoirs of veterans (1999, 18). From the World War I soldier who, after first using a trench mortar, found the "satisfactions of scientific research, of a successful public activity, of authority, of love" paling in comparison to the joy of seeing the impact of mortar strikes on the bodies of enemy soldiers (quoted in Bourke 1999, 19), to the soldier in Vietnam who admitted that there is a "certain joy you had in killing, an exhilaration that is hard to explain" (quoted in Baker 2002, 144) soldiers in wars throughout history have confessed to the pleasures of taking life, and those involved in World War II are no exception.

Historians Sönke Neitzel and Harald Welzer (2012) recently uncovered a series of transcripts of conversations among German prisoners of war covertly recorded by the British intelligence service that reveal the excitement and pleasure the soldiers took in killing. The phrase "great fun" is repeated frequently, with one prisoner using this phrase to describe an attack on a town that ended in the slaughter of livestock and civilians (quoted in Neitzel and Welzer, 58). Another describes killing as "our before-breakfast amusement" (45). But it was not only German soldiers who found the war fun. War correspondent Ernie Pyle, the subject of Wellman's film, *The Story of G.I. Joe* (1945), observed that "[s]ome of us, even over here, are having the time of our lives" and that "war is vastly exhilarating" (Pyle [1943] 2004, 246). The visual media discussed in previous chapters are mournful paeans to the Greatest Generation that highlight the nobility of fighting for "the man next to you" and emphasize the masculine bonds of brotherhood formed as a result of combat or, alternatively, position the citizen soldier as the main victim of war. But despite the overall impression generated by the current configuration of the transmedia structure of World War II, fear, horror, sorrow, and brotherly love are not the only emotions found in combat. Satisfaction, joy, and fierce exhilaration are equally valid emotions, sometimes existing in conjunction with those less difficult to explain. As Glenn Gray points out, "[W]ar compresses the greatest opposites into the smallest space and the shortest time" ([1959] 1998, 12).

The idea of war as a traumatic experience for soldiers has become normalized in the transmedia structure of World War II. By focusing on the mechanisms of war itself rather than on the citizen soldier, *World at War* illustrates the tension between acknowledging that, as Ed Halter points out, "war is hell . . . but in video game form, it's also fun as hell" (2006, 254). The FPS offers the opportunity to engage with those emotions left unexplored by other representations of World War II. Roebuck and Reznov may act as emotional mentors and guides through the game in single-player mode, and social bonds may be cemented through online gaming "clans" in multiplayer, but there is very little sense of the evocative bond of brotherhood as the primary reason for engaging in combat. Instead of fighting for your brother in arms or for abstractions such as freedom and democracy, the pared-down structure of the simulation of *World at War* suggests other reasons for fighting—survival in the Pacific, for example, or for home and country in the Russian campaign, or even simply for the joy of fighting. Fighting for the fun of it is illustrated by the "reward" for finishing *World at War* in single-player mode—the unlocking of a bonus level involving Nazi Zombie soldiers, a neat combination of the two elements Scott Sharkey (2009) describes as "things we can guiltlessly cap in the head." *World at War* acknowledges and trades on the exhilaration of warfare, allowing gamers to indulge in the thrill of combat without any risk. While some may argue that it is precisely the engagement with the joys of war without jeopardy that desensitizes gamers to real-world violence, the FPS's cycle of dying and respawning to fight once more provides a valuable counterbalance to the narratives of self-sacrifice and trauma that pervade the transmedia structure of World War II and reminds us that the primary objective of the soldier in war is to kill, not to die. As William Broyles (1984) puts it, "War is a brutal, deadly game, but a game, the best there is. And men love games."

CONCLUSION: BRUTAL GAMES, BRUTAL TRUTHS

The diverse range of environments and weapons available in World War II provides a particularly rich source of material for developers of the FPS, and the conflict has maintained a vital presence in the mediascape of the so-called Gamer Generation since the 1980s. As game writer Ken Smith puts it, "the war to keep the world free may have been fought by the Greatest Generation, but it has been won many times over by the Gamer Generation" (2010). A commercial for *Call of Duty: Black Ops* produced by Advertising Agency TBWA/Chiat/Day in 2010 gives some indication of the widespread demographic that the franchise targets. The commercial's use of civilians, including a smartly dressed businesswoman, who steps delicately over the rubble of the battleground with an M16 assault rifle slung over the same shoulder as her handbag, to the background of the Rolling Stones track "Gimme Shelter," is a reminder that it is not only men who love games and that the appeal of the FPS extends beyond the Gamer Generation. *World at War* removes the character of the citizen soldier, with his burden of sacrifice, sorrow, and trauma, from the narrative of World War II and replaces him with the "ordinary" civilian, whether that be an adolescent male, a rabbi, or a businesswoman. For journalist Winda Benedetti (2010), the FPS is therefore "more honest" than other forms of media in its representation of war precisely because it removes the soldier and reveals "who it's all really about—us."

Gameplay demands that gamers encounter the gameworld of *World at War* as a fluid and dynamic lived space. While navigating the spaces of the gameworld and simultaneously operating an array of weapons, gamers develop embodied habit memories that incorporate both the gaming platform's interface and a range of responses created by their personal experiences of the game. The individual nature of these experiences creates a powerful sense of *having been there*, which is a characteristic of simulations. The sense of presence, together with the emotional shading of the cutscenes and the guidance provided by mentors Roebuck and Reznov, allows gamers to feel empathy for soldiers who fought in World War II. However, because fun is an essential component of gameplay in *World at War*, the FPS also allows the gamer to experience the push-and-pull tension between the ideas that "war is hell" but also "fun as hell." *World at War* consequently exposes aspects of the experience of combat obscured elsewhere in the transmedia structure of the World War II. Most significantly, by introducing "play" into the transmedia mnemonic structure of the war, the FPS forces a confrontation with the disturbing truth that both men and women might love war just as much as they hate it.

World at War breaks down the visual construction of World War II into its component parts. The game's configuration of the spaces of conflict facilitates a particular kind of gaming experience that involves moving through controlled narrative channels to achieve specific objectives. Spectacle and machinery therefore have a different purpose in *World at War* than they do elsewhere in the transmedia structure of the war. In the FPS, spectacle and the machines and weapons of war are essential components of gameplay that enable sensory connections between the gamer's body and the gameworld in which each affects the other. Weapons take on personal significance for gamers because their choice of gun in the FPS affects the way they play the game. Virtual weapons influence the shape of individualized narratives and memories that gamers construct in *World at War*, and knowledge of World War II weaponry has real-world social implications in gaming communities. *Call of Duty*'s trademark style of play, which involves relentless movement through weaponized spaces filled with the thrilling effects of mechanized warfare, radically intensifies the polarization between war and peace in the transmedia structure of the war. Civilians have been steadily marginalized throughout the evolution of the transmedia structure of the war, but *World at War* completely eradicates noncombatants from the spaces of war, and the game therefore also intensifies the concentration on combat as the defining experience of World War II. The absence of civilians and of friendly fire in *World at War* supports the perception that it is possible to wage a "just" war. Although the removal of the citizen soldier and the introduction of the Russian campaign in *World at War* obscures some of the ideological trappings associated with the reverence for America's Greatest Generation that pervades the remainder of the transmedia structure of the conflict, the game nevertheless preserves the idea of World War II as a "good war" in the very structure of its gameworld.

The ways in which *World at War* both remediates and recalibrates elements of the transmedia mnemonic structure of World War II are indicative not only of the FPS's relationship to other media but also of the form's contributions to the structure as a whole. Despite release dates timed for Remembrance Day and the significance of the *Call of Duty* franchise in the current mediascape, the FPS is not accorded the same sense of importance as film or television in the discourse that accompanies commemorations and in general academic discussions of World War II. Yet just as it is important to honor the sacrifices and trauma of war, it is equally important to remember war's appeals because these are part of the perpetuation of warfare. As William Broyles (1984) notes, "it may be more dangerous, for both men and nations, to suppress the reasons men love war than to admit them." Recalling Tim O'Brien's observation from the Introduction to this book, "War is hell, but that's not the half of it," the FPS restores the other half of the memory of World War II to the transmedia structure of the conflict: the brutal truth that war is not only about brotherly love, sacrifice and trauma, but also about fierce exhilaration and joy in combat and killing.

NOTES

1. The intricacies and complexities of the relationship between the digital gaming world and that of the military are outside the scope of this book; however, it is important to note that the US military has been an enabling force in the development of digital games from the outset. The US Department of Defense, along with various affiliated agencies, has been one of the most significant sponsors of research into computer games, either directly or indirectly, since the beginning of World War II. In addition to *Doom*, the military also showed interest in Atari's *Battlezone* (1980), which was also modified for the Army's use.
2. The decision to sell DreamWorks Interactive was one Spielberg later regretted, although he admits that EA was better suited to make the game a commercial success (Gaudiosi 2009).
3. In 2013, EA announced it would not produce another *Medal of Honor* game, following disappointing sales of *Medal of Honor: Warfighter* (Activision, 2012), a game with a modern setting.
4. I have excluded rereleases and expansion packs from this number.
5. For one example, see Shoemaker (2003).
6. The importance of the latter innovation for gamers cannot be overstated. Tom Bissell describes the act of saving the game as "an imperative as biologically intense as food or sleep" (2010, 28)
7. The game engine is software that provides the core functionality of the game (including graphics, sound, and, in a physics engine, effects like impact detection) and abstracts it from platform dependency, thereby allowing games to be run across various operating systems. The game mechanics are the procedures and constraints governing the functionality of the gameworld as prescribed by the game engine. For a detailed description of a game engine, see Jeff Ward, "What Is a Game Engine?" on www.gamecareerguide.com.
8. "Spawning" refers to the creation during gameplay of characters (such as enemy soldiers) or items. "Respawning" refers to the resurrection of a character after it has been killed or destroyed.
9. For one example, see "*Call of Duty: World at War* Real Weapons." Accessed September 25, 2014. Posted December 17, 2008. www.youtube.com/watch?v=dss2sw-PD3o
10. For one example, see "*Call of Duty: World at War* Weapons." Accessed September 25, 2014. Posted December 21, 2008. www.youtube.com/watch?v=VWUuW0YPOac
11. Subsequent games, such as *Call of Duty: Modern Warfare 2* (Activision, 2009), include scenes with civilians.
12. Vivienne Pattison, director of Mediawatch-UK, for example, told Sky News that "these games dehumanise violence" (Bonnett 2010).
13. See the comments on Ebert's blog (2010) for a representative overview of the general response.

REFERENCES

Aarseth, Espen. 1998. "Allegories of Space: The Question of Spatiality in Games." University of Jyväaskylä, Department of Arts and Culture Studies, Collection: 152–171. Accessed December 13, 2010. http://cybertext.hum.jyu.fi/articles/129. pdf

Aarseth, Espen. 2004. "Genre Trouble: Narrativism and the Art of Simulation." In *First Person: New Media as Story, Performance and Game*. Noah Wardrip-Fruin and Pat Harrigan, eds.: 45–55. Cambridge, MA: MIT Press.

Alexander, Leigh. 2010. "Who Cheers for War?" *Kotaku*, June 30. Accessed October 18, 2010. http://Kotaku/5576332/who-cheers-for-war?skyline=true&s=i

Anderson, Craig A., and Karen E. Dill. 2000. "Video Games and Aggressive Thoughts, Feelings, and Behavior in the Laboratory and in Life." *Journal of Personality and Social Psychology* 78, no. 4: 772–790. DOI: 10.1037//0022–3514.78.4.772

Baker, Mark. 2002. *Nam: the Vietnam War in the Words of the Men and Women Who Fought There*. London: Abacus Books.

Baudrillard, Jean. [1981] 1994. *Simulacra and Simulation*. Sheila Faria Glaser, trans. Ann Arbor: University of Michigan Press.

Beck, John, and Mitchell Wade. 2004. *Got Game: How the Gamer Generation Is Reshaping Business Forever*. Boston: Harvard Business School Press.

Benedetti, Winda. 2010. "Outrage over *Call of Duty* Ad Outrageous." *NBC News: Technolog Blog*, November 10. Accessed September 26, 2014. http://technolog-discuss.nbcnews.com/_news/2010/11/10/5443472-outrage-over-call-of-duty-ad-outrageous

Bissell, Tom. 2010. *Extra Lives*. New York: Pantheon Books.

Bonnett, Tom. 2010. "Shoot 'Em Up Video Games 'Are Good For You.'" *Sky News*, September 14. Accessed September 15, 2010. http://news.sky.com/home/technology/article/15727525

Bourke, Joanna. 1999. *An Intimate History of Killing: Face-to-Face Killing in Twentieth Century Warfare*. New York: Basic Books.

Boxer, Steve. 2011. "*Call of Duty: Modern Warfare 3* Gets Gamers Fired Up: Video Game Stores Open Especially to Sell Follow-Up to *Black Ops*." *The Guardian*, November 7. www.www.guardian.co.uk/technology/2011/nov/07/call-of-duty-modern-warfare-3-on-sale?intcmp=239

Breuer, Johannes, Ruth Festl, and Thorsten Quandt. 2011. "In the Army Now—Narrative Elements and Realism in Military First Person Shooters." Paper presented at the Fifth International Conference of the Digital Research Association, "Think Design Play," Utrecht School of Arts, Utrecht, September 14–17. www.digra.org/dl/db/11307.54018.pdf

Broyles, William Jr. 1984. "Why Men Love War." *Esquire*, November. Accessed August 1, 2011. http://public.wsu.edu/hughesc/why_men_love_war.htm

Connerton, Paul. 1989. *How Societies Remember*. Cambridge: Cambridge University Press.

Computer and Video Games (CVG). 2008a. "The 10 Ways *Call of Duty* Changed War Games Forever." Special issue, *CVG Presents* Call of Duty 4: 121–123.

Computer and Video Games (CVG). 2008b. "Hank, Military Man." Special issue, *CVG Presents* Call of Duty 4: 50–55

Computer and Video Games (CVG). 2008c. "Breaking the Sound Barrier—Sound in *Call of Duty: World at War*." Special issue, *CVG Presents* Call of Duty 4: 58–59.

Crogan. Patrick. 2003. "Gametime: History, Narrative, and Temporality in *Combat Flight Simulator 2*." In *The Video Game Theory Reader*. Mark J.P. Wolf and Bernard Perron, eds.: 275–301. New York: Routledge.

De Groot, Jerome. 2009. *Consuming History; Historians and Heritage in Contemporary Popular Culture*. Oxon: Routledge.

Deterding, Sebastian. 2010. "Living Room Wars. Remediation, Boardgames, and the Early History of Video Wargaming." In *Joystick Soldiers: The Politics of Play in Military Video Games*. Nina B Huntemann and Matthew Thomas Payne, eds.: 21–38. New York: Routledge.

Ebert, Roger. 1998. "*Saving Private Ryan.*" *Sunday Times*, July 24. Accessed October 18, 2010. http://rogerebert.suntimes.com/apps/pbcs.dll/article?AID=/19980724/REVIEWS/807240304/1023

Ebert, Roger. 2010. "Video Games Can Never Be Art." *Roger Ebert's Journal* (blog), April 16. Accessed September 26, 2014. www.rogerebert.com/rogers-journal/video-games-can-never-be-art

Elliot, Phil. 2008. "Turning Dreams into Reality." *GamesIndustry.biz*, February 5. Accessed December 29, 2010. www.gamesindustry.biz/articles/turning-dreams-into-reality

Entertainment Software Association. 2005. "2005 Sales, Demographics and Usage Data. Essential Facts About the Computer and Video Game Industry." Accessed April 23, 2010. www.tntg.org/documents/gamefacts.pdf

Entertainment Software Association. 2014. "2014 Sales, Demographic and Usage Data. Essential Facts About the Computer and Video Game Industry." Accessed September 25, 2014. www.theesa.com/facts/pdfs/esa_ef_2014.pdf

Fahs, Travis. 2009. "*IGN* presents: The History of *Call of Duty.*" *IGN*, November 6. Last updated October 13, 2010. Accessed September 28, 2014. http://uk.ign.com/articles/2009/11/06/ign-presents-the-history-of-call-of-duty?page=1

Ferguson, Niall. 2006. "How to Win a War." *New York Magazine*, October 15. Accessed November 9, 2010. http://nymag.com/news/features/22787/

Flynn, Bernadette. 2008. "The Navigator's Experience: An Examination of the Spatial in Computer Games." In *The Pleasures of Computer Gaming: Essays on Cultural History, Theory and Aesthetics*. Melanie Swalwell and Jason Wilson, eds.: 118–146. Jefferson, NC: McFarland and Company.

Frasca, Gonzola. 2003. "Simulation Versus Narrative: Introduction to Ludology." In *The Video Game Theory Reader*. Mark J. P. Wolf and Bernard Perron, eds.: 221–235. New York: Routledge.

Funk, John. 2008. "Review: *Call of Duty: World at War.*" *Escapist Magazine*, December 11. Accessed October 21, 2010. www.escapistmagazine.com/articles/view/editorials/reviews/5564-Review-Call-of-Duty-World-at-War

Garratt, Patrick. 2012. "*Medal of Honor* Interview: Greg Goodrich on Controversy." *VG24/7*, September 11. Accessed September 25, 2014. www.vg247.com/2012/09/11/medal-of-honor-interview-greg-goodrich-talks-controvery/

Gaudiosi, John. 2009. "Spielberg Makes Videogames to Keep His Family Happy." *Reuters*, May 14. Accessed December 29, 2010. www.reuters.com/article/idUSTRE54D2H420090514?pageNumber=1

Gray, J. Glenn. [1959] 1998. *The Warriors: Reflections of Men in Combat*. Lincoln: University of Nebraska Press.

Green, Shawn C., Alexandre Pouget, and Daphne Bavelier. 2010. "Improved Probabilistic Inference as a General Learning Mechanism with Action Video Games." *Current Biology* 20, no. 17 (September): 1573–1579. Accessed September 26, 2014. http://dx.doi.org/10.1016/j.cub.2010.07.040

Grossman, Lt. Col. David. 2000. "Teaching Kids to Kill." *Killology Research Group*. Accessed January 2, 2011. www.killology.com/article_teachkid.htm

Halter, Ed. 2006. *From Sun Tzu to Xbox: War and Video Games*. New York: Thunder's Mouth Press.

Herz, J. C. 1997. *Joystick Nation: How Videogames Ate Our Quarters, Won Our Hearts, and Rewired Our Minds*. London: Abacus.

Hitchcock, William I. 2009. *Liberation. The Bitter Road to Freedom: A New History of the Liberation of Europe*. New York: Free Press.

Hocking, Clint. 2007. "Ludonarrative Dissonance in *Bioshock*. The Problem of What the Game Is About." *Click Nothing: Design from a Long Time Ago* (blog), October 7. Accessed October 23, 2010. http://clicknothing.typepad.com/click_nothing/2007/10/ludonarrative-d.html

IGN. 1999. "Medal of Honor Society Endorses Game. Congressional Medal of Honor Society Officially Endorses EA and DreamWork Interactive's PS Game." *IGN*, December 9. Accessed October 14, 2010. http://uk.psx.IGN/articles/073/073075p1.html

Ivan, Tom. 2009. "*Call of Duty* Tops 55 Million Sales." *Edge*, November 27. Accessed September 25, 2014. www.edge-online.com/news/call-duty-series-tops-55-million-sales/

Jenkins, Henry. 2004. "Game Design as Narrative Architecture." In *First Person: New Media as Story, Performance and Game*. Noah Wardrip-Fruin and Pat Harrigan, eds.: 118–130. Cambridge, MA: MIT Press.

Jenkins, Henry, and Mary Fuller. 1995. "Nintendo® and New World Travel Writing: A Dialogue." In *Cybersociety: Computer-Mediated Communication and Community*. Steven G. Jones ed.: 57–72. Thousand Oaks, CA: Sage Publications, 1995.

Jones, Gerard. 2002. *Killing Monsters: Why Children Need Fantasy, Super Heroes and Make-Believe Violence*. New York: Basic Books.

Kennedy, Sam. 1999. "PS *Medal of Honor* Ships." *Gamespot*, November 10. Accessed September 25, 2014. www.gamespot.com/articles/ps-medal-of-honor-ships/1100-2446813/

King, Richard, and David Leonard. 2010. "War games as a New Frontier: Securing American Empire in Virtual Space." In *Joystick Soldiers: The Politics of Play in Military Video Games*. Nina B Huntemann and Matthew Thomas Payne, eds.: 91–105. New York: Routledge.

Klevjer, Rune. 2002. "In Defence of Cutscenes." Paper presented at the Computer Games and Digital Cultures Conference, Tampere, Finland, June 6–8. http://folk.uib.no/smkrk/docs/klevjerpaper.htm

Lahti, Martti. 2003. "As We Become Machines. Corporealized Pleasures in Video Games." In *The Video Game Theory Reader*. Mark J.P. Wolf and Bernard Perron, eds.: 157–170. New York: Routledge.

Landsberg, Alison. 2004. *Prosthetic Memory*. New York: Columbia University Press.

Lukas, Scott. 2010. "Behind the Barrell. Reading the Video Game Gun." In *Joystick Soldiers: The Politics of Play in Military Video Games*. Nina B Huntemann and Matthew Thomas Payne, eds.: 75–90. New York: Routledge.

Martin, Matt. 2008. "New *Call of Duty* Outsells *CoD4*." *Gamesindustry.biz*, November 18. Accessed September 25, 2014. www.gamesindustry.biz/articles/new-call-of-duty-outsells-cod4-by-more-than-2-to-1

Neitzel, Sönke, and Harald Welzer. 2012. *Soldaten: On Fighting, Killing, and Dying*. Jefferson Chase, trans. New York: Alfred A. Knopf.

Newman, James. 2002. "The Myth of the Ergodic Videogame: Some Thoughts on Player–Character Relationships in Videogames." *Game Studies: The International Journal of Computer Game Research* 2, no. 1. Accessed September 25, 2014. www.gamestudies.org/0102/newman/

Newman, James. 2004. *Videogames*. London: Routledge.

NPD Group Press Release. 2009. "2009 U.S. Video Game Industry and PC Game Software Retail Sales Reach $20.2 Billion." NPD Group, May 20. Accessed July 9, 2010. www.npd.com/press/releases/press_100114.html

NPD Group Press Release. 2010. "More Americans Play Video Games Than Go Out to the Movies." NPD Group, January 14. Accessed July 9, 2010. www.npd.com/press/releases/press_090520.html

O'Brien, Tim. 1991. *The Things They Carried*. London: Flamingo.

Payne, Matthew. 2010. "'F*ck You, Noob Tube!': Learning the Art of Ludic LAN War." In *Joystick Soldiers: The Politics of Play in Military Video Games*. Nina B Huntemann and Matthew Thomas Payne, eds.: 206–222. New York: Routledge.

Penney, Joel. 2010. "'No Better Way to "Experience" World War II': Authenticity and Ideology in the *Call of Duty* and *Medal of Honor* Player Communities." In *Joystick Soldiers: The Politics of Play in Military Video Games*. Nina B Huntemann and Matthew Thomas Payne, eds.: 206–222. New York: Routledge.

Perry, Doug. 1999. "*Medal of Honor. Goldeneye* for the PlayStation Has Finally Arrived." *IGN*, November 18. Accessed September 25, 2014. http://uk.ign.com/articles/1999/11/19/medal-of-honor

Plunkett, Luke. 2009. "Rabbi Overcomes Fear of Nazis, Courtesy of *Call of Duty*." *Kotaku*, March 6. Accessed November 9, 2010. http://Kotaku/5165862/rabbi-overcomes-fear-of-nazis-courtesy-of-call-of-duty

Pyle, Ernie. [1943] 2004. *Here Is Your War: The Story of G.I. Joe*. Lincoln: University of Nebraska Press.

Robinson, Andy. 2008. "*World at War* Review." *Computer and Video Games*, November 14. Accessed October 21, 2010. www.computerandvideogames.com/article.php?id=201616

Robinson, Martin. 2008. "*Call of Duty: World at War* UK Review. War Never Changes." *IGN*, November 14. Accessed October 23, 2010. http://uk.ign.com/articles/2008/11/17/call-of-duty-world-at-war-uk-review

Sharkey, Scott. 2009. "Why WWII? A Look at Videogames and Wars of the 20th Century." *1UP*. Accessed November 9, 2010. www.1up.com/do/feature?cId=3175558

Shoemaker, Brad. 2003. "*Medal of Honor: Rising Sun* Review." *Gamespot*, November 13. Accessed January 14, 2011. www.gamespot.com/reviews/medal-of-honor-rising-sun-review/1900-6083408/

Smith, Ken. 2010. "Top Five World War Two Games." *Msnbc.com*, April 12. Accessed July 6, 2010. www.msnbc.msn.com/id/23712168/ns/technology_and_science-games/

Stuart, Keith. 2011. "Modern Warfare 3 Smashes Entertainment Launch Records." *Games Blog*, November 11. Accessed September 25, 2014. www.guardian.co.uk/technology/gamesblog/2011/nov/11/modern-warfare-3-breaks-sales-records?intcmp=239

Thorsen, Tor. 2008. "*CoD5* Invading 'New Theatre,' Next 007 CoD4-Powered." *Gamespot*, May 8. Accessed September 25, 2014. www.gamespot.com/articles/cod5-invading-new-theater-next-007-cod4-powered/1100–6190641/

Torgovnick, Marianna. 2005. *The War Complex: World War II in Our Time*. Chicago: University of Chicago Press.

Watters, Chris. 2008. "*Call of Duty: World at War* Video Review." *Gamespot*, November 12. Accessed October 23, 2010. www.gamespot.com/reviews/call-of-duty-world-at-war-review/1900-6201026/

Wendig, Chuck. 2010. "The 12-Year-Old English Kid Who Carried Us to Victory." *Escapist Magazine*, September 7. Accessed October 21, 2010. www.escapistmagazine.com/articles/view/issues/issue_270/8060-The-12-Year-Old-English-Kid-Who-Carried-Us-to-Victory.3

Whitehead, Dan. 2008. "*Call of Duty: World at War*: Still Soldiering On," *Eurogamer*, November 13. Accessed September 26, 2014. www.eurogamer.net/articles/call-of-duty-world-at-war-review

Wright, Will. 2007. "Keynote Speech." Keynote Delivered at the SXSW (South by Southwest) Interactive Festival 2007, Austin, Texas, March 13. Transcription on ww.3pointd.com. Accessed September 26, 2014. www.3pointd.com/20070313/sxsw-xcript-will-wright-keynote/

XBOX *The Official Magazine*. 2008. "Preview: *Call of Duty: World at War*." *XBOX: The Official XBOX Magazine*, July 8. Accessed September 25, 2014. www.oxm.co.uk/5084/previews/call-of-duty-world-at-war/?page=1

KEY GAMES

Battle for Midway. Personal Software Services, 1984.
Beyond Castle Wolfenstein. Muse Software, 1984.
Call of Duty. Infinity Ward, Activision, 2003–present.
Castle Wolfenstein. Muse Software, 1981.
Doom. ID Software, 1993.
Marine Doom. U.S. Marine Corps, 1996.
Medal of Honor. DreamWorks Int., EA Games, 1999–present.
Night Gunner. Digital Integration Ltd., 1984.
Wolfenstein 3D. ID Software, 1992.

Conclusion
Stories without End

The "truths" of war are contradictory and elusive. In Tim O'Brien's words, "Order blends into chaos, love into hate, ugliness into beauty, law into anarchy, civility into savagery," with the result that in any story about war, "nothing is ever absolutely true" (1991, 78). O'Brien concludes that the only way to tell a "true" war story is to keep on telling it (80). The story of World War II has been told in innumerable ways through a range of media. Only by understanding that every mediated iteration of the memories and narratives of World War II is part of a continually evolving and integrated network of texts is it possible to begin to gain a sense of some of the truths of the war's mnemonic identity. Understood as media of memory and memory of media, the transmedia, transgenerational structure of World War II connects both media and individuals to the past, present, and future. Examining the ongoing development of World War II as a transmedia mnemonic structure in this book has illuminated the procedural and diachronic dimensions of the system of memory in which media interact, intersect, complement, and/or contradict one another.

Coordinated and influenced by organizations such as the Office of War Information during the war, the American wartime generation's media, while not necessarily speaking with one voice as did the media of Germany and Japan, were certainly more synchronized than any time before or since in order to support the war effort. The foundations of three elements that would become the organizing framework of the transmedia structure of World War II—the citizen soldier, the "good war," and the war's visual construction—were established in the wartime generation's highly integrated mediascape and then repurposed in the media of their progeny, the Baby Boomers. Although no longer as united in purpose, the media in operation in the current generation's mediated milieu do not function in isolation.

The commercial success of *Saving Private Ryan*, for example, which is itself connected to other media through photographs, newsreels, documentaries and written histories, produces ripples throughout the transmedia structure of World War II. As a master mediation, *Saving Private Ryan* effectively premediates subsequent representations. *Flags of Our Fathers* and *Letters from Iwo Jima* thus remediate the wartime media's configuration of the organizational framework of the war, as well as the "template" of war memory established by *Saving Private Ryan*. Industrial connections between the film and television industries facilitate the ongoing circulation of "cultural debris," to use Judith Burnett's term, through the mnemonic structure of the war, which then provide the building blocks for future mediations. Connections between these industries also led to the development of *Band of Brothers* and *The Pacific*, both of which function as brand extensions of *Saving Private Ryan* and remediate cinematic memories of World War II according to the affordances of televisual narratives. The games industry similarly includes references to film, television, and news media as a measure of authenticity, but, by introducing the element of play into the memory of World War II, it occasionally contradicts and challenges the elegiac tone that infuses representations in other media. The films, television series, and digital games discussed in this book remediate and reconfigure the citizen soldier, the "good war," and the visual construct of the time in response to the commercial, industrial, and cultural needs of the present, but each component also has aspects that resist recalibration. In summary, just how are the citizen soldier, the "good war," and the war as a visual construct emerging within the current configuration of the transmedia mnemonic structure of World War II?

Widely described by the media of the wartime generation as a "people's war," World War II in America's current mediascape is very much a soldier's war. More specifically, World War II is the American soldier's war, to the exclusion of other members of the Allied forces, resistance fighters, and civilians who were all involved in the conflict. To a certain extent, World War II first-person shooters mitigate this perspective by regularly featuring members of other nations, but even within digital games, US soldiers are the largest group of protagonists to feature across all military-themed FPSs.[1] That American-produced media should primarily be concerned with American characters and stories is understandable. However, the exclusion of other nationalities is indicative of what historian Norman Davies (2007, 478) identifies as an "Americocentric" view of World War II in which "the world," as the tagline on the DVD special edition box set (November 2002) for *Band of Brothers* puts it, depended on American citizen soldiers to save it from tyranny and aggressive imperialism.

The white racial identity of the citizen soldier is its most consistent attribute throughout the development of the transmedia construct of the war. I am not suggesting that no films or television productions tell the story of the experiences of African Americans or Native Americans in the transmedia structure of World War II, only that these are exceptions that prove the rule. *Miracle at St. Anna* (Spike Lee, 2008), for example, is Lee's direct response to the lack of heroic African American figures in representations of World War II in general and to the lack of African Americans in Eastwood's *Flags of Our Fathers* in particular.[2] *Miracle at St. Anna* tells the story of a squad of African American soldiers who venture behind enemy lines in Italy.

Windtalkers (John Woo, 2002) deals with the experiences of the Navajo code talkers in the Pacific, and in 1995 HBO produced a made-for-TV film on an African American squadron of fighter pilots, *The Tuskegee Airmen*, a story repeated more recently on a larger scale in the film *Red Tails* (Anthony Hemingway, 2012). Edward Zwiek's *Defiance* (2008), meanwhile, departs completely from the citizen soldier's perspective to tell the story of the Bielski partisans in German-occupied Belarus. Despite the occasional deviation, however, in the first decades of the new millennium, the experiences of the white American soldier remain the principle framework through which memories of World War II are organized in the transmedia structure of the war in the US.

In its current incarnation, the World War II citizen soldier is rarely an isolated figure. The national solidarity so critical to wartime depictions of the citizen soldier morphed into an exclusive "brotherhood" forged in combat in more recent representations of the war. Protecting other members of the brotherhood is the fundamental reason why soldiers fight and die in the current configuration of the citizen soldier, but the "justness" of the US involvement in World War II and the importance of the fight for freedom and democracy remain implicit within the structure. Obscured in part by the uncertainties that fractured the construct as it cycled into the media of the Baby Boomers, current representations of the war resurrect self-sacrifice as an essential design feature of the citizen soldier's architecture. The citizen soldier has become symbolic of the Greatest Generation. According to the films and television series discussed in this book but also evident elsewhere in the commemorations of events from the war and in the discourse that accompanies such events, subsequent generations of Americans owe their lives and lifestyles to the soldiers of the Greatest Generation. The moral ambiguities that entered the makeup of the citizen soldier in the wake of the wars in Korea and Vietnam are plastered over in current representations. The World War II soldier is once again a defender of democracy, as represented in the brotherhood of soldiers, and of liberty, as represented by the freedoms enjoyed by subsequent generations. Acknowledgment of any atrocities committed by GIs during World War II is still relatively rare or, as *The Pacific* demonstrates, is mitigated by positioning the soldiers as victims of war's brutalizing influence. The dark, bitter humor so intrinsic to the American GI that it was represented in wartime media despite restrictions on content and became emblematic of an idiosyncratic national spirit is all but completely lost in the current configuration of the citizen soldier, perhaps because it sounds a jarring note in the reverential tone of the widespread drive to "honor" the generation that fought in World War II.

The structure of the citizen soldier is only partially realized in its representation in film and television, however. Digital games constitute a vital element of the mediascape at the turn of the millennium, and the first-person shooter introduces different shades of meaning into the soldier's design. Although the *Medal of Honor* franchise (EA Games, 1999–2013) acknowledges the sacrifice and nobility of the citizen soldier, the FPS in general serves as a critical reminder that the primary function of citizen soldiers on the battlefields of World War II was not to die but to kill. The FPS also introduces a disturbing and difficult element into the structure, previously only hinted at: that the citizen soldier might at times have enjoyed killing and the more destructive aspects of the "work" of war. Only one film in the last decade suggests something similar. Quentin Tarantino's *Inglourious Basterds* (2009) recalls the tone and structure of films like *The Dirty Dozen* (Robert Aldrich, 1967). Lieutenant Aldo Raine (Brad Pitt) echoes Lee Marvin's Major John Reisman as he gleefully orders his "bushwhackin'" guerilla squad to "disembowel, dismember and disfigure" as many Nazis as they can. That nobility, pathos, sorrow, and sacrifice coexist with unadulterated fury, exhilaration, and bloodlust does not necessarily imply instability within the contemporary design of the citizen soldier. On the contrary, the citizen soldier in today's transmedia structure of the war can be understood as revealing the contradictory emotions and responses that war elicits in soldiers. In the words of Glenn Gray, any examination of war must, in the end, attempt to grapple with both "gods and devils in the form of man" ([1959] 1998, 242). The FPS thus provides an essential balance to the mediated construct of the soldier.

However, the central position occupied by the white, male US citizen soldier in the transmedia structure of the war displaces the experiences of others involved in World War II. As a consequence, a gap crucial to the development of the idea of World War II as a "good war" not only has been maintained but has significantly deepened in the contemporary configuration of the structure. Although it is difficult, if not impossible, to access exact figures, civilian deaths make up over half the figures for the mortality rates of World War II, a statistic "hiding in plain sight," to adopt Marianna Torgovnick's term for those aspects of war memory that are readily accessible but rarely acknowledged (2005, 41). The chaos and devastation that accompany total war prompted Glenn Gray to reflect that "[n]o change in the character of warfare seems as crucial as this modern blurring of all distinctions between combatants and non-combatants" ([1959] 1998, 221). The understatement of the human cost and complexities of the process of liberation in wartime media, followed by the political necessities of sustaining America's moral integrity as the righteous defender of democracy during Cold War conflicts, progressively minimized the "blurriness" of the boundaries between soldiers and civilians in terms of the impact of World War II. In current representations throughout the mediated structure of the war, World War II is depicted as a war involving and affecting soldiers, above all others. Increasingly graphic depictions of the battlefield acknowledging the impact of industrial warfare on the bodies of soldiers have not destabilized the concept of the "good war." On the contrary, the ignobility of technological warfare is ennobled in the films and television series discussed in this book through the concept of sacrifice. The sacrifices made by America's citizen soldiers overshadow the effect of the war on civilians, allowing for a perspective of war itself that feeds into a way of understanding all wars and of the role of the US in the world.

In 1942, Henry Luce wrote that the "task" of the US was to "win the war and create a family of nations" in which the US would serve as the "elder brother" because American ideals of democracy and freedom could provide a blueprint for the way peace should be implemented across the world (91). The consistent elision of the complexities and substantial human cost involved in the pursuit of "liberating" the world for democracy during World War II—an endeavor that, it should be remembered, ended with much of Europe consigned to yet another totalitarian regime in the form of the Soviet Union—underwrites the perception of the US as the benevolent "elder brother" in the "family of nations." The possibility that the US concepts of democracy and of freedom might not be applicable to, or appropriate for, every country in the world, either during World War II or in present conflicts, has never significantly troubled the notion of the "good war." It is largely due to the idea of a "good war" that World War II remains the touchstone for American conflicts, from its invocations by the Bush administration throughout the second Gulf War through to President Barack Obama's more recent justification for American intervention in Libya's civil war in which he remarked that "some nations may be able to turn a blind eye to atrocities in other countries. The United States of America is different" (quoted in Kirsch 2011). The idea of World War II as a "good war" not only confirms America's national identity as "different" but also endorses the perceived moral integrity of the country's actions.

Over half a century after the conflict, Adam Kirsch (2011) questions whether World War II can still be regarded as a "good war" in the light of a "new wave" of histories that reassess the moral implications of different aspects of the war and counter the vicarious nostalgia in the work of popular historian Stephen Ambrose. Norman Davies, for example, emphasizes the significance of the war on the Eastern Front and suggests that in light of the differences between the Eastern and Western Fronts in size and impact, it is difficult not to see the latter as anything more than a "sideshow" (2007, 23–25). William Hitchcock explores the complexities of the liberation of Europe in the hope that "[w]e now have the evidence, and perhaps the critical distance, to develop a richer, more complex history of the 'good war' that incorporates both its glories and its misfortunes" (2009, 373). In television, Oliver Stone, together with historian Peter Kuznick, released a documentary series entitled *The Untold History of the United States* (Showtime, 2012) to specifically counter what Stone describes in a talk at the Illinois Institute of Technology (2013) as the "worship of World War II" and the idea of the Greatest Generation generated by the work of Stephen Ambrose, Tom Brokaw, and Steven Spielberg. The ten-part series emphasizes the role played by the Soviet Union in the war (but understates the darker side to

Stalin's regime) and reframes the decision to drop the two atomic bombs as a demonstration to the Communist bloc of US military might.

Overall, the series and accompanying book by the same title issue a challenge to the notion of the actions of the US in World War II as heroic and altruistic, therefore attempting to undermine the notion of the "good war." That the series provoked passionate debates in the US media is indicative of the enduring power of World War II as a measure of American national identity.[3] Similarly, David Ayer's film *Fury* (2014), one of the most recent films set in World War II at this time of writing, promises to reveal the "ugliness in the heroes of World War II" by acknowledging that US citizen soldiers crossed moral boundaries (Cieply 2014).[4] It is as yet too early to tell, however, whether such histories will in any fundamental way destabilize the notion of the "good war" or whether the information they provide will simply continue to hide in plain sight without in any significant way filling the spaces in the transmedia structure of the war that allow the "good war" to persist. Until "active absences," such as the impact of war on civilians, register significantly across the transmedia structure of World War II, the "good war" will continue, as Marianna Torgovnick suggests, to have a space in which to "loop back into the present" (2005, 4).

The distinctive elements of the visual construction of the war define how World War II is received and interpreted every time it cycles back into the present. David Hockney once observed that "we've come to think the world looks like a photograph. That's how mad it's got" (quoted in Moeller 1989, 16). World War II's visual construction is drawn from a range of visual media and not just photographs, but it can be similarly suggested that we have come to think that World War II looks like its mediated representations. David Ayer, director of *Fury*, for example, recounts how he examined "actual photographs" from World War II in order to develop a visual esthetic that does not repeat "someone else's World War II movie look" (interview in Lesnick 2014). Yet Ayer also admits that *Fury* replicates "the look and feel" of World War II newsreel footage (quoted in Weintraub 2014). What is significant about Ayer's comments is not that he researched archive material of the war but that it suggests a perception of wartime visual media as offering an unmediated glimpse of the past. This book has shown that the visual construction of World War II during wartime was the result of complex interactions between conditions of combat and the dominant strategies of representation of the time, which combined to create a visual signature for the war that gave combat footage priority and that focused on the citizen soldier and on the esthetic building blocks of spectacle and machinery. *Saving Private Ryan* transformed the "satisfaction of the astonishing" into a "spectacular-authentic" esthetic—a hypermediated combination of the "look" of wartime footage with contemporary cinematic techniques such as computer-generated imagery, designed to create an under-the-helmet perspective that provides insight into the soldier's experiences and memories of combat. Just as the spectacle of warfare played an important role in showcasing particular technologies, such as widescreen cinema in the 1960s and 1970s, the spectacular-authentic depiction of war in contemporary representations is employed today to showcase the capabilities of DVD and Blu-ray players and home theater systems. No more than 25 percent of those serving in the US Army ever came under enemy fire, yet the combat experiences of ground forces remains the central mainstay of the visual construction of the war (Dunnigan [1982] 2003, 292).

Because the spectacular-authentic esthetic of current representations of World War II relies so heavily on the wartime media's visual construction of the war, they preserve and in some cases heighten the ideological filters embedded in the look of the war. Wartime media's concentration on the soldier's experience of combat as the defining moments of World War II created extreme binaries between war and peace, us and them, good and evil in the transmedia structure of the war that continue to be enforced in current media, most notably in the FPS, where war is rendered as *nothing but* combat. As extraordinary landscapes filled with spectacle, wonder, and intense emotions, the spaces of war contrast sharply to those of the home front. The deep divisions inherent in the visual construction of the war preserve the appeal of World War II as a display of military virtue, excitement, and intensity, in contrast to the humdrum day-to-day life in the spaces of peace. The divisions between home and war in the war's esthetic composition are generated in part by the fact that, with the exception of the attack on Pearl Harbor, the US was largely spared the devastation to cities and countryside that spread across much of the rest of the world during World War II. As a result, the chaos of war is associated with "strange and faraway land[s]," as the character of Ernie Pyle puts it in Wellman's *The Story of G.I. Joe* (1945), while the order of peace is implicitly connected to the US, with the profound implication that the latter can reasonably be maintained by the former. The polarized perspective of war in general has proved to be one of World War II's lasting legacies, as George Roeder predicted, and it remains a central feature of the transmedia construct of the conflict today.

In this book, I concentrated on the industries and products of three media that can be considered as particularly significant in the current mediascape. However, film, television, and digital games are not, of course, representative of all the media that contribute to the transmedia structure of World War II. Technologies of digital media in particular are transforming the structure in ways that have yet to be fully assessed. A variety of historical material once inaccessible except through archives and private collections is now available through the World Wide Web, and a range of mediations of World War II have been given a new lease of life through Web 2.0 applications. For instance, *Victory at Sea* has a dedicated website (http://victoryatseaonline.com/) featuring stills and photographs from the series, as well as complete episodes, courtesy of YouTube. Fragments of World War II combat footage as well as entire films circulate on YouTube, while online archiving projects such as the Internet Archive (www.archive.org/) incorporate films such as

The Battle of Midway and make them freely available for viewing. *Band of Brothers* and *The Pacific* have pages on Facebook (https://www.facebook.com/bandofbrothers; https://www.facebook.com/thepacific), ensuring that those who have chosen to "like" these pages (and over two million people have done so with *Band of Brothers*) are constantly reminded of them through regular status updates of quotes, images, and pieces of historical information from both series, integrating the series even further into personal memory. Furthermore, Facebook gives advertising space to *Band of Brothers* tours, one of many such tours that blend history, war memory, and cultural practices of commemoration with television fandom.[5]

In addition, digitization has made media content far more easily malleable than in the mediascape of the past. Posts on sites such as YouTube echo the reverence inherent in the representations of World War II produced by Baby Boomers such as Ambrose, Spielberg, and Hanks—such as the numerous "fan trailers" consisting of user edits of footage of *Band of Brothers, Saving Private Ryan,* and *The Pacific* occasionally intermingled. Others, however, combine media forms in unexpected and sometimes irreverent ways. For example, *"Call of Duty*: Secret Spielberg Level Unlocked," posted on comedy website funnyordie.com (FoDTeamUK 2009), re-presents the landing sequence from *Saving Private Ryan* as a "secret level" of a *Call of Duty* Xbox online death match, complete with comical gamer chatter. In other examples, there are a number of YouTube videos of recreations in Lego stop-motion animation of various battles from World War II, as well as moments from World War II films and series (including *Letters from Iwo Jima* and *Band of Brothers*), all giving an entirely new and literal interpretation of Jeanine Basinger's description of genre as a kind of "Lego set" ([1986] 2003, 15). These kinds of representations are a powerful indication that the transmedia mnemonic structure of the war is subject to an infinite variety of individual interpretations and remediations.

Although this book took World War II as its focus, the concept of transmedia structures can be extended to those networks of texts that accrue around other moments of social and historical significance. We are currently witnessing the emergence of a transmedia structure of the War on Terror in the news footage, documentaries, films, television series, FPSs, soldiers' blogs, and videos associated with the conflicts in Iraq and Afghanistan, for example. Questions can be asked about how the practice of embedding journalists influences the visual construction of these wars not only in news footage but also in television series such as HBO's *Generation Kill* (2008), which is drawn from *Rolling Stone* reporter Evan Wright's experiences with the 1st Recon Marines. An "active absence" with the potential to define the future understanding of these wars is already apparent in the structure. From *Generation Kill* to films such as *The Hurt Locker* (Kathryn Bigelow, 2008) and documentaries such as *Gunner Palace* (Petra Epperlein and Michael Tucker, 2004), the enemy is practically invisible, and blends seamlessly into the civilian population—a way of representing the enemy that may become the source of profound divisions between notions of us and them. The ubiquity of digital cameras enables soldiers to shoot a great deal of combat footage themselves, in many cases presenting a far more intensive and easily accessible under-the-helmet perspective of battlefields than in any other war, which in turn raises questions concerning the role and continued significance of the soldier's experience of combat as the most significant of all the views and memories of warfare. The increasing resemblance between such footage and the first-person perspective of the FPS, together with the overlap between the digital displays and readouts of weapons and their controlling systems with game footage, has already contributed to a distinctive visual esthetic in representations of these wars that may well shape ideological perceptions of war in the future. How the transmedia structure of World War II will intersect with that of the War on Terror is yet to be determined.

In 1962, film critic Bosley Crowther made an "educated guess that there will not be another motion picture about World War II on the scale or with the power intensity in re-enactment" of Darryl Zanuck's *The Longest Day*. Twenty-four years later, Jeanine Basinger (1986, 197) hazarded a similar guess about *The Big Red One*. And twenty-four years after that, Brian Crecente (2010) speculates that World War II "seems to have lost its attraction for video game developers." After *Call of Duty: World at War*, both the *Medal of Honor* and *Call of Duty* franchises turned to games set in modern conflicts. Such predictions not only demonstrate the persistence with which World War II cycles back into the present in each generation's mediascape but also indicate the impossibility of forecasting with any certainty whether the conflict has seen its final incarnation or when and in what medium it may return. What role World War II might play in the next generation's mediascape is uncertain, but the transmedia mnemonic structure of the war is a sizable and powerful presence that will not dissipate easily. As an ongoing process, the evolution of World War II within generational media is open to further investigation. It is a "long-running" story, with no sign as yet of an ending.

NOTES

1. American soldiers make up 82 percent of the ethnicities in all war-themed FPSs, according to Breuer (Festl and Quandt 2011).
2. Prior to the release of *Miracle at St. Anna*, Lee engaged in a widely publicized and heated exchange with Clint Eastwood over the lack of African Americans in *Flags of Our Fathers* and *Letters from Iwo Jima*.
3. The discourse surrounding Stone's documentary is a particularly rich network of paratexts that reveals the appropriation of World War II by various political ideologies, as well as attitudes toward the relationship between media and history, and ideas over who has the "right" to communicate history. For reviews that cover all these aspects, see Radosh (2010) and Wiener (2012).
4. Whether the film will actually do so is unclear because it was not yet released at the time of writing. However, the trailer for the film, which has as its tagline, "In the depths of war, each man is only as strong as the man beside him,"

suggests that the film rehearses arguments regarding the brutalization of war on soldiers and calls on the idea of the brotherhood of soldiers.

5. For the best example of such tours, see stephenambrosetours.com, which promises that "you'll stand with Easy Company veterans in the very foxholes and precise locations where they fought in some of the most climactic battles of World War II" and offers replica airborne jump jackets as "worn by the cast in the HBO miniseries."

REFERENCES

Basinger, Jeanine. [1986] 2003. *The World War II Combat Film: Anatomy of a Genre*. Middletown, CT: Wesleyan University Press.

Breuer, Johannes, Ruth Festl, and Thorsten Quandt. 2011. "In the Army Now—Narrative Elements and Realism in Military First Person Shooters." Paper presented at the Fifth International Conference of the Digital Research Association, "Think Design Play," Utrecht School of Arts, Utrecht, September 14–17. www.digra.org/dl/db/11307.54018.pdf

Cieply, Michael. 2014. "*Fury*, Starring Brad Pitt, a Raw Look at Warfare." *New York Times*, July 30. Accessed September 26, 2014. www.nytimes.com/2014/08/03/movies/fury-starring-brad-pitt-a-raw-look-at-warfare.html?_r=0

Crecente, Brian. 2010. "Video Games Bid Adieu to World War II." *Kotaku*, June 4. Accessed January 28, 2012. http://Kotaku/5555349/black-opsvideo-games-bid-adieu-to-world-war-ii

Crowther, Bosley. 1962. "No More Worlds: Peak for War Films Hit by *Longest Day*." *New York Times*, October 7. Proquest Historical Newspaper: *New York Times* (1851–2008).

Davies, Norman. 2007. *No Simple Victory: World War II in Europe, 1939–1945*. New York: Viking Penguin.

Dunnigan, James F. (1982) 2003. *How to Make War: A Comprehensive Guide to Modern Warfare in the Twenty-First Century*, 4th ed. New York: HarperCollins.

FoDTeamUK. 2009. "*Call of Duty*: Secret Spielberg Level Unlocked," November 13. Accessed September 26, 2014. www.funnyordie.com/videos/32d666a5cd/call-of-duty-secret-spielberg-level-unlocked

Gray, J. Glenn. [1959] 1998. *The Warriors: Reflections of Men in Combat*. Lincoln: University of Nebraska Press.

Hitchcock, William I. 2009. *Liberation. The Bitter Road to Freedom: A New History of the Liberation of Europe*. New York: Free Press.

Illinois Institute of Technology. 2013. "Oliver Stone and Peter Kuznick Discuss the *Untold History of the United States*." Illinois Institute of Technology (ILT), Department of Humanities. Filmed at the McCormick Tribune Campus Center, February 1, 2013. Posted February 7, 2013. www.youtube.com/watch?v=uGwwkl2EdeM

Kirsch, Adam. 2011. "Is World War II Still 'the Good War'?" *The New York Times*, May 27. Accessed January 3, 2012. www.nytimes.com/2011/05/29/books/review/adam-kirsch-on-new-books-about-world-war-ii.html?pagewanted=all

Lesnick, Silas. 2014. "From the Set of David Ayer's *Fury*, Starring Brad Pitt," *Comingsoon.net*, July 1. Accessed September 26, 2014. www.comingsoon.net/news/movienews.php?id=119863

Luce, Henry. 1942. "America's War and America's Peace." *Life*, February 16. Accessed September 17, 2014. http://books.google.co.uk/books/about/LIFE.html?id=R1cEAAAAMBAJ

Moeller, Susan D. 1989. *Shooting War: Photography and the American Experience of Combat*. New York: Basic Books.

O'Brien, Tim. 1991. *The Things They Carried*. London: Flamingo.

Radosh, Ron. 2010. "I Thought Howard Zinn Was Bad Enough. Now We Have to Learn Our History from Oliver Stone." *PJ Media*, January 12, 2010. Accessed September 26, 2014. http://pjmedia.com/ronradosh/2010/01/12/i-thought-howard-zinn-was-bad-enough-now-we-have-to-learn-our-history-from-oliver-stone/

Torgovnick, Marianna. 2005. *The War Complex: World War II in Our Time*. Chicago: University of Chicago Press.

Weintraub, Steve. 2014. "Director David Ayer Talks Fury, Telling a Different WWII Story, Cast Boot Camp, Reshoots, Using Shia LaBeouf as His 'BS Detector,' and More." *Collider*, July 2, 2014. Accessed September 26, 2014. http://collider.com/david-ayer-fury-interview/

Wiener, Jon. 2012. "Oliver Stone's *Untold History*." *The Nation*, November 14. Accessed September 26, 2014. www.thenation.com/article/171210/oliver-stones-untold-history

Index